DIPLOMACY IN
IRON
The Life of Herbert von Bismarck

DIPLOMACY IN IRON

IRON

The Life of Herbert von Bismarck

By

LOUIS L. SNYDER

ROBERT E. KRIEGER PUBLISHING COMPANY
MALABAR, FLORIDA
1985

Original Edition 1985

Printed and Published by
ROBERT E. KRIEGER PUBLISHING COMPANY, INC.
KRIEGER DRIVE
MALABAR, FL 32950

Printed in the United States of America

Library of Congress Cataloging in Publication Data

Snyder, Louis L.
  Diplomacy in iron.

  Bibliography: p.
  Includes index.
  1. Bismarck, Herbert, Fürst von, 1849-1904.
2. Diplomats – Germany – Biography.   3. Germany – Foreign relations –
1871-1918.   I. Title.
DD218.93,S65 1985   943.08′092′4 [B]   84-17175
ISBN 0-89874-794-5

To
Nancy, Mark, Erin Hayley, and Meredith Ann Snyder,
Rhea Belle and Dr. Rick,
and in loving memory of brother Nemo

TABLE OF CONTENTS

FOREWORD

"What a sad creature was Herbert Bismarck! His inner life atrophied to bitterness and unfulfilled hopes. How little love he gave, how little he received.... His life was like a coruscating rocket that we see rise swiftly and then suddenly fall into the individual glimmering particles before our eyes in the dark.... This unsatisfied mortal fought for his dreams with ever-growing passionate energy, more fiercely than ever, as he found himself passing his prime."

Prince Philipp zu Eulenburg-Hertefeld

PREFACE

After Shakespeare the greatest English dramatist of his age was Ben Jonson, who boldly stated three centuries ago: "Greatness of name in the father often overwhelms the son. They stand too near one another. The shadow kills the growth."

The story is as old as primogeniture. Sons of famous fathers carry unconscionable burdens throughout their lives because they are always being compared with their more distinguished sires. Again and again it is the tale of the psychically wounded son who, longing to stand on an equal footing with his famous father, suffers tortures of psychological agony. One needs only consider the case of Winston Churchill, quintessential British hero of the twentieth century, and his sometimes obnoxious offspring, Randolph. Here, as elsewhere, the son reacted and suffered in the shadow of his illustrious father.

Herbert Bismarck too, son of the great Chancellor Otto von Bismarck, was never able to emerge from the burdensome shadow. He also could not cope with the task of living with a giant of a father. The pattern is a predictable one. Prince Bismarck exaggerated his son's ability and closed his eyes to flaws of character. Whereas the normal parent prepares his son for independence, the German Chancellor unconsciously kept his son Herbert at a four-year-old level, to be loved, cherished, and pampered. He would have his adored son take on the mantle of Bismarckian power.

In the process Herbert suffered severe psychological damage. He was pulled in two directions, dangerous for the human psyche. He was subservient and loyal to his revered father and solicitous for him, on the one hand. On the other hand, he sought to find ways of expressing his own free status as an independent human being. The resulting conflict left emotional scar tissue, plaguing him for life. Herbert Bismarck turned to the bottle as did Randolph Churchill as one means of easing his inner turmoil.

There are, of course, exceptions. William Pitt the Elder, first earl of Chatham, known as the Great Commoner, transformed Britain into an imperial power in the mid-eighteenth century. His son, William Pitt the Younger, prime minister during the French Revolutionary Wars, led his country successfully during the Napoleonic Wars. Although a dominant, forceful orator, William Pitt the Younger always remained in his person a shy, lonely man, bearing the burden of a great father.

My interest in the Bismarcks began with the publication in 1932 of a doctoral dissertation, *Die persoenlichen und politischen Beziehungen Bismarcks zu Amerikanern*. After that came publication of such studies as *From Bismarck to Hitler* (1935) and *The Blood and Iron Chancellor* (1967), as well as articles on phases of Bismarck's career. The name of Herbert Bismarck emerged again and again in these studies. Thus far there has been no full-length study of his life.

I should like to express my thanks to the New York Public Library, the library of the City University of New York, the British Museum, and the libraries at the universities at Bonn, Cologne, and Frankfurt-am-Main in West Germany. It is to be regretted that some of our leading university libraries in the United States have adopted a policy of closed access to non-campus researchers, a blow to the cherished American freedom of scholarship.

To Ida Mae Brown Snyder, my career-long collaborator and editor, I owe not only warm thanks but a sense of gratefulness for her remarkable work in improving this manuscript. It is a humbling experience to write the perfect sentence and then find that it needs revision after all.

Princeton, N.J.

Louis L. Snyder

DIPLOMACY IN IRON

IRON

The Life of Herbert von Bismarck

1
THE BISMARCK DYNASTY HAS AN HEIR

The fiery, headstrong thirty-two-year-old squire of Schönhausen, Otto Eduard Leopold von Bismarck, was thoroughly bored by his rural occupation, compounded as it was of agricultural administration, bookkeeping by double entry, and dreams at night about threshing, manure, and stubble fields. To relieve the monotony he sought satisfaction in riding, swimming, duck-shooting, gambling, drinking, and whoring. Apparently he had not outgrown his student life at Göttingen, where he was remembered as a duelist and general hell-raiser. When some friends failed to meet him for an appointment in the early morning, he galloped off to their home. Finding the door barricaded with a chest of drawers, he fired a shot through the open window so that the plaster would shower down on them. Neighbors were shocked by his insatiable appetite for food and drink, as well as by his disgraceful appearance. Clothes meant nothing to him.

No wonder that Bismarck's unsavory reputation led to the amusing appellation of "Mad Junker"* and to several broken engagements. This Pomeranian eccentric was noted for wildness and arrogance in an area where pietism was fashionable.

Yet, despite head-shaking predictions, the marriage of Bismarck to the

---

*Junker: landowning class of Prussia and east Germany, which, during the German Empire (1871-1918), maintained considerable political power. Politically, Junkers were strongly conservative, monarchist, and supporters of military tradition.

quiet and pious Johanna von Puttkamer turned out to be a singularly happy one. That it took place at all indicated the kind of persistence that was to characterize Bismarck throughout his entire eventful life. He met Johanna, daughter of a landowner, at a friend's manor house. Small, dark, and slight, graceful and natural, she had been brought up in the Revivalist circles of her Pomeranian home and educated in a spirit of rigorous piety. Nevertheless, she was instantly attracted to the "monster of Schönhausen." Her mother was dismayed when she learned that Johanna proposed to marry the mad Bismarck. But the wily young Junker knew what to do. He wrote Heinrich von Puttkamer, Johanna's father, an extraordinary letter, ingeniously calculated to impress the recipient. Employing ecclesiastical phraseology altogether foreign to his usual mode of life, he confessed the errors of his past, and sprinkled the entire letter with plentiful references to God. He would not, he wrote, dwell upon his own feelings and designs in regard to the young lady, for the step he was taking spoke more loudly and eloquently than words. He would not try to further his cause by promises, for the untrustworthiness of the human heart was well-known. His only guarantee "for the welfare of your daughter is to be found in my prayer for the blessing of the Lord."

The pious father was most reluctant to give his daughter to one of whom he had heard so much evil and so little good. His answer was noncommittal. Thereupon, having prepared the way, the suitor visited the home of the parents, displayed his talent for charm, and within a short time conquered the entire household. He waltzed with his Johanna, drank champagne with her father, and earnestly discussed religion with his future mother-in-law. It was the kind of frontal attack, suitably planned, which was to distinguish the irrepressible Junker throughout his life.

Otto and Johanna were married on July 28, 1847, shortly after a new phase in his career had begun. At the beginning of 1847, Frederick William IV had summoned the States General for the first time, and, as a representative of the lower nobility, young Bismarck had to attend the meeting in Berlin. It was the start of an extraordinary political career.

A daughter, Marie, was born to the couple on August 21, 1848. Bismarck happily welcomed his first child – he would have been satisfied, he said, even if it were a kitten, and on bended knee he thanked God that Johanna's ordeal was safely over. In October 1849 Johanna, again pregnant, came to Berlin where her husband, now a deputy in the Prussian *Landtag*, had taken a house at Behrenstrasse 60, corner Wilhelmstrasse.[1] In a small, ground-floor apartment the couple lived in *gemütlich,* almost Bohemian, fashion. Johanna served her food-conscious husband beefsteaks on wooden platters with peasant's bread and the grease of broiled goose, plus liberal supplies of Pomeranian wine. Often during meals Johanna would get up to see after the baby – the Bismarcks could not yet afford a maid.

Johanna took weekly piano lessons, a pursuit interrupted on December 28, 1849, by the addition of a son to the small family. [2] It was a difficult birth. Johanna, always frail, became very ill. Ordinarily kind and considerate, she became moody and quarrelsome, arguing constantly with her distraught husband. Of these difficult days she wrote in her diary: "The whole day nagging, two days silence!" Bismarck saw it and tore out the offensive page.[3]

On February 11, 1850, Bismarck wrote a formal request to Pastor Gossner to baptize his son:

> Although I do not have the honor to know you personally, nevertheless, because we have many friends in common, I hope that you will not refuse to baptize my first-born son. I permit myself the humble request that Your Reverence will come to discuss this holy ceremony, day after tomorrow, Wednesday the 13th at about 11:30 in the morning at my dwelling in the Dorotheanstrasse 37. If you agree I request that you allow me to visit you tomorrow afternoon or evening at your home so that I can discuss the matter further with you.
>
> With sincere respect for Your Reverence,
>
> VON BISMARCK-SCHÖNHAUSEN, ABG. II.[4]

The formal ceremony took place in Berlin's Jerusalem Church. The infant heir was christened Nikolaus Heinrich Ferdinand Herbert von Bismarck-Schönhausen. The name Herbert was taken after that of the first known Bismarck, Herbert von Bismarck, who in 1270 was Master of the Guild of Clothiers in the city of Standhal.[5] The special name of Nikolaus was in honor of the Russian Emperor, who was regarded by Bismarck as the strongest advocate in the world of the royalist and conservative order.[6]

The rising young Junker, although concerned about the health of his wife, was deliriously happy with his chubby infant son. To Gustav Scharlach, who had been his fraternity brother at Göttingen, he wrote that the greatest happiness had come through his marriage, which had brought him unclouded sunshine and two wonderful children.[7] He credited his wife with the remarkable change in his way of living: "The happy married life and the children God has given me are to me as the rainbow that gives me the pledge of reconciliation after the deluge of degeneracy and want of love which in previous years covered my soul."[8]

Bismarck ruled his brood with affectionate and benevolent tyranny. The

5

DIPLOMACY IN IRON

thoroughness of the future German Chancellor can be detected in this letter of the newly married Bismarck to his wife in which he gave detailed instructions for the rearing of Herbert:

> My Dear: After I had written this morning, I got your letter, which disturbed me because of the complaint about the young fellow. I went to Bücking, and I shall give you his advice and see that it goes to you this evening by train. He says, a loss in flesh, constipation, and, as a result, a loss of appetite is a natural thing after the weaning, and will be worsened when the child, because of the use of sugar in his bottle, will suffer from sour stomach. His advice is to give him only unskimmed cow's milk immediately after milking in the stalls, to bring him daily into the open air, even if he gets a cough and sniffles from it, only not when it rains and even less in the wind. Fresh air is the important thing, even in the room. Heated air is too dry for children....

> In addition to the cow's milk, he should have lean beef, if you have it, but no gravy soup. For drugs B. [Bücking] recommends chamomilla: give it to him in tea form when there is restlessness or sleeplessness. No purgatives, all of which weaken the stomach, no wheat rolls, no sugar, which will give him acid stomach and loss of appetite.

> This whole change of diet he wants to be used at once, because the little fellow has not been doing too well. He must be sponge-washed each day – cold water on the back. However, above all, fresh air, outside of rain and strong wind, and plenty of air in the nursery. If he cries for a few days, don't give him too much sugar, for only a strong stomach can take it. Also, if he is constipated for a few days, that is no misfortune. B. says that if you carry all this out he will guarantee success, if the child has a healthy constitution, and that he has.[9]

Herbert, however, was a sickly infant and child, even if plump. He was a constant source of anxiety to both parents. During the first six years of the child's life, he was ill on many occasions. Again and again Bismarck urged his wife to see to it that the boy did not catch cold: "Take *great* care – *more* than seems necessary."[10] He even advised against too frequent bathing: "I am afraid of it; dirt is always better than sickness."[11] From Berlin he wrote on February 18, 1851: "I have spoken to Simon again about our youngster; he says the gland swellings are entirely without danger, and that nothing should be done except to poultice them when they are ready to burst; therefore, let the infamous iodine alone, otherwise the boy will suffer the after-effects for years, in his teeth and elsewhere. Even if the glands become hardened, that will pass off without the aid of medicine."[12] He complained that his children had been weakened by the "exaggerated fearfulness" of the women in the household,[13] conveniently forgetting that he was guilty of more anxiety than they. When the children were in comparatively good health, he praised God that they were well "despite the cold and the bad heating of the house."[14]

The young father protested humorously against the responsibilities of parenthood, and especially against the parading of his domestic life before the public. When the whole family had to travel together, he was both annoyed and amused, as indicated in this letter to his sister: "I already picture myself with the children on the platform at Genthin, then both of them in the railway carriage, incontinently satisfying their needs and making a nasty smell. The other travellers sniff pointedly, Johanna is ashamed to give the baby the breast, and he screams until he is blue in the face.... Yesterday I was in such despair at the prospect of all these annoyances, that I positively made up my mind to give the idea of the journey the go-by. Then, in the night, Johanna attacked me, carrying the baby in her arms, and, making use of all the feminine arts which cost our race the privilege of living in paradise. She was naturally able to take me over, so that we have gone back to our original plan. But I seem to myself a person to whom a terrible injustice has been done. Next year, I shall certainly have to travel with three cradles, nurses, swaddling clothes, and so on....If only my allowance as deputy were larger because I am a family man! Fancy squandering the remnants of a once fine property upon travelling with a pack of infants! I am very unlucky!"[15]

This was all tongue-in-cheek complaint, without substance, for the truth was that Bismarck was entranced with his first-born son. He dutifully recorded that one day, while he was working at his desk, the two-year-old Herbert came in with a girl's "infamous" cap on his head, put his fat hands on the table, and asked: "Papa, what are you writing?[16]

After the second son William was born on August 1, 1852, the concerned father had his hands full. He complained, when they were youngsters. "They make too much noise for me, and give each other bloody noses."[17] Bernhard von Bülow, who later became the German Chancellor, knew Herbert and his brother Bill when he was a boy in Frankfurt-am-Main (Bismarck was then Prussian envoy at the German *Bund* from 1851-58). "My earliest memory of Herbert," Bülow wrote in his memoirs, "is of playing with him in Frankfurt and with his brother Bill, and our little friend Christa Eisendecher, who was to change her name to Eickstedt-Peterswaldt. There was a streak of brutality in both brothers. Herbert and Bill wanted to make Christa kiss a fat toad. My brother Adolf and I defended her, and this led to a pitched battle."[18]

Bismarck was careful to preserve what he believed to be the complete independence of his sons. Although Johanna protested against the practice, he never asked his sons, or allowed them to be asked, where they were going. Even when they were only six years old he permitted them to act freely for themselves.[19] But he did not extend this freedom to their studies, which he carefully guided. Every Saturday morning they had to come to him with their schoolbooks and give him an account of all they had learned during the week. He then examined them painstakingly on their scholastic knowledge.[20] The boys were uninhibited savages at play, but they were serious in their scholastic work.[21] When they wrote letters to their father he expected them "to read the letters through with great care before they are mailed, so that they can be certain as to where they have left out words and mixed them up, so that they can correct them — that much time they must take."[22]

Bismarck carried on a happy correspondence with his eldest son. The tenor of these communications from Paris may be judged from this typical letter sent to Herbert, who was then twelve and one-half years old:

My dear Herbert: I was very happy when I awoke and found your letter and Bill's. I am delighted to hear of all your daily experiences, especially about your studies, how far you have gotten in your work, what pleases you and what displeases you.

Day before yesterday I got a letter from Mama and also from Grandmother. I was just about to go to Fontainebleau to the Emperor. Therefore, I had to get up early and read the letter on the train, as well as one from Aunt Malwine from Landek. I read them as I rode the long way to the station, along the Seine and over the Place of the Bastille, where there is now a great victory column.

In Fontainebleau there is a great castle, to which many kings of France have added sections, from Louis the Pious on. The Emperor led me around the place and showed me, among other things, the mailed armor which Mondaldeschi wore under his clothes, when Queen Christine had him murdered. After some 200 years you could still see the blood stains on it as well as the holes which had been bored in the back between the chains in order to kill him.

Then we went to the pretty garden, with its mile-long forest with many deer. At breakfast I sat with the Empress, who is very attractive and charming.

Day after tomorrow I go for several days to England. I had wanted to go today, but I got too busy. We leave at 9 tomorrow, and shall be in London at 6 in the evening by way of Boulogne. On Thursday I hope with God's help to be back here again.

Tomorrow I send a courier to Berlin, for whom I have written so much that my fingers are tired. Now it is 12 and I shall go to bed. Give the enclosed to Mama. Now good night. May God protect you as much as He has up to now. Give all my heartiest greetings, also Bill, whom I shall answer next. Eat and drink moderately and do some work daily, if your tutor is away. Also do not forget your French!

Your Father,

v B.[23]

Both Herbert and William attended the old Werdeschen *Gymnasium.* A fellow student, Paul Zauleck, tells how the two Bismarcks, then eighteen and fifteen and one-half at the end of January 1868, performed in a Schiller play. "Count Bismarck attended the performance and applauded stormily. We were surprised when eight days later Herbert Bismarck invited us on behalf of his parents to dinner. We were happy and proud to visit the Bismarck home. Herbert presented us to his good, genuinely womanly mother and his sister. When we came into the salon after dinner, Bismarck called to the officer who was present: 'Friend, come here a moment, we must certainly establish who is the tallest in our party today. Herbert is taller than I, that I know, and you are taller than Herbert. But Herr Zauleck seems to be taller than you.' We two rivals then had to stand back to back, and Bismarck laughed happily when by the examination I carried the day. Then our host offered us Manila cigars, urged us and his sons to sit down in the salon, and, as the rest of the company retired to the living room, he began graciously to tell us of his own student days."[24]

Undoubtedly, Bismarck told his young guests of his experiences as a student at the University of Göttingen, but, in view of his care in supervising the education of his sons, it is questionable how much of the truth he told on this occasion.[25] In the summer of 1832 the citizens of staid Göttingen took the young nobleman, Otto von Bismarck, for an escaped lunatic. He wore a cap embroidered in crimson and gold, a dressing gown of many colors strapped tightly around his loins with a leather girdle in which were thrust two horse-pistols and which supported a long, basket-hilted *Schlä- ger*, or duelling sword. On his feet were a pair of red Turkish slippers, while his legs were bare from the ankles to the knees. In one hand he brandished an oaken cudgel and in the other he carried a small notebook, in which he recorded the dates of approaching duels. The young man was preceded by a *Deckel (Dachshund),* a hound with a long body and short legs and a tail as graceful as a pig's. Bismarck tied a wreath of artificial flowers around the dog's neck and decorated its tail with fancy-colored ribbons. In this guise the young Junker strode through the streets of Göttingen, heedless of spectator reaction. But when any student laughed, that unfortunate was required to apologize to Bismarck's dog ("who does not understand words") by keeping him company in jumping over a stick. Either this, or a duel!

The anxious father who wanted his sons to study hard had paid little attention to his own studies at Göttingen. One of his professors noted on Bismarck's scholastic papers that he had never seen Herr von Bismarck in his lecture room, although the young Junker was registered for the course. On one occasion Bismarck hurled an empty beer bottle from his lodgings at the head of an innocent passerby – a professor, of course, as a result of which the cantankerous Bismarck had to spend some time in the student jail.[26]

In the winter of 1832, Bismarck, his American friend, John Lothrop Motley,[27] and Count Keyserling, continued their studies at the University of Berlin, where Bismarck's bizarre behavior continued. One day the three comrades, finding themselves without money, repaired to the corner of Unter den Linden and Friedrichstrasse, the busiest corner in Berlin, donned dark glasses, drew tin cups from their pockets, and began to whine the familiar beggar's tune. In a short time the three hungry students had enough funds for a magnificent beefsteak dinner.

The three friends regarded a certain Baron von Ropp, a cousin of Bismarck's, as a Philistine because he studied too zealously. Von Ropp would lock himself in his room in the afternoons in order to avoid the company of the three disturbers. The latter avenged themselves by painting a sign on von Ropp's door: *"Hier sind zwei junge Elefanten zu sehen – Eintritt frei!!* ("Here are two young elephants on exhibition – entrance free!!") The result was that the earnest young student was almost driven out of his wits by the pounding of visitors seeking a free look at two young elephants.

The reformed Bismarck probably carefully edited his experiences when he described them to his impressionable sons. On March 3, 1869, they completed their preparatory work by passing the *Abiturienten* examination, and were promptly registered at the University of Bonn.[28] A few days later, as a reward for passing their examinations, the two young Bismarcks were sent on a vacation trip to London. Although they were asked to stay at the German Embassy, they preferred the Grosvenor Hotel. Friedrich von Holstein, who later was to become one of the most important political personalities in Germany after Bismarck,[29] reported on the boys' behavior in London: "For the last eight days the young Bismarcks *[Herbert and Bill]* have been here with Eisendecher....[30] The two youngsters amuse themselves, it seems to me, altogether unbelievably. My two friends,

Southwell and Digby, go to a lot of trouble to teach them the English way of doing things, with riding, driving four-in-hands, rowing, boxing, etc. Yesterday and the day before yesterday we rowed from Windsor to London, the five of us, 40 English miles, for a part of the time against the tide and wind. Since I haven't done this for a long time, my hands are in a curious state. Bernstorff[31] doesn't like all this; he would rather see them in society, but after the first attempt they couldn't be brought back again. He doesn't know that their favorite occupation is, above all, boxing. They even get up early in order not to miss their lessons. The teacher, a former boxer by profession, is astonished by their progress."[32]

After Herbert and William had registered at the University of Bonn, they became active in the Borussia, the crack local fraternity corps, to which, since its infancy, members of the Prussian royal house had belonged in their university days. Although their father had attended the Universities of Göttingen and Berlin, at this time he was apparently impressed by Bonn's aristocratic *numerus clausus,* and by the fact that it was widely considered to be "an intellectual nursery of hereditary monarchism, of intense loyalty, and of approved political principles generally."[33] The beautiful little university town, nestled among the wooded hills and castle ruins of the Seven Mountains, had taken the place of Heidelberg as the preferred choice of royal and aristocratic students. Prince Albert of Saxe-Coburg, who later became the husband of Queen Victoria, had set the fashion, along with his brother, Ernst. A long series of royal and princely students enrolled at Bonn. Frederick William, later Emperor Frederick III, attended the university from 1849 to 1851.

The two young Bismarcks quickly found themselves at home in Bonn. They took part with much delight in the drinking and singing meetings characteristic of fraternity life and managed to show a more than average capacity for beer and other beverages. Herbert, especially, was proud of his father's duelling record at Göttingen. The elder Bismarck had fought twenty-five duels in his first three terms at Göttingen, and was only once wounded, probably a deliberate loss in order to carry the duelling scars throughout his life. As a Prussian aristrocrat, Herbert regarded student duels as a means of acquiring a degree of firmness he would need in later life.

In late November 1869 the Bismarcks received the shocking news that Herbert had been wounded in a duel. The wound itself was not serious, but a blood infection had set in. Frau Bismarck hurried to the side of her son, who was unable to leave his bed during the month of December.[34]

Meanwhile, Bismarck sent agitated letters to his wife:

Berlin, Dec. 7, 1869: Of the poor weak boy I can find little that is assuring in your reports, though still my reliance on God's help is firm. How recklessly they must have neglected him! Greet my beloved youngster heartily, and keep him right quiet; he will still be patient and weak, but if his strength, with God's help, begins to return, great caution will be needed to keep him from presuming on it....Love to the dear children, comfort Herbert, keep him quietly patient and spare yourself.

Berlin, Dec. 13, 1869: God be thanked that your letters are of comforting tenor. The retiring disease still rises and falls perhaps, but on the whole keeps on the ebb, and through your accounts of the situation there breaks now and then a comforting bit of humor, which indicates that the spirit of joy is uppermost in your heart....

With all Herbert's good prospects, I cannot yet but fear the he will not be able to travel at Christmas. Will it suit you if we keep the holiday together in Bonn, or is the poor boy so weak that it would be inadvisable?...The journey would not hurt me; there must be lodgings to be found there, so that Herbert will not be disturbed....If Herbert could leave his room, by that time there might be a place near Bonn – Rolandsbeck, Honnef, or the like – where we could spend a few days quietly together.[35]

The distraught family spent Christmas at Bonn. On the last day of 1869 the parents decided to take Herbert back to Berlin, where he recovered from his wound. He then enrolled at the University of Berlin for further study.

Herbert's career as a son of an extraordinary father was well under way. There it was – a story as old as the human race: over-indulgent father, fascinated by the very existence of his son, his greatest pride, and determined to push him to heights he would achieve in his own career; spoiled brat of a son, wild and carefree, slavishly devoted to his father, contemptuous of others. In his role as heir-apparent he would carry a heavy psychic burden throughout his life. His intimate collaboration with Bismarck Sr. would serve to hamper his own sense of manhood.

The formula persisted throughout Herbert's childhood, adolescence, and manhood: always the coarse and venomous attitude toward those he did not like and especially to anyone who was unlucky enough to incur his hatred. Even as an adult he could revert to childish behavior. One object of his scorn was Gerson von Bleichröder, his father's trusted banker, who remained "that stinking brute Bleichröder." Berlin was abuzz with stories about Herbert's deliberate rudeness to his father's financial advisor. As a grown man he was to indulge in such infantile pranks as setting off firecrackers while the blind Bleichröder was waiting in the Chancellery.[36]

Two British poets came to the same conclusion about the phenomenon. In the seventeenth century John Milton wrote in *Paradise Regained:* "The childhood shows the man, as morning shows the day." And in the nineteenth century William Wordsworth stated in *My Heart Leaps Up When I Behold:* "The child is father to the man."

Kikeriki, August 15, 1870

THE BERLINER PEACOCK

"No wonder he is proud!"

All the world was astounded by the quick Prussian victories after the opening of the Franco-Prussian War. The caricature shows Bismarck as a peacock strutting proudly. The main feathers are titled after Prussian victories. The final stunning victory came at Sedan two weeks after the publication of this cartoon.

Figaro, March 5, 1870

BISMARCK CRACKS THE WHIP IN THE NORTH GERMAN REICHSTAG

14

GOOD WEATHER   CHANGEABLE   STORM

"No Minister or Ambassador should
be without this guide"

In *Kladderadatsch*, the German satirical magazine, 1881. Bismarck's
three hairs became the cartoonists' delight.

Kladderadatsch, 1883

BISMARCK DEFENDS THE TRIPLE ALLIANCE

In 1882 Bismarck completed the formation of the Triple Alliance, including
Germany, Austria - Hungary, and Italy. The cartoonist shows how the alliance
provided "warmth for cold blood."

Kladderadatsch, 1887

BISMARCK AS FAUST

Faust: I greet you, thou only phial
      Which I with devotion bring down

     Show thy master thy favor!

   A cartoon shows Bismarck as Faust reaching for a *Wählurne* (ballot box) and asks for it to work its magic for him. This is an election commentary.

Kladderadatsch, 1890

THE RETIRED CHANCELLOR TURNS IN HIS THREE HAIRS, 1890

   Throughout Bismarck's career the satirical German magazine, *Kladderadatsch*, had depicted Bismarck again and again with his three hairs. In the issue of March 1890 Bismarck is shown relinquishing his insignia as he departs for Friedrichsruh.

16

Punch, March 29, 1890

DROPPING THE PILOT

One of the most famous political cartoons of all time shows Bismarck, the pilot, leaving the ship of state. The young Emperor, William II, now in responsible command, leans over to witness the departure.

2

FROM WAR TO CHANCELLOR'S AMANUENSIS, 1870-81

"Not by speeches and majorities will the great questions of the day be decided – that was the mistake of 1848 and 1849 – but by iron and blood."

On September 30, 1862, shortly after his appointment as Minister-President of Prussia, Otto von Bismarck made this remark before thirty members of the budget commission of the Prussian Lower House. The words spread throughout the country with the rhythm changed to "blood and iron." They may well have been a slip of the tongue, but they adhered like pitch to Bismarck's name. He never repudiated his words. He explained somewhat lamely that by this allusion he meant that the weapons of war had first to shed human blood before great decisions became possible.

In fact, Bismarck was summarizing a historical trend of the nineteenth century. This recognition of the power of might in human affairs was to become a trend of the times. For Germany it provided a guiding light for Bismarck's three wars of national unification, against Denmark in 1864, Austria in 1866, and France in 1870-71. The hard-bitten Prussian Junker always insisted that these wars were forced upon him – the innocent diplomat. Many historians reject Bismarck's view and claim that the three wars were consequences of his openly professed "iron and blood" policy.

In defense of his position, Bismarck pointed out that he had two growing sons and he had no desire to sacrifice them in an unwanted war. But if war came they would do their duty. His sons were always on his mind. As early as January 2, 1861, when William I ascended the throne of Prussia, Bismarck, then envoy at St. Petersburg, sent his Majesty a long telegram of congratulations, concluding with this sentence:

...MAY GOD GIVE YOUR MAJESTY A LONG AND BLESSED REIGN AND MAY HE ALLOW ME TO RAISE MY SONS JUST AS FAITHFUL SERVANTS OF THE EXALTED ROYAL HOUSE AS I HAVE ALWAYS STRIVEN TO BE.

VON BISMARCK[1]

It was a typical gesture: Bismarck was preoccupied with his sons, especially with matters concerning their health and their performance as Prussians. Robert von Keudell told how Bismarck was with his king on a hilltop near Königgrätz on July 3, 1866, during the war with Austria: "Bismarck was mounted on a huge chestnut-colored horse. Wearing a great cloak, his great eyes gleaming from beneath his steel helmet, he was a wonderful sight, and reminded me of the tales I had been told in childhood about giants of the frozen north." The mythological hero soon vanished, to be succeeded by a father worried about his own offspring: "After several minutes we came to a spot where several shattered corpses lay. Bismarck turned to me and said in low tones: 'It makes me sick at heart, when I think about it, that Herbert may be lying like this some day.'"[2]

Bismarck's hopes and fears were both justified upon the outbreak of war against France on July 15, 1870. Both Herbert and William promptly left the University of Bonn and volunteered as Dragoons in the Cuirassiers of the Guards, serving in the ranks in the same regiment whose uniform their father was entitled to wear.[3] Father Bismarck took enormous pride in this action of his two sons[4] and boasted that there was no nepotism in the Prussian Government when his two sons were serving as privates.[5] Journalist Moritz Busch, who accompanied Bismarck on his battlefield tours, recorded that he repeatedly remarked to officers: "You can see that there is little nepotism among us. Bill has served now for almost twelve months and has not yet been promoted to *Fähnrich* [*officer aspirant*], although others have made it in four weeks. I don't know how it came about. I have inquired whether he had gotten drunk and the like, but it seems not. His conduct has been good. At Mars-la-Tour...he had his horse shot out from under him. No nepotism is certainly a good thing, but being kept from promotion is indeed bitter."[6] The father was suffering for his sons.

At the outset of the war against France, Bismarck issued specific orders to his sons, added as a postscript in a letter to Herbert:

Mainz, August 6, 1870

My beloved Boy: Hearty thanks for your letter of two days since, received today; where this will find you I do not know. We go with the King tomorrow morning to the border; I should like to meet there the dear blue colors.

The beginning, under God's blessing is good; would it might keep so to the end. From Weissenbourg, 400 French prisoners came through here today, and 400 through Darmstadt. At Saarbrück today the retreating marauders, who fired this unfortified town in their wantonness, were overtaken by Göben and [*Froissard's corps*] utterly routed. Within a few days the same, with God's help, will be the case with the main army. I have good news of your mother, only throw in the mail frequent letters for her, when you can. I hope she will soon be at Nauheim.

Hearty love to Bill, and join me and your mother in prayer that God will reunite us all in health, but, above all, that He will give us victory of His grace.

Faithfully, your father,

V. BISMARCK

Should either of you be wounded, telegraph me at this King's headquarters as quickly as you can. But not to your mother first.[7]

Anxious to see for himself what was happening during the opening weeks of the campaign, Bismarck stayed close to the front. Wherever he went he repeatedly expressed to officers the hope that he would by chance meet his sons.[8] He kept his wife informed. On August 14, 1870, he wrote to Johanna: "I would be very happy if I could get just one word from Bill and Herbert. The Dragoons are 6-8 miles from here; today on the other side of the Mosel, between Metz and Nancy. God protect the young ones from sickness and wounds."[9] Two days later he wired his wife: "Herbert and Bill were seen very well today."[10] That same day he wrote from Pont-à-Mousson "My dear: I have sent a telegram today to you in which I reported that a Dragoon had seen Herbert and Bill in good health just four miles from here."[11]

Bismarck was not aware of it at the time, but his sons were to take part that same day in one of the bloodiest and costliest battles of the war. On August 16, 1870, at Vionville, also called Mars-la-Tour, Prince Frederick Charles led a desperate encounter with a French force nearly twice as large as his own. There were two cavalry charges, in the first of which Bismarck's sons took part and which, in the opinion of one historian, was fully equal to the charge of the Six Hundred at Balaklava.[12] The losses on both sides were tremendous. The bloody days of Mars-la-Tour and Grave-lotte placed in mourning nearly every noble family in Prussia.[13]

Bismarck was with the King nearby in the early morning after the battle when an officer came up and in low tones reported to General von Moltke. When the general looked alarmed, Bismarck instantly asked whether the matter concerned him or not. The officer replied that in the last attack made by the First Dragoon Guards, Count Herbert Bismarck had fallen and Count William had been mortally wounded. When the shocked father asked for the source of the news, he was informed that it came from the general in command of the Tenth Corps, von Voigts-Rheta.[14]

Visibly distressed, Bismarck had his horse saddled, rode off without a word, and, in the company of his cousin (Count Theodor von Bismarck-Bohlen) began to search the field hospitals about an hour's ride away. Eventually, he found Herbert at a farm house near Mariaville, where there were many other wounded soldiers. The men were under the charge of a surgeon, who had been unable to obtain a supply of water and who was reluctant to appropriate for the use of his patients the turkeys and chickens that were running around the yard. "He said he could not," Bismarck recounted later, "and all our arguments were in vain. I then threatened to shoot the poultry with my own revolver and afterwards gave him 20 francs to pay for fifteen. At last I remembered that I was a Prussian General and ordered him to do as I told, whereupon he obeyed me. However, I had to look for the water myself and to have it fetched in barrels."[15]

Apparently, the situation was not as bad as it had been reported to the frantic father. William had come out of the fiery gulf unharmed – his horse had been shot from under him and he had fallen, only to get up and continue forward. He brought back with him a wounded comrade, whom he had thrown on a horse at the risk of being captured himself.[16] Herbert escaped by what seemed to be a miracle: one bullet struck his watch, another went through his coat, but a third wounded him. "It's not bad," William reported to his father, "Herbert has only a wound in his thigh."[17] The bullet had not touched the bone, but had gone clear through the young man's thigh.

Relieved, and delighted by the performance of his sons in battle, Bismarck dispatched a telegram to his wife Johanna:

I HAVE JUST SPOKEN TO HERBERT AND BILL. BILL'S HORSE WAS SHOT FROM UNDER HIM, HE HIMSELF IS VERY WELL. HERBERT HAS RECEIVED A WOUND THROUGH THE THIGH,

NOT DANGEROUS, BONES UNINJURED. HE WILL COME TO ME
THIS EVENING. THEN I WILL DIRECT HIM TO NAUHEIM, SO THAT
YOU CAN GO THERE! PHIPP IS WELL.

BISMARCK[18]

That same day Bismarck sent a detailed letter to his wife:

Pont-à-Mousson,

17 August, 1870

My dear: The main facts I telegraphed you. We were alarmed today
at three in the morning, rode for four miles where I heard by accident
that the 1st Dragoon Guards had many losses, rode two miles across
fields with many challenges and little danger, found Herbert with 250
wounded in a farmhouse, Bill visiting him under the excuse of looking
for another horse; he really found a lean mare.

Herbert lay near Szerdahely [*2. G.Drag.*], and he seemed to be all
right, only two well bandaged holes in his left thigh, where the bullet
went in and came out. I had my wagon stopped there, and remained
for four hours waiting for him, and when he came he found that sitting
down was painful and the heat was too great.

I left him with the Chancellory servant, Krüger, requisitioned an
ambulance, in which he will come here when it gets cooler in the
evening. He also had two shots through his clothing, one of which
smashed my black wooden watch. I took it with me and left with him
my 10-franc watch which I had bought in St. Avold. I am bringing the
black one for you, and we shall buy another one here.

For Herbert, the campaign is now over, and he, if God doesn't will
any further misfortune, is protected against further danger, since it
will take him several weeks to recover. I shall send him immediately
by rail to Germany. How would it be if you nursed him in Nauheim?
If he does not get the cross, I shall never wear any decorations
again.

Wesdehlen, Westarp, Reuss, Kleist are all right. Auerwald was shot
in the abdomen and badly wounded; he also lies there. The three
squadrons which attacked lost 12 officers, other men uncounted.
Everyone a hero!... [19]

Herbert was brought into headquarters and a bed was prepared for him
in his father's room.[20] His wound quickly became black and infected, leading his father to believe the bullets (French *mitrailleuse* – machine-gun
bullets) were covered with a poisonous substance.[21] For the next week
Bismarck's interest in the war was tempered by his concern for Herbert,
who, although cheerful was in great pain. The father dutifully reported to

his wife every detail of the early days of convalescence, noting that Herbert's desire to smoke had returned, that purulent discharge of the wound had begun, that his fever had gone down, and that the father had to obtain trousers for him because he now had none.[22] When the Crown Prince, who was to become Frederick III, visited headquarters at Vacouleurs on August 20th for a council of war with Generals von Moltke and von Roon, he noted in his diary that he had "paid a visit to the Minister Count von Bismarck, in whose anteroom lay his eldest son Herbert, badly wounded in the leg at Mars-la-Tour."[23]

On August 24th Herbert was placed on a troop transport and sent to Nauheim. It was now Johanna's turn to report on the condition of Herbert. "Thursday evening Herbert was brought here," she wrote to her husband. "I arranged everything for your child and always sit at his bed. I am very happy to have him and to watch over him, but am very much disturbed because he has so much pain. I get very much afraid when I see the two big wounds in his poor thigh, where the French bullets went in and out, so that he often whimpers pitifully."[24]

Herbert's first attempt to walk failed; the wound began to bleed freely. Complications set in and he again became feverish. The solicitous mother bitterly excoriated the French for what they had done to her son, denouncing them in terms that Gothic and Frankish women must have used when the horns of battle were blown. "Not one stone must be left above another in France," said Johanna.[25] Convalescing Herbert, however, animated by excellent claret, struck up his favorite ditty in a loud voice – Scheffel's song about the Swabian Duke, Krock, who sallied forth from Böblingen to lay waste the whole of Gaul.[26]

There was joy in Bismarckdom! The sons had performed well in combat. Their parents were grateful they had been spared. The Chancellor's knightly sentiment as a Junker needed the certainty of having male heirs. He could not forget that he had lost his composure in the presence of the King at Gravelotte, when he heard that his sons were in the midst of battle. Now he felt that they had had enough, and he took care to see that they were not ordered to the front again. He asked Johanna not to worry about Bill: "A regiment such as the Dragoons which has suffered so much will not without urgent need be placed under fire again."[27] William was finally transferred to General von Manteuffel's army command, where he was free of all danger. For the father there was no nepotism here: William had done his share of fighting.

Bismarck's combination of feelings – pride in his sons and concern for Herbert – was expressed in two letters sent to Herbert in September 1870:

Reims, September 7, 1870

My dear young fellow: Today while dining the King informed me that you had been named to officer, Bill to officer-aspirant.[28]...I am happy that you won it in combat and after so brilliant a military action as that of the regiment on the 16th. May God give you long years to think back on it, with thanks for the grace that protected both of you in this blood bath. The other ministers were more unfortunate with their sons; of Itzenplitz you know; Roon's good young son was shot through the abdomen by a rifle shot[29] and died on the 3rd in the evening. My poor old Roon is sick with grief and lies in bed; he told me that Leonhardt also lost his son. There will be very few families at home without sadness....On the 1st we took some 90,000 prisoners, 60 generals, and 6000 officers or men in officer's grades....God protect you, my old fellow, and may He soon give you back your leg. Heartiest greetings.

Your father,

v.B[30]

Ferrières, 23 September, 1870

(Today, eight years ago, I recall, I became Minister.)

My dear young fellow: I received today two letters from your mother of the 15th and 16th, from which I learn with sorrow that it still doesn't go well with your wound. You have had a bad year physically, but, nevertheless, I praise God for helping you through the charge of your regiment on the 16th of August, for it was not given to many to live through that charge and can tell about it today. With God's help your leg will not become stiff, but the movement will be kind of rusty for some time, say the doctors; the tearing of the muscles is too great; the replacement of tissue and the working of the new cartilages proceed very slowly. Roon's wound was a lighter one. Despite all this, God has willed that we shall make many rides together in the Varzin forests. There's not much riding to be done here so the Crown Prince asks me to tell you, for he was here when I got your mother's letter and read the motherly complaints....

I hope and beg God for a quick end and complete recovery for you, the son of my heart [*Herzensjunge*], with a thousand greetings.

v.B.[31]

Bismarck was anxious that his sons be decorated for valor. "For my part," he wrote to his wife from Versailles on October 8, 1870, "I cannot demand the cross for my sons, but they have earned it without doubt."[32]

In his letter to Johanna, written on August 17th, directly after he had found his wounded son, Bismarck underlined part of the sentence: *"If he does not get the cross,* I shall never wear any decorations again."[33] At Christmas, Bismarck sent Herbert a fine sword, apparently his own substitute for a medal. But he carefully avoided saying anything to the King about a decoration. In the meantime, William was awarded the Iron Cross. Later, at dinner, Bismarck told the journalist Moritz Busch that it would have been better had his eldest son been given the decoration, because he had been wounded in the famous cavalry charge at Mars-la-Tour. "It is an accident," he remarked. "Others, who were not wounded could have been just as brave. But for the wounded it is indeed a distinction, a kind of equalizer....I remember when I was a young man that a certain Herr von Reuss ran around Berlin, and he also had the Iron Cross. I wondered what he had done, and learned that he had had a Minister as an uncle and had served as an office boy for the General Staff."[34]

Despite the sarcasm, Bismarck was pleased when he received a telegram on February 5, 1871, informing him that the King-Emperor had bestowed upon his son, Herbert von Bismarck, Second Lieutenant of the First Dragoon Guard Regiment, the Iron Cross Second Class.[35] Bismarck sent the telegram to his wife with the remark: "Finally, at last, but Herbert earned it in August and he should have had it while he was in the hospital."[36] Nevertheless, the award gave the father great satisfaction.

On November 6, 1870, Herbert sent a despairing letter to his father, complaining that, now that his wound had healed, he had been transferred to a depot on what amounted to inactive service. All he had had out of the whole war, he wrote was a fortnight's ride with his regiment and then three months on his back. Bismarck sent assistant Moritz Busch to Minister of War von Roon to see if anything could be done. Von Roon, however, dissuaded him with tears in his eyes – he had once interfered in a similar way and had lost his son in consequence.[37]

The performance of his sons in the Franco-Prussian War of 1870-71 remained a favorite source of conversation for the Iron Titan throughout the remainder of his life. But, on one occasion, his joy in relating the incident at Pont-à-Mousson backfired in an exchange with his wife which was not without political significance. In 1885 Bismarck was discussing the battle with Professor Ludwig Aegidi, who had met the distracted father at Pont-à-Mousson when he was searching for his sons. After telling his version of the story, Bismarck turned to his wife and said: "Imagine, if I telegraphed you that Herbert had fallen on the battlefield, without seeking to verify the news." "Then," answered Princess von Bismarck, "I would never have forgiven you for having started the war." This remark, reported Professor Aegidi, set Bismarck into a high degree of excitement. "What?" he exclaimed. "*I* began the war, I who three years beforehand had shown my love of peace so much in the Luxembourg question?" [38] German nationalist historians have always regarded the three wars of German unification (1864, 1866, and 1870-71) as having been forced upon a reluctant Bismarck, a point of view apparently not shared by Johanna von Bismarck. The great Chancellor was inured to diplomatic triumphs over foreigners, but not over his wife Johanna. With her, a mother's love came first.

What was to be done about Herbert now that the Second German Empire had been established? The father decided on a diplomatic career for his eldest son. He approached that task with characteristic German thoroughness [*Gründlichkeit*], placing Herbert at the bottom rung of the diplomatic ladder and then watching carefully as he advanced in his profession. In 1873, at the age of twenty-four, Herbert began service in the Foreign Office and was sent to Dresden and Munich to gain experience. The next year he was taken on by his father as private secretary, in which post he served intermittently, with probationary status at various other positions.

In March 1876 Herbert passed the State diplomatic examination. Then came a scintillating career. After working at the German Embassy at Berne, he was stationed in the winter of 1876-77 at the Embassy in Vienna. In 1882 he was made Councillor of the German Embassy in London; in January 1884 he was sent to St. Petersburg, and in July 1884, he became Ambassador at The Hague. At Christmas, 1884 he was called back to the Foreign Office, and in 1885 he again became Councillor of the Embassy in London. In 1885 his father made him Under-Secretary of State for Foreign Affairs, and in 1886 obtained the secretaryship for him. Between 1886 and 1890 he was his father's right-hand man in the Wilhelmstrasse. In December 1887 he was made a *Wirklicher Geheimer Rat* (Actual Privy Councillor), and in April 1888 he was given the additional post of State Minister in the Prussian State Ministry.

Nepotism? There is room for a difference of opinion on the role of favoritism in Herbert Bismarck's steady advancement. Throughout Herbert's career the anti-Bismarck camarilla denounced the Chancellor bitterly for the way he promoted the career of his eldest son. In an unguarded moment Bismarck admitted his special interest. In a conversation with the sculptor Professor K. Keil on September 7, 1876, Bismarck said in Herbert's presence: "The inclination of the heart is always a call of fate! For Herbert, who later will always be outside there, I will see to it that he gets a very satisfactory place."[39] Fritz von Holstein, who became Director of the Political Section of the Foreign Office, and who later was detested by both Bismarcks as "the blind worm" and "His Gray Eminence," concluded that "Bismarck, egotist to his finger-tips, sees in his eldest son the prolongation of his own ego."[40]

Although scarcely an objective observer, Holstein may well have been correct in his opinion. At any rate, during the period from 1874 to 1881, the Chancellor was convinced that he could place absolute reliance only upon his eldest son.[41] He felt that there was no one else on whom he could rely to understand his most secret thoughts and intentions and who could implement the great decisions he was always being called upon to make.[42] He had need of such loyal and discreet help, for had not Louis XIV once said that State secrets must be entrusted to the fewest possible hands?[43] Lord Ampthill, the observant British Ambassador in Berlin, reported back to Lord Granville on November 26, 1881: "Prince Bismarck adores this son, who is a remarkably clever youth, and hopes to make a great Statesman of him. He has often told me in confidence that Herbert, young as he is, would already make an abler Ambassador than all the Members of the German Dip. Body taken together!"[44]

Herbert's duties as his father's amanuensis and secretary consisted of a wide variety of tasks, which became increasingly important as time went by. They varied from minute personal matters to significant affairs of state. When in 1874 the Chancellor's weight reached 240 pounds and he decided to go to Kissingen for the cure, Herbert was called upon to obtain quarters for him and to arrange the baths in the house for him.[45] Herbert, as his father's direct intermediary with the Foreign Office, received the long coded telegrams and quickly prepared them for the Chancellor's attention.[46] He acted as his father's right hand, stretched out as a buffer against the hordes of busy officials and private persons who clamored to see him.

All these tasks the younger Bismarck performed with absolute loyalty and minute attention. The following excerpts from a letter sent by Herbert on November 10, 1879, to Lucius Freiherr von Ballhausen reveal how carefully the young diplomat regarded the instructions of his father:

> My father received Your Excellency's letter and has asked me to send you his thanks....
>
> My father is sorry that Herr von Benningsen was not elected.
>
> My father had wished Benningsen's election.
>
> My father is in complete agreement with your Excellency's suggestions.

For my father the railroad question before the *Landtag* session is
the most important....

The condition of my father, has praise God, become so much better
that my mother this morning left for Berlin.[47]

Always "My father." That was exactly the kind of attention the elder
Bismarck desired. The wear and tear of battles of state often sent him
home to Varzin in a nervous condition. He hesitated to come to Berlin
because he was afraid that the Emperor and others would give him too
much to do there.[48] On such occasions, he became furious and threatened
to resign, but generally gave orders to his son to handle irritating matters
in a precise way.

Foreign diplomats recognized the necessity of dealing with Bismarck
through his son, as evidenced by this letter sent by Saburov to Giers,[49]
Berlin, June 13, 1881:

Up to the receipt of your telegram of 20 May, I kept quiet, maintaining
complete silence with regard to Prince Bismarck. I confined myself
to saying to his son that his withdrawal from the negotiations would
without doubt make a sad impression in St. Petersburg. Two days
later Herbert Bismarck confided to me that his father had just telegraphed to Schweinitz ordering him to give the Emperor the assur-
ance that the solid ground for his decision had been the obstinacy
of Baron Haymerlé.

...I had to negotiate with a Chancellor, sick, invisible and not allowing
any business to reach him.

I resolved then to get hold of Herbert Bismarck and make use of him
as an intermediary between his father and myself. The cooperation
of this intelligent young man has been very useful to me, and I ought
to say that it is in our talks of the last few days that all the difficulties
have been overcome.

I began by asking him to hand to his father the letter of which I sent
you a copy.[50]

While, on occasion, foreign diplomats regarded Herbert as a convenient
tool in seeking the way to the Chancellor's attention, many governmental
figures inside Germany resented the necessity of penetrating the iron
curtain of Herbert's judgment. There was much bickering and gossip in
both court and governmental circles. The younger Bismarck was criticized
and feared as "the Boss's son," as one who had enormous influence on
the old man, and as one who could make or break careers. A typical
example of the resentment against Herbert may be found in a discussion

between Moritz Busch and Lothar Bucher, both journalists of note, who had been taken into public service and both of whom worked very closely with the Chancellor. Bucher had written two articles, "Bismarck as a Junker" and "Bismarck and Religion," which he had sent to Varzin for the Chancellor's approval. Herbert replied to the effect that the Prince had read the articles through but that he could not remember a statement that he had "brought about three wars." Herbert added his personal opinion that nothing more ought to be written about his father, and if he had any influence with Bucher he would use it in that direction. Bucher described the incident to Busch, who explained that if the Prince himself had asked him not to publish anything more about him, he should most *probably* forbear to do so, but that Herbert had no claim to any influence on him. "What is Hecuba to me?" he concluded.[51]

In Berlin there was much ado about something. Herbert's co-workers resented his now cascading career. Even in foreign countries there were tales of Herbert's influence. It was generally believed that Herbert prevailed upon his father to promote his own friends.[52] While serving as Legations Secretary to his father, he was instrumental in having his presently close friend Philipp zu Eulenburg[53] excused from an oral diplomatic examination because of an excellent thesis.

"I congratulate you heartily," Herbert wrote, "and believe that this news will come to you as a fine Christmas present.... I wanted to tell you that it gave me special pleasure to be the bearer of such good tidings to so good a friend.... Please tell no one, because I am not supposed to send you the news, which you will receive officially soon.... The only vacancy is the third secretary in Paris. I hope you will get it."[54] In 1881 Eulenburg was appointed to the position.

Herbert's responsibilities increased as his period of probation ended. By 1878 the Chancellor was ready to place greater burdens upon the shoulders of his elder son, not yet thirty. The European political situation was critical. A year earlier the Turks led by Abdul Hamid II, once described as a creature half-fox, half-rat, had slaughtered Bulgarians in a series of atrocities that shocked the world. Russia declared war on Turkey as a means of obtaining the outlet to the sea she so greatly desired. By the Treaty of San Stefano (March 3, 1878), signed by Russia and Turkey, Turkish rule was virtually obliterated in Europe. England refused to sit by tamely and watch Turkey dismembered to the advantage of Russia. There was no doubt that England would go to war again to prevent Russian penetration through the Dardanelles to the Mediterranean, as England had done once before in the Crimean War (1853-56).

In this dangerous situation a congress of the Powers met in Berlin with Bismarck as President and *ehrlicher Makler* (honest broker) between Russia and England.[55] Disraeli represented England and Prince Gortschakov was the leading Russian delegate. The Treaty of Berlin took away half of Turkey's European territory, and then solemnly guaranteed her "integrity." For England it was "peace with honor," for Bismarck it meant the peace of Europe but the eventual loss of Russia as an ally.

The Chancellor entrusted Herbert with the mass of details in organizing and holding the important Congress. The young man drew up each necessary prospectus and agendum, attended to matters of protocol, and wrote out in longhand reports on the sessions of the conference. "I wrote so much during those four weeks," he said, " that my fingers became almost crippled."[56]

But, more significant than these details, the Chancellor entrusted his son with the important task of negotiating the occupation and administration of Bosnia and Herzegovina. Herbert performed this to the entire satisfaction of his father, although it is questionable whether either Bismarck at the time recognized the critical nature of the problem. By Article twenty-five of the Treaty of Berlin (July 13, 1878), Austria-Hungary was given the right to occupy and administer parts of the provinces of Bosnia and Herzegovina, as well as the right to annex them eventually, provided that the Great Powers were notified beforehand. On October 6, 1908, Vienna suddenly announced the formal annexation of Bosnia and Herzegovina, ignoring the agreement and apparently taking advantage of the general European confusion and Russia's weakness after her war with Japan. This was a critical move – leading to the European crisis of 1908, which helped prepare the way for World War I.

The old man was pleased with his son's performance at the Congress. Herbert himself was even more delighted. Sitting next to his friend Bülow at the final banquet of the Berlin Congress, he suggested a toast. Bülow described the moment: "Full of excitement and with a proud expression he said to me: 'This is a great day. Four years ago that wretched cooper's apprentice, Kullmann, shot at my father and wounded him on his right wrist. Today my father has signed the Berlin Treaty. In 1814 the European Congress gathered at Vienna. In 1856 the Peace of Paris was signed. Now it's the Berlin Congress and today the Peace of Berlin. *Prosit,* old Bülow!'"[57]

In the meantime, between the termination of the Congress and the formal signing of the Treaty of Berlin, Herbert decided to stand for election to the *Reichstag* as a Conservative deputy from Lauenberg. His campaign was singularly inept, characterized as it was by overconfidence and a somewhat tactless treatment of the voting public. There are records of two of his campaign speeches, one at Ratzeburg and another at Aumühle.[58]

Herbert came to Ratzeburg on July 14, 1878, three days before the election, and addressed a political meeting. He informed his listeners that it was his "heart's wish" to represent them in the *Reichstag,* especially since he expected later to live among them as a neighbor. He would not burden them with a political program – he would merely give them a view of the current situation. Because of vicious attacks on the Government, he said, the *Reichstag* had been dissolved on June 11th and the Government had now appealed to the nation for a new mandate. Between the two attempts on the Emperor's life[59] the *Reichstag* had rejected the Government's proposed Exceptional Laws against the Socialists. Either the Chancellor had to resign or the *Reichstag* had to be dissolved. Herbert then launched into a spirited defense of the proposed laws against disturbers of the public order: Look at the practical Englishmen who, so they say, enjoy the greatest liberties – had they not in their battle against the Fenians decreed a whole set of exceptional laws? A band of conspirators guilty of accursed crimes, exemplified in two attempts to assassinate the Emperor, now existed in Germany, and the citizens had to be protected against them.

Concluding his short talk, Herbert then identified his candidacy with his father's views: "As to my other views, you know all about them, my position relative to my father, the Reichs Chancellor, and you will understand that I identify my political position with him. That is well-known to you. I won't bore you with clarifying my program and I won't ruin your lovely Sunday afternoon."[60]

There were "Bravos!" Then an attorney in the audience named Barlach took the floor and asked the speaker whether he supported or accepted the vile and slanderous newspaper campaign of the Conservatives against his opponent, Dr. Hammacher. Count Bismarck was portrayed in the press as "clean as gold and white as snow," while his opponent was insulted and abused. Barlach then demanded that the candidate make his views known on such vital matters as the proposed higher taxes on tobacco, the budget, etc.

Angered, Herbert replied that he had been working night and day at the Congress of Berlin on important matters concerning the Great Powers of Europe and had no time to read the advertisements in the Lübecker and Ratzeburger journals. The matter of slander would be taken up by the courts. As for the higher taxes on tobacco, if this distressed the working man let him forego his smoking for one or two days. The candidate was insulting his proposed constituents, scarcely the way to victory!

The next day Herbert was queried at an election rally held at Aumühle. When a member of the audience asked for his opinion on the May Laws,[61] he replied that only time could solve this problem and "the crown of Prussia will not bow before the arrogance of Roman priests or before the striving of priestly rule."[62] The Bismarck obstinacy was at work – and the Catholic vote lost.

Herbert's campaign was clearly clumsy and ineffectual. Although the Conservatives were greatly strengthened in the elections of July 17, 1878, Herbert went down to defeat. It was a close contest – 3,894 votes against the winning National Liberal candidate, Dr. Hammacher, who polled 4,276 votes.[63]

Ignoble defeat was hard for the Bismarcks to bear. Somewhat chastened, Herbert went back to his post as secretary to his father. He remained a sturdy fighter for his master in the struggle against center and left. In a letter to Lucius Freiherr von Ballhausen, he urged that "our side must continually use as the basis for our agitation the theme that the election of such people as the Forchenbecks, Stauffenbergs, Laskers, and Richters mean much the same as free trade, industrial misery, and high direct taxes.[64]

On March 22, 1880, Herbert was made Councillor of Legation, whereupon his father sent a flowery letter of thanks to the Emperor:

> I thank Your Majesty respectfully for the gracious manner in which Your All Highest has thought of my son. It is a great joy to me that Your Majesty has shared that grace, which you have given to me, with my son....You may be assured that this will be an incentive to him to work faithfully in the service of Your All Highest....[65]

By this time Bismarck was considering his son as a possible Secretary of State. In discussing the position, the Chancellor remarked to Moritz Busch on March 20, 1880: "There is my eldest son, who has been working under my guidence for seven years, and who promises well – but that would not do, as he is only thirty."[66] Lothar Bucher became resigned to the fact that Paul Hatzfeldt would not remain in his position. On November 9, 1881, Bucher informed Busch: "[*Hatzfeldt*] will not remain. He comes at two o'clock and disappears again at five, attends to nothing beyond the interviews with foreign diplomatists and troubles himself very little with other business....He will be replaced by Herbert, that haughty and incapable fellow, and more than one of the officials will leave."[67] It was an accurate prophecy.

From 1881 to 1886 Herbert represented the electoral district of Lauen-berg in the *Reichstag* as a member of the *Reichspartei*. Skeptical of parliamentarianism in general, he nevertheless paid close attention to his *Reichstag* duties, promoting a vigorously conservative policy and defend-ing Bismarckian proposals with energy and enthusiasm. His work in the *Reichstag* later assumed greater significance, upon his election as a dep-uty in 1893.[68]

Thus far the career of the younger Bismarck seemed to be progressing nicely. He had served his Fatherland honorably in the crucible of war. His political career, despite setbacks, appeared to be going well.

Most important of all, the old man was more than pleased by the budding career of his son. In his eyes, Herbert could do no wrong. Let the stupid fools condemn Herbert's reckless behavior, his love for puerile pranks, his obstinacy and arrogance. Much could be excused – he was a Bismarck.

All seemed well, but there were shadows in the rosy picture.

3

GERMANY'S DR. JEKYLL AND MR. HYDE

Throughout his short life Herbert Bismarck suffered much due to his position and personality. Clues to his misery may be found in his early life.

Herbert idolized his mother Johanna as the perfect example of motherhood. "My father," he said, "could not take his heavy life if he did not have my good mother."[1] For him she meant kindness and gentleness. As a Prussian mother she was restricted to *Kirche, Küche, und Kinder* (Kirk, Kitchen, and Kids), but at the same time she tried to give her children the kind of love they needed.

The dominant father was lord and master in the hectic Bismarck household, as was traditional among the Prussian aristocracy. The old man believed in the essential Prussian virtues of discipline, obedience, loyalty, order, and respect for authority – the *Obrigkeit*. If his children misbehaved they felt the sting of his strap or switch. On one occasion he chastised both Herbert and Bill when they took some hazel nuts and ran away from the pursuing ranger. "It was not on account of the nuts," he related later, "but because they had obliged the old man to run after them through bush and briar until I caught them and gave them a good thrashing, at which the ranger seemed to be greatly surprised."[2]

On the surface there seemed to be a mutual adoration between father and son. The older Bismarck made no secret of his pride in his son: to his personal physician Dr. Eduard Cohen he confided that he was deeply satisfied with Herbert, "whose ability and earnestness make him indispensable [*unentbehrlich*]."[3] It seemed to be a normal and happy relationship, but underneath were rumblings of stress. Whereas other children sought emancipation from their parents, moving away to build a life of their own, Herbert was unable to break away from his father. He never severed the iron bond.

Something had gone wrong with the delicate balance of power in the Bismarck household. Herbert absorbed his father's personality into his own, recapitulating his parent's sense of authority, arrogance, and bluntness. His ego was unable to set up adequate defenses against parental authority. Denied the necessary freedom for adolescent and adult adjustment, he remained psychologically crippled for the rest of his life. In the process he developed illogical and exaggerated feelings of fear and guilt – a vague inner sense of unworthiness.

As the years went by, Herbert seemed to become a remarkable clone of his distinguished father. To those who heard him speak before the *Reichstag* at the age of forty, it seemed as if the old man were speaking again.[4] To the world the Bismarcks presented a solid front. Father merged into son.

Herbert saw his father as a god. For him he sacrificed health, first love, and career. In Berlin, French Ambassador Jules Cambon observed how tenderly Herbert spoke of his father.[5] The great man could do no wrong in his son's eyes.

But below the surface a crippling neurosis was already at work. It is perhaps a reflection on the Bismarck family that all three children developed personality difficulties. All, like their father, were burdened by lack of moderation. All displayed the Bismarckian egoism. Daughter Marie became more and more neurotic as time elapsed. Her father described her as essentially lazy, thinking only about her children, her husband, and her nearest relatives. Absent-minded, of a scoffing disposition, she was impractical and untidy. Visitors to her home found on their bed a dozen cane chairs on which were three half-eaten cakes, and all over the place a litter of birds, guinea pigs, and bandboxes.[6] A family friend judged her as "peculiar rather than attractive," becoming outwardly more ungainly, and inwardly more stupid, as the years went by.[7]

Herbert's younger brother Bill was affected in a similar way. His potential was undeveloped because he too was inordinately lazy and drank too much. Bill also was destined for a short life, dying in 1901 at the age of forty-nine.

Herbert turned out to be the classic case of a split personality. In *The*

Strange Case of Dr. Jekyll and Mr. Hyde (1886), Robert Louis Stevenson presented a powerful psychological allegory on the duality of man's nature, with its alternations of good and evil impulses. Dr. Jekyll, highly respected London physician, a good and kindly man, in his youth had an inclination for evil, which for a time he was able to suppress. In experiments with drugs he chanced upon one which enabled him to change his external form into Mr. Hyde, a repulsive dwarf, the very embodiment of evil.

Herbert needed no drugs beyond alcohol to induce the duality of his own nature. Without the exaggeration of his fictional counterpart, he became indeed the Dr. Jekyll and Mr. Hyde of German diplomats. On the one hand he was agreeable, charming and friendly, on the other side, rude, obstinate, and tactless. There seemed to be two people coalesced into one individual.

This split personality recapitulated similar characteristics of the elder Bismarck. On occasion, the Chancellor was all cordiality and charm; at other times he was overbearing and self-assertive, in a way that either frightened or alienated people. Much of this was expertly calculated – the great Chancellor was not only a master of diplomacy but also a shrewd manipulator who used his own personality for furtherance of his notion of *Realpolitik.* Everyone expected harshness from the great Bismarck. Like father, like son. But in Herbert, with his considerably lesser talent, it became an almost unendurable quality.

The attractive side of Herbert when he was in his middle twenties (1875) was described by Bülow: "The first to congratulate me after my diplomat examination was Herbert von Bismarck. As he knew I was not up to the mark on account of my headache, he had been waiting in a room close by. There was not a nicer, more distinguished young man anywhere in those days than Herbert Bismarck."[8] A decade later, on October 14, 1885, Bülow wrote to Eulenburg from St. Petersburg: "Herbert leads our foreign policy most beautifully, with tremendous will for work, fire, energy, and for one of his age and temperament with marvelous prudence and self-possession. He is a darling of the gods; may the nation hold on to him."[9] Later on, when Bülow chose the side of the young Emperor in the Bismarck-William II feud, his opinion of Herbert underwent a radical transformation.

A similar judgement was expressed by Eulenburg, who for many years was close to the Bismarck family. Describing a visit to Kissingen on August 20, 1883, Eulenburg wrote: "I was deeply pleased to see Herbert Bismarck again. I have taken him to my heart. His fresh manner, his meaningful knowledge, which he gained through zealous work with his father for many years, have made him a very able official....I am happy to observe his vital energy and the absolute naturalness of his nature.[10] Although as a subordinate, journalist Lothar Bucher disliked Herbert,[11] he gave him grudging admiration: "He is very diligent and not unskillful. It will not be pleasant to work under the young man, but work will be done and things will not be allowed to drag on in such a slow and slovenly manner. Herbert has also a good memory."[12]

Herbert made a good impression during his earlier visits to England in 1884 and 1885, despite the bluntness of his manners. Foreign Secretary George Granville said that "it was impossible for anyone to be more genial and easily pleased."[13] Charles Wentworth Dilke, who remained his friend, referred to him as "this personally friendly fellow."[14] In March 1885 Gladstone described him: "He spoke in a modest and thoroughly friendly manner....I cannot presume to answer for any practical result, but nothing could be more rational or more friendly than the conversation."[15] English statesmen may have resented Herbert's conception of diplomacy, but at first they were personally attracted to the young Prussian giant. They were seeing the charming side of their German visitor.

So much for the Teutonic Dr. Jekyll. But there was another side to Herbert's character, a contempt for humanity which could turn him instantly from ingratiating personality into angry, snarling martinet. His friend Bülow recognized the trait: "Herbert is a man of many moods — dependent on the state of his nerves at the moment. He is more responsive to attentions than one would expect in a man who has been so spoilt. He is far too intelligent to run his head against a wall, once he knows it to be solid and permanent. We, who love Herbert so much, can only deplore many of his failings, the worst of which is, I think, his contempt for humanity. This feeling alone makes him a bad judge of human nature....Herbert thinks all other people *canaille,* attributes every possible bad motive to them, and so discourages and demoralizes just the best in them. Therefore, he soon mistrusts where he ought to trust, and puts faith in many a swindler. We would gladly see Herbert less cynical, better balanced, and more considerate. Herbert is still the best Secretary of State as long as his father is still alive."[16]

Herbert was an incessant talker, to the annoyance of his friends. Eulenburg reported that Herbert spoke in an energetic, pontifical manner, which he learned from his father, and often wounded people by his lecturing tone. "Herbert," added Eulenburg, "is not exactly the silent kind."[17] His lack of tact, especially as a diplomat, was notorious. When visiting Bülow in Paris in May 1884, he was taken to Versailles, where Bülow showed him the regal courtyard where the statue of the *Roi-Soleil* (Louis XIV) was surrounded by statues of sixteen French generals. Bülow mentioned the unquenchable ambition of Frenchmen, the indestructible French vitality, and especially the passionate French patriotism. To this Herbert said: "All this here is nonsense! There are *tempi passati*. We mustn't allow the French to bluff or impress us. They are really done forever."[18] In contrast to his father, Herbert was inclined to make sweeping political generalizations. This attitude made him unpopular among co-workers. Hohenlohe described a luncheon at Berlin on January 21, 1891: "After lunch the conversation became general. All present were highly indignant with Herbert Bismarck, and all kinds of instances of his want of refinement were related."[19]

The dualism in Herbert Bismarck's character was recognized by his English friend, Sir Charles Dilke: "On January 20th *[1882]* Herbert Bismarck dined with me – a man to whom I took a liking. I had not seen much of him before this date, but from this time forward we had continual meetings – a man of far stronger ability than that for which the public gives him credit. He had a special aversion to being called 'Herbert' and insisted upon being called the Count of Bismarck-Schönhausen. On Sunday, January 22nd, I dined with the German Councillor of Embassy…and met Count Bismarck again. I wrote in my diary on this day: 'Bismarck is a chip off the old block: not a bad sort of brute, with a great deal of humour of a rough kind. He saw through ____, an Austrian, who is a toad-eater, in a moment, and stopped a pompous story of his about….As soon as we were told by the narrator, with a proper British shake of the head, that he 'drank,' Bismarck shouted at the top of his voice, 'Well, that is *one* point in his favour.' *[The other]*, disconcerted, went on and said: 'He fell from a landing and was killed,' 'Ah!' cried Bismarck, 'what a wretched constitution he must have had.'

"In an aside to me Count Bismarck violently attacked Papists, and broke out against the Confessional in the tone of Newdegate, or of Whalley, or of General Grant. To the whole table he stoutly maintained that it was right that no Jew should be admitted into the Prussian Guards or into clubs. One man at the table said: 'But you had a Jew in the Guards'; to which Bismarck replied: 'We precious soon hunted him out.' The man hunted out was the son of Prince Bismarck's banker, the Rothschild agent, British consul at Berlin, and Bismarck's confidential adviser at the time of the treaty of Versailles. I added in my diary of young Bismarck: 'He is only 'sham' mad.'"[20]

Members of the anti-Bismarck camarilla were delighted with each display of Herbert's "obnoxious" conduct and particularly with reports of his drinking bouts, all of which made for gossip in court and diplomatic circles. Count Waldersee was critical of Herbert's entire personality, accusing him of acting as if he were his father "but unfortunately he lacks the understanding of the father, and also the fine sense of tact." "If Herbert," said Waldersee, "would act tactfully in his present position, and use his influence to soothe instead of to annoy, as he does now, he would have a great future before him; by his present conduct he must ruin himself completely."[21]

There is a question as to the effect of Herbert's split personality on Anglo-German relations. In his personal contacts with British statesmen, he turned on the charm and made himself well liked. But on diplomatic matters of importance he adopted an iron attitude that caused much friction. Maximilian von Hagen declared that the elder Bismarck was acting from the point of view of general policy and wanted to placate England by moderation.[22] Herbert's extraordinary frankness and sharp criticisms in dealing with British statesmen may well have contributed to the final estrangement with England. Paul Knaplund, also struck by the duality syndrome, judged Herbert to be "a Doctor Jekyll and Mr. Hyde, hindering instead of promoting the growth of relations between Britain and Germany."[23] The elder Bismarck, who seldom made a political error, may well have allowed his emotional attachment to his son to blind him to political reality.

One thing was certain – Herbert drank too much. But, as he could not match the political genius of his father, neither could he hold his liquor as well as the old man. The drinking habit may well have begun in a household notorious for its lack of moderation in food and drink. Visitors were astonished to see the amount of food consumed by the Chancellor and his children, the lion and his cubs. The entire family was indiscreet in matters of both food and drink. When his doctor ordered an invalid diet, the Titan was content, after his soup, to eat a plump trout, some roast veal, and three large sea gull's eggs, all washed down by abundant draughts of Burgundy. Because he believed that he could sleep only after libations of beer, he ate great amounts of caviar and other highly spiced foods in order to promote thirst.[24] At a time when he was complaining of a disordered digestion, loss of appetite, and neuralgia, he partook of the following dishes one after the other: soup, eels, cold meat, prawns, lobsters, smoked meat, raw ham, roast meat, and pudding. When he was complimented on his healthy looks, he rejoined: "I wish I looked ill and felt better!"[25]

All this Lucullan splendor had a dangerous influence on Herbert, who developed the same habits of eating and drinking but could not prevent his own descent into alcoholism. Though physically a giant as was his father, he was weakened by the Puttkamer strain on his mother's side. His constitution had already been assaulted during his early years. Both his father and mother were disturbed by the illnesses which upset Herbert from youth to manhood. In 1886, just as he was about to be named Secretary of State, his mother wrote to Eulenburg: "Let us hope that God stays with us, for our hearts tremble for our beloved Herbert, who has suffered so much from this horrible pneumonia....My dearest Herbert is miserable and our worry is great....I am writing from beside his sick room and I hear his horrible coughing. I can think of nothing else, and I scarcely know what this pen is writing."[26] Emperor William I had already signed Herbert's appointment as Secretary of State, but he withheld public announcement pending the outcome of Herbert's illness.[27]

For a man of such weak constitution, coupled with severe hypochondria, alcohol was sheer poison. But the family considered the ability to drink and tolerate alcohol a mark of masculinity. When father and son discussed the possibility of appointing Freiherr von Eckardstein to the diplomatic service, the elder Bismarck remarked: "The fellow is over six feet tall, he can drink without getting drunk, and is otherwise suitable, so we'll make a diplomat of him."[28] Both Bismarcks were delighted by the rumor that while in Würzburg Eckardstein had drunk some hundred Bavarian soldiers under the table.[29] When Italian Minister-President Francesco Crispi visited Friedrichsruh in 1887 and complimented Prince Bismarck on the excellence of his Bordeaux and Mosel wines, the latter said: "Direct your compliments to my son, who supervises my cellars. I must say that he performs this task superlatively well."[30]

Herbert not only supervised the cellars, but he enjoyed the gargantuan drinking, unaware of the toll it was taking on his health. His drinking bouts, some lasting through the night, became the talk of Berlin. He was proud of his capacity. To a dinner partner he advised in French: "Drink the wine, Madam, it is enough to resurrect the dead."[31] He loved to sing at the top of his voice when under the influence. Friend Bülow professed his amazement at Herbert's ability to drink without apparent effect. Bülow's report about a visit to Paris in May 1884 states: "Herbert astonished me by the staying power he displayed, sitting up till all hours, in the Café Anglais or at Voisins, drinking heavy Romanée-Conti and extra-dry champagne, to appear at lunch the next morning in the best of condition and finish a bottle of port....The Frenchmen admired the drinking capacity of this young German giant."[32] Equally as impressed were Herbert's British friends on the occasions of his visits to London.[33] When in 1889 Bavarian Ambassador Count Hugo Lerchtenfeld made sarcastic remarks about Baron Fritz von Holstein, at that time Herbert's close friend, Herbert, with loyalty animated by wine, violently rebuked him: "Holstein is as true as steel. Whoever says a word against Holstein will have to answer to me!"[34] Herbert would later change his mind about Fritz Holstein.

In both court and official circles Herbert's drinking was a favorite topic of conversation. When on November 17, 1889, Eulenburg sent a letter to William II suggesting a hunting trip, he appended a list of guests to be invited, with descriptions such as – "Count Hochberg, sings; Lieutenant von Chelius, plays; Landrat von Varnbüler, draws caricatures; Herbert Bismarck, drinks."[35] Gen. Alfred Count von Waldersee, leader of the anti-Bismarck clique, described a party that broke up at 4 A.M.: "Herbert Bismarck carried on like a student, certainly not the type of behavior one expects from a Secretary of State."[36]

Herbert was aware of his reputation for overdrinking, but he cared little what others thought. Nothing, not even the Bismarck heritage, could save him from the consequences of his addiction to drink.

The story of Herbert von Bismarck is one of extremes. One looks in vain for the saving grace of stability or restraint and finds only the violent fluctuations of a dual personality. On the Dr. Jekyll side there were sentimentality, puckishness, and romanticism, on the Mr. Hyde side, arrogance, snobbishness, and cold hatred. The public face, all toughness and all Bismarck, was carefully cultivated in the Junker mold to impress lesser breeds.

But behind the coarseness and bluntness was a persistently low self-esteem, the sickness of many a great man's son. The show of exuberance was less an expression of the natural man than a mask used to hide the little boy's urgent search for parental approval.

Herbert's entire life revolved around the axis of his awesome father's personality. He would work himself to exhaustion merely to attain a nod of approval. He would face the contempt of the mob rather than risk disloyalty. But, unable to resolve his subconscious frustrations, he turned to the bottle for an outlet. He longed to believe that its magic potions could transform him into a tough and true Bismarck, blessed by Nordic gods.

Disagreements between father and son were invariably settled by triumph for the father. At the age of thirty-two, starting on a promising career, although already in the grip of alcoholism, Herbert felt ready for marriage. He thought he could make the decision himself. But then came a harsh and acrimonious clash from which he never recovered.

4
MARRIAGE TRAGEDY: THE RELUCTANT CAD

"Normal (nor'mâl) *adj.* [*L. normalis* fr. *norma* rule, pattern, carpenter's square.] According to, constituting, or not deviating from, an established norm, rule or principle; standard, regular, natural....*Psychol.* a. Of or indicating average intelligence or development. b. Free from mental disorder; not insane or neurotic."

Few words in the realm of semantics have caused as much confusion as the word "normal." Psychologists and psychiatrists battle among themselves for clarity. What is normal behavior? Where is the line between the normal and the abnormal?

Otto von Bismarck wanted "normal" children – and was rewarded with two alcoholic sons and an eccentric daughter. Herbert wanted a "normal" marriage – and fell into a grotesque situation which left him shattered and even more dependent on alcohol.

The key element is the gradual "normal" inurement of the child to the vicissitudes of the world. It must be prepared for a life of its own – specifically, it must be treated so that one day it can leave the nest. This is the crux of what is called normality. The development is standard and well known: the infant becomes a child and begins its struggle for independence. The child goes off to school, where allegiance and trust tend to be transferred to the teacher and to peers. The adolescent endures the miseries of growing up. The young adult seeks to break away from parental control and then turns to the opposite sex. This is the way of the "normal" human being.

Trouble arises when either parent attempts to hold on too long. Some mothers are unable to accept the necessity for independence; for them the child remains eternally an infant, that squiggly center of delight. Some fathers also refuse to relinquish the reins held on their helpless youngsters who must not be allowed to escape masculine guidance. In both cases the child may suffer severe psychological damage. Being denied independence can cause ego problems for the rest of one's life. No matter what the age, the offspring remains in a childhood trance, overwhelmed by the mother's love or the father's authority. Wounded egos turn to the soothing lure of alcohol or some other substitute.

Such was the case with Herbert Bismarck. The father, mighty titan of diplomacy, had pushed his way to world renown as the greatest German of them all. Always the authoritarian, in political life as well as in interpersonal relations, he was obsessed by a need to maintain his hold on both Fatherland and family. He would make Herbert his successor in a Bismarck dynasty. He would train his son in the wiles and wilds of diplomacy and give substance to the Bismarck name. He would not allow Herbert to go off on his own: as a Bismarck clone he must function inside the mold set by the old man himself.

It was of prime importance to the hard-bitten Chancellor that Herbert not be allowed to enter the camp of political enemies, the ever-present anti-Bismarck cabal thirsting for the Chancellor's fall. Also important – there must be no "wrong" marriage to wreck the old man's plans. No, Herbert must not leave the nest. But, when ready for marriage, Herbert chose a partner who could be described best as a ward of the anti-Bismarck faction in German society. For the father it was a catastrophic choice. He would not allow it – and no argument would change his mind. The son must bend to the father's will. From this tragic circumstance, Herbert emerged dismayed and depressed, with the reputation of an unspeakable cad.

The lady in question was beautiful and charming, depicted in a painting by Gustav Richter with dark brown hair and magnificent blue eyes. The much-loved daughter of Prince Hatzfeldt-Trachtenberg, she was a member of what many regarded as an eccentric and bizarre family. She was married to Prince Carolath-Beuthen, but it had been an unhappy union. Herbert Bismarck had met her in the late seventies and was promptly smitten. Her marriage made no difference to the young Bismarck. He was determined to have her for his own. Courting her with Bismarckian passion, he urged her to divorce her husband and become his wife.

Elizabeth Carolath was both delighted and flattered by the attention given her by the dashing Herbert. Bored with her husband and ambitious to make her way even higher in German society, she responded carefully to Herbert's fiery courtship. For her the possibility of marrying into the Bismarck family and becoming the daughter-in-law of the great Bismarck was extremely attractive.

There was, however, a disquieting element in the situation, for which Elizabeth Carolath was not responsible, but which complicated her plans to join the Bismarcks. By birth and by family marriage she was allied to the anti-Bismarck camarilla, which infuriated the Chancellor. The male Hatzfeldts were longtime critics of Otto von Bismarck. Female members of the family absorbed by osmosis an acid contempt for the older Bismarck. For the ambitious Elizabeth Carolath at first this seemed to be a minor block on the path of her future, but it turned out to be an obstacle which she was never able to overcome.

There were additional difficulties. One of Elizabeth Carolath's sisters was married to Baron Walther von Loë, and the other to Count Alexander von Schleinitz, treasurer of the court household. Both brothers-in-law were bitter enemies of the Bismarcks. It was a solid trinity of critics – Prince Hatzfeldt-Trachtenberg, Count von Schleinitz, and Baron von Loë. For the Chancellor, the Hatzfeldt-Schleinitz-Loë faction was composed of dangerous political enemies who intended to destroy his career. The prospect of his son marrying into this nest of conspirators dismayed and angered him to the point of fury. Never, but never, would he allow his son to venture into the camp of the enemy!

Behind Bismarck's violent reaction to his son's contemplated marriage was an additional worry for the Chancellor. He saw the Hatzfeldt-Schleinitz-Loë faction as an offshoot of the Augusta party, the real fronde against Bismarck. At this time, 1881, Augusta was Queen of Prussia and German Empress.[1] There was a long-standing feud between the two – the Queen and Bismarck. From 1848 until his death the Iron Chancellor had to bear what he called Augusta's "intolerable accessory and opposition government." He spoke of his conflicts with the Queen as "the hardest-fought battle of my life." He was never able or willing to heal the breach. Nor did the implacable Queen ever relinquish her contempt for the man who, despite his political successes, angered her to the point of distraction.

Born the Princess of Saxe-Weimar, Augusta remained a woman of great beauty, but always sensitive to her royal heritage. She was dictatorial in manner. Her feud with Bismarck went back more than three decades to the Revolution of 1848. At that time Augusta had been married for nearly twenty years to Prince William of Prussia, brother of King Frederick William IV (1795-1861). As the monarch's madness became more obvious, Augusta hoped, because he was childless, that her husband, Prince William, would ultimately ascend the throne of Prussia. In March 1848, however, following an unfortunate affair in which troops he had once commanded fired on the people, Prince William fled to London.

The young squire of Schöhausen, Otto von Bismarck, an ardent royalist, came to Berlin with some ill-armed peasants and offered his services against the revolutionaries. He found his monarch in a hopeless state of confusion. In his brusque way he moved to obtain active orders from Prince William. He was referred to the Princess. Bismarck then went to Potsdam, where he collided head on with a conspiracy already under way. Augusta, convinced that both the monarch and her husband had irretrievably lost any prospect for power, decided to obtain the accession for her son. Grasping at any opportunity, she was in the process of negotiating for help from Georg von Vincke, leader of the moderate Liberal party in the Prussian Chamber.[2]

The meeting at Potsdam between Bismarck and Augusta was an acrimonious one which left both parties with contempt for the other. There are many versions of that fateful confrontation.[3] In his memoirs, published some fifty years later, Bismarck gave his own description of the meeting. When he asked Princess Augusta about the whereabouts of her husband, she declined to answer. It was her duty, she said excitedly, to defend her son's rights. Bismarck wrote: "In the name of his party, and apparently under instructions from higher quarters, Vincke was anxious to obtain my support for a move to induce the *Landtag* to ask the King to abdicate. The Prince of Prussia was to be passed over, presumably with his own consent. The Princess of Prussia was to be regent for her son during his minority. I...declared that I would counter any such proposal with one to take proceedings against its authors for high treason."

Bismarck continued: "I never told Emperor William anything about this affair, not even at a time when I could not help look upon Queen Augusta as my opponent, although to remain silent was the hardest test to which my sense of duty and my nerves were put at that time of my life."[4]

Bismarck thus painted himself as the patriot *par excellence.* But there may well have been other ideas in his mind. Although not an adovcate of the bare-faced lie, as was Adolf Hitler, he was a past master in the use of the diplomatic half-truth, the carefully structured statement intended to confuse a political opponent. Witness his ingenious and utterly unscrupulous edition of the Ems Dispatch on July 13, 1871.[5] In that fateful meeting with Augusta at Potsdam in March 1848, it was probable that he came to Augusta on behalf of Prince Charles, a younger brother of the stricken monarch. Charles was a reactionary who, in Bismarck's view, was just the man to take over leadership of the counterrevolution at a critical time. Augusta, with some indignation, declined. She never forgave Bismarck for what she believed to be intrigue on behalf of Charles.[6] She wanted her own son on the throne.

After this embittered encounter, the ambitious Junker squire and the strong-willed Augusta became bitter enemies. While Bismarck remained on cordial terms with King William I, who became Emperor William I in 1871, he never managed to win the forgiveness nor the friendship of Queen Augusta. The grateful King worked hand-in-hand with his chief minister in the business of uniting the German Fatherland under Prussian auspices. The two worked with a minimum of friction in the three wars of national unification. But the angry Queen never forgave – nor forgot.

Bismarck was well aware of Augusta's contempt and hatred for him. Again and again in his letters and conversations he attacked the woman he regarded as an obstacle both to himself and to the progress of Prussia-Germany. When he was transferred in 1858 from his desirable post at Frankfurt, as Prussian representative to the German *Bund,* to St. Petersburg in far-off Russia, he was certain that this was all due to Augusta's machinations.[7] According to Max Lenz, Augusta even opposed Bismarck's appointment as Minister-President in 1862 because of "his attitude in the March days of 1848, his reactionary views as diplomat and politician, and his frivolous and arrogant personality."[8] In 1866, when Bismarck was about to embark on his war with Austria, Augusta and her clique came out against the war with Austria and worked feverishly to prevent it. Bismarck complained that Augusta's tactics and those of her friends at that time were decidedly anti-national.[9] In 1871, after the victory over France, the entire country was convulsed in a display of joy: the great Bismarck had done it again and Prussia's arms were victorious! But Augusta, in an outburst of pique and alienated by the attention paid to Bismarck, held up the victory celebration in Berlin for some five weeks while she took the cure at Baden-Baden. The pause was an expensive one for the national treasury, but Augusta in her own way was expressing her contempt for the squire of Schönhausen.[10]

The personality feud continued during the early foundation years of the German Empire. The Chancellor suspected that the Queen was mixing in political affairs and he would have none of it. On May 14, 1875, in a letter to Count Georg zu Münster, German Ambassador in London, Bismarck complained about Augusta's private correspondence with Queen Victoria. She was playing politics, he said, in a way that was not consistent with her royal duties, and she was hampering the work of responsible ministers.[11] The Chancellor suspected Augusta of passing on state secrets to Princess Victoria, wife to Frederick, heir to the throne, and he was certain that Victoria would send them to her mother, the Queen of England. To Bismarck this was uncomfortably close to treason.

Augusta sought for help wherever she could find it in court circles. Her feud with Bismarck gathered momentum when she joined forces with Alexander von Schleinitz, her personal advisor, to support the anti-Bismarck fronde. Schleinitz was already working with two of Bismarck's most active opponents – Ludwig Windhorst, parliamentary leader of the Catholic Center in the *Reichstag,* and Count Harry von Arnim, pro-French and pro-Catholic diplomat.[12] Augusta was attracted by all three – Schleinitz, Windhorst, and Arnim – precisely because they opposed Bismarck's policies and did everything in their power to thwart him. The persistent Queen turned out to be a powerful enemy of the Chancellor and his family, including Herbert.

Bismarck well understood what was going on. He was certain that Augusta and her clique were out to destroy his political career. He fought back with all the strength at his command. He was inexpressibly shocked when he learned that his son wanted a marriage which would link him to the Augusta camarilla. He would not allow it. In his estimation nothing was worse than this contemplated union with the camp of his enemies.

Not only was the Princess Carolath a divorced woman, but she was also a Catholic. For the Protestant Bismarck this was anathema. Already engaged in a serious conflict with the Catholic Church, he angrily opposed its infiltration into his family. No sooner was the German Empire proclaimed in 1871 than Bismarck embarked upon a battle against what he decribed as "enemies of the Empire." In 1864 Pope Pius IX had issued his *Syllabus of Modern Errors,* including among such "errors" civil marriage and secular education. In 1870 the Vatican Council announced that the pope was "infallible" when speaking *ex cathedra* on matters of faith and morals. Both proclamations annoyed Bismarck, but because he needed Catholic support at the time, he decided to wait a more propitious moment to meet the "challenge."

Bismarck's struggle against the Catholic Church began in earnest in 1871 after national unification had been won. The ever-combative Chancellor turned from foreign to domestic foes. His hated opponents the Liberals joined the conflict, which they called a "fight for civilization" *(Kulturkampf).* Bismarck boasted that *he* would not go to Canossa, as Henry IV had done in 1077, and submit to the papacy. In 1872 he put through an imperial law expelling the Jesuits from Germany. In 1873-74 he promulgated the May Laws in the Prussian *Landtag*, by which the state took control over marriage and education, muzzled the Catholic press, confiscated church property, and prosecuted recalcitrant priests, monks, and nuns. Archbishops, bishops, and priests were deposed, imprisoned, or expelled, The inevitable result was the emergence of the Catholic Center Party as a new and vital political force and the appearance of Ludwig Windhorst as parliamentary gadfly. Bismarck was losing the battle. The accession in 1878 of the moderate Pope Leo XIII provided the Chancellor with an opportunity to end the conflict. Convinced that the growth of socialism in Germany was even more dangerous – that the "red international" was a greater enemy than the old "black international" – Bismarck abandoned the *Kulturkampf*. He began to seek clerical support in his struggle against the Socialists, though he still resented the Catholicism that had defeated him.

The wounds remained. In 1881, when Herbert announced that he intended to marry the Catholic Elizabeth Carolath, his father reacted violently. No son of his would enter into a union with the Augusta-Hatzfeldt-Schleinitz-Loë cabal. These political enemies, Bismarck insisted, had conspired against his political program. They had slandered the Bismarck family by circulating false rumors in the press. He, the object of their plots, would not allow this hated camarilla to invade the sanctity of his home. It was too much to bear.

Johanna, the Princess Bismarck, added her bit. "I'll fight tooth and nail," she said, "to see to it that the society of Loë, Schleinitz, and Hatzfeldt does not come to our table!"[13] The desertion of his mother meant additional woe for the distracted Herbert. Why would his parents not accept the choice of his heart? His intended bride had already indicated her willingness to become a Protestant. What more could they ask?

Herbert, caught in a vicious dilemma, could not undertand why such a simple matter as marriage with the woman he loved should awaken his father's angry disapproval. Elizabeth Carolath was not a political figure and should not have been blamed for the political views of members of her family. Herbert was torn in two directions – love for his intended bride and adoration of his great father. He hoped against hope that his parents would relent and allow him to proceed with the marriage. Yet, he sensed that eventually he would have to accept their decision.

The elder Bismarck, too, suffered in the clash of wills. Highly emotional by nature, he was adamantly opposed to this assault on his family. When Dr. Eduard Cohen, his family physician, visited him on April 8, 1881, he found the

Chancellor suffering from a bad catarrh and in a high state of nervousness. The doctor attributed it to Bismarck's misunderstanding with his son.[14] For the father it was more than mere misunderstanding – it was an absolute demand that Herbert drop his marriage plans.

And what about the lady in the delicate situation? In early April Elizabeth Carolath learned to her dismay about the firm opposition of Herbert's father. Shocked by the news, she fled to Venice, where she collapsed. In despair, she turned to Prince Philipp zu Eulenburg.[15] "I was so sick," she wrote to him on April 14, 1881, "that it was believed I wouldn't live and even now am so weak I can scarcely take a few steps....I shall try to regain my life and seek to begin a new life."[16]

At the same time, the aggrieved lady maintained an embarrassed correspondence with Herbert. On April 20 Herbert begged Eulenburg to write to the Princess "because the poor woman has no one she can talk to from the heart."[17] He added that in May he intended to go to Venice and see Elizabeth. "When I come back, I shall make a final attempt with my father. My present feeling is that it is a matter of life and death, and what will happen God only knows! I seem to be faced by the absolute impossibility to devote to the Princess what remains to me of life."[18]

The sixty-six-year-old unyielding father and the thirty-two-year-old beseeching son now had several painful interviews, which left both shattered and miserable. The first meeting took place on April 28. The father, with tears in his eyes, told his son bluntly that he was absolutely determined not to go on living if this unwanted marriage took place. It was an ultimatum – Herbert would obviously be responsible for the death of his father. Herbert pleaded in vain, insisting that it was far too late for an honorable man to withdraw his promise.

Two days later, in an equally uncomfortable and embarrassed interview, Bismarck warned his son that it was incompatible with his honor that his name be connected through marriage with those of Hatzfeldt, Carolath, Loë, and other of the Catholic cabal, against him. He urged Herbert to remember that he did not bear the Bismarck name for himself alone. Anything which concerned his father's name was of importance not only to him but also to his brother William.[19] The father then repeated Johanna's admonition: he too would oppose Herbert's marriage *"mit Zähnen und Nageln"* ("with tooth and nail").[20]

A master at diplomatic maneuvering, the Chancellor was determined to use everything in his power to win the battle of wits with his son. He could place additional pressure on Herbert. He now asserted that, as Herbert's superior in the government, his permission was necessary for the marriage. He even hinted that Herbert might be disinherited if he went through with the marriage. This was a new development. Herbert told of it in a plaintive letter to Eulenburg on April 31:

> In the meantime, I am forbidden to leave the service. Therefore, I cannot marry without permission (there is no legal possiblity until after the lapse of ten months). In addition, I must remember that I have nothing to offer the Princess, since, according to the terms of the law of primogeniture, as recently changed with the Emperor's approval, any son who marries a divorced woman is automatically disinherited. Since my father has nothing except the two great entailed estates, I should have no inheritance whatever. This would be all the same to me, since I would not live very long after the marriage anyhow; the split with my parents and their ruin would be the death of me.[21]

In the same letter Herbert wrote that his father had said again that "if the Princess were to bear his name, it would drive him to suicide."

Meanwhile, an impatient Elizabeth was waiting in Italy. A week later, on May 6, she wrote to Herbert that she expected him in Venice by the middle of May. She told him that she did not wish to live any longer. Herbert's father, she wrote, had no heart. Sensing the impact on a pious family, she quoted the Bible: "For this cause a man shall leave his father and mother, and shall cleave unto his wife."[22] She would bring the man to his senses: he was an adult and he had the right to make up his own mind.

The Chancellor had his own sources of information – little of importance could take place in Prussia-Germany without his knowledge. He quickly learned about the contents of Elizabeth Carolath's letter and her summons to Herbert to come to Venice. Infuriated, he demanded that his son pledge on his honor not to go there. If he made that pilgrimage, he would have to accept the company of his father. The parent was again holding on to the child: "I have your own fortune and the prevention of marriage more at heart than the whole empire."[23]

Herbert was thoroughly shaken and unhappy. He was aware that it was impossible to keep secret a journey to Venice and that a hegira to his exiled love would attract the "vermin" of the press. Moreover, the anti-Bismarck camarilla would exaggerate his trip out of all proportion. Herbert feared ridicule of his family, probably with such cartoons as an agitated Chancellor speeding in a gondola to rescue his son from the arms of a designing woman! He was pulled in two directions – wanting to preserve his honor in his relations with Elizabeth, while trying to prevent his adored father from becoming a laughingstock in the hostile press.

Herbert bared his soul in letters to Eulenburg, to whom he confided his innermost thoughts:

– "I wonder whether or not I have lost my reason."

– "I feel that I am one of those unfortunates being torn apart by four horses."

– "I regard it as a point of honor that I should marry her, even though my love for her were gone."

– "I blame myself for all that has happened, and am loathsome to myself."

– "The rest of my life stretches out before me in prospect like an interminable avenue of trees leading through a flat, sandy waste."[24]

Eulenburg was sympathetic. He understood the agony of his friend, who was obviously deeply troubled by what he regarded as a point of honor. Eulenburg responded as tactfully as possible. He hoped to do what he could to resolve the dilemma. In the final analysis, however, he urged Herbert not to separate himself from his parents. That would be a mistake, he warned. He even equated filial loyalty with patriotism: "In all seriousness," he later wrote, "I feared for the life of Prince Bismarck, whose health was degenerating. If the marriage took place, it would mean the withdrawal of the Chancellor from all affairs of state, and his retirement to Friedrichsruh to await death....I did my duty with a bleeding heart."[25] Eulenburg's "duty" was to advise Herbert to end his plans for the marriage – for the good of the country. National good should come before private welfare. It was the kind of advice of which the agitated Chancellor thoroughly approved.

No fury like that of a woman scorned! In the end it was Elizabeth Carolath herself who broke off the marriage plans. By this time she was thoroughly disillusioned. In her eyes Herbert had turned out to be a weakling, still holding on desperately to family strings. He was unable to make a rational decision for himself. Her grief turned to biting scorn. She wrote Herbert a final letter, informing him coldly that she despised him. She let him know through others that she would have nothing further to do with the house of Bismarck. Never again did she send word, letter, or greeting to the man who had deserted her, and who, in her estimation, had besmirched her good name by his puerile actions.

Bernhard von Bülow, later to become German Imperial Chancellor and Prussian Prime Minister, described Elizabeth Carolath in Italian exile: "Suffering the fate of Ariadne, she was left to languish on Naxos."[26] She was said to have retained the beauty and charm which orginally had attracted the attention of Herbert Bismarck. She became the leader of a brilliant social circle in Venice. Venetians liked to point her out to visitors as she skimmed through the canal waters in her private gondola propelled by gondoliers in her special gold and black livery. Natives whispered that she was "the lady scorned by the Bismarcks." For some thirty-three years she lived in her Palazzo Modena, surviving until January 1914.

The anti-Bismarck cabal reacted as expected. It denounced Herbert as the weakling son of a brutal family despot, as a "shameful lout" who had arranged Princess Elizabeth Carolath's divorce and then betrayed her, and, contemptuously, as "a thoroughgoing cad." Baron Walther von Loë, a general in the armed forces, saw the situation from the viewpoint of a military man. "If Herbert were not the son of the almighty Chancellor, he would be brought before a court of honor and it would be a farewell appearance for him."[27]

The Chancellor emerged triumphant from the fray – he had defeated the anti-Bismarck fronde and he had retained the loyalty of his son. The victory was won. Now it was necessary to forget all about it and to buckle down to real work. In a letter dated December 27, 1881, written to A.W. Hildebrandt, a former servant, the Chancellor spoke of his sons, but carefully avoided details: "Herbert is at the embassy in London, and the youngest works here with me. Both, thank God, are in good health, which, unfortunately, I cannot say about my wife."[28] For the Iron Chancellor the disagreeable matter was closed.

The real loser in the marriage tragedy was Herbert Bismarck. The outcome left permanent scars. He had been a clever, confident diplomat rising in the service of his country, but now he became a hard misanthrope who hated intensely and was hated in return. He was never able to rid himself of a sense of guilt.[29] Bülow recognized the change: "I am still convinced that the struggle through which he fought his way left permanent traces upon Herbert, that the wound in his heart was never entirely healed."[30]

Bülow was correct in his observations then and later. Four years after the marriage fiasco he met Herbert at a dinner and told him of his plan to marry the Countess Marie Dönhoff. It was an embarrassing moment. Bülow later described it: "Herbert was dumbfounded. He had two conflicting emotions: (1) he wanted to show that he was my friend; and (2) he was convinced that I was to know a happiness denied him. He had loved Princess Elizabeth Carolath passionately. He loved her still, and, I believe, never ceased to love her. He could never rid himself of a feeling that he had failed in the first great love of his life, that his behavior in this crisis had been neither wise nor correct."[31]

Bülow went on to describe the meeting. Herbert tried to change Bülow's mind about his marriage to Marie Dönhoff. The lady, Herbert admitted, was "gifted, truly good, and uncommonly charming," but, unfortunately, she was a foreigner, and German diplomats should not wed foreigners. "Besides, she is a Catholic....She is a friend of people who hated my father. I do not think that my father will give his consent to such a match. I cannot even advise him to. I shall even advise with all my energy against it."[32] Herbert was still caught in the net cast around him by his father.

Bülow, however, was made of stronger stuff than was Herbert. He listened patiently to his friend. He could not, however, tolerate this interference in his personal life. He spoke plainly to Herbert: "If consent to my marriage is withheld – a marriage from which I hope not only life's happiness but that of the woman I love – I shall resign." Herbert wrinkled the skin of his forehead. That reply brought unpleasant memories. He retreated: "My father will ask His Majesty's consent in person. As soon as this is granted the Empress will receive your wife in a special audience."[33]

Bülow was probably right in his estimate of Herbert's unhappiness. Indeed, Herbert had loved Elizabeth Carolath passionately, and, as Bülow guessed, had never ceased to love her. The marriage tragedy was one more reason for turning to the solace of alcohol. The father had made an unholy mess of the son's life – and the son of the great man was expected to take it as the price of loyalty.

Herbert never managed thereafter to live down his reputation as "an unspeakable cad," a weakling who had tarnished the name of his intended bride. He was discredited not only in the eyes of his spurned love, but also at court, among the citizenry and, worst of all, in his own estimation. From this time on Herbert could lay no claim to Alfred, Lord Tennyson's "grand old name of gentleman."

5

THE BISMARCKS GUIDE GERMANY'S SURGE INTO AFRICA

The months following the breakup of his marriage plans meant a time of trial for Herbert Bismarck. Deeply in love, he had urged Elizabeth Carolath to divorce her husband on his promise of marriage, and then, responding to his father's violent reaction, he had deserted her.

Alcohol was one means of relieving the pain and shame. Another solution was work. He resolved to immerse himself in his diplomatic career and justify the confidence his father had in him. Fortunately, there was a continent to occupy his attention. For the remainder of the 1880s he devoted his energy to the task of ensuring Germany's penetration into Africa. He became the spearhead of his father's drive in the vast African hunt.

There was opportunity for the Second German Reich fashioned by Otto von Bismarck. The Dark Continent had already attracted the interest of major European powers – spoliation was already under way. The opening up and partition of Africa was a story of gold, glory, and God – in that order, compounded by greed, adventure, and missionary zeal.[1] In the process the invaders stripped the continent of its wealth, while piously proclaiming they were interested only in suppressing slavery, tribal warfare, superstition, and disease. They were bringing the blessings of Western civilization to backward peoples. Gold, rubber, diamonds, and cotton, they said, were of secondary importance. It was truly an exercise in glorified hypocrisy.

In the early nineteenth century, French, British, and Portuguese traders set up small posts on the African coastline, but did not venture into the interior. In November 1855 David Livingstone, a Scottish missionary, explored East and Central Africa, and discovered Victoria Falls. He returned to the area in March 1866 "to blaze a trail for the gospel." When contact with Livingstone was lost by the outside world, James Gordon Bennett, owner of the New York *Herald*, sent the British journalist Henry Morton Stanley to find the lost missionary-turned-explorer. The two finally met at Ujiji on Lake Tanganyika in November 1871, since identified with the memorable phrase, "Dr. Livingstone, I presume."[2]

The effect throughout Europe was electric. Tales of riches in the vast continent aroused the attention of European businessmen, adventurers, and clerics. This was the promised land! Hundreds, fired equally by enthusiasm and greed, hit the African trail to seek gold, trade, prestige, and converts. Belgians, British, French, Portuguese, Spaniards, and Italians moved in. There was no planning – all was chaos and confusion. New boundaries were settled on the basis of simple power. The invaders paid little attention to the tribal patterns: they mixed natives indiscriminately in the hectic grab-all.

Explorers, traders, and promoters brought with them blank treaties, sometimes only printed forms. They would seek out a willing chief who seemed to have some influence over his people and who would give them the right to convey sovereignty, sell land, or grant concessions.[3] Few native chiefs knew exactly what they were doing.

Leopold II, King of the Belgians, among the most avaricious of the intruders, organized his own Congo Free State, which was recognized reluctantly by the Great Powers. In the process he acquired an enormous personal fortune from rubber and ivory. His treatment of natives in his quest for profits aroused such universal condemnation that in 1908 his private domain in the heart of Africa was abolished. His private estate later became the Belgian Congo.

There was some variation in European behavior. The British worked subtly, efficiently, and tactfully to win the lion's share of the spoils, bringing with them cricket, roast beef and Yorkshire pudding, and magistrates' courts. Wherever profit was to be made, there British traders appeared as if by magic. French invaders graciously allowed natives to speak French and wear red military pantaloons, while at the same time demanding sub-servience to French control. Later, in September 1898, British and French interests were to clash at Fashoda in the Sudan on the west bank of the Upper Nile, where a confrontation between British and French forces nearly led to war.

The Germans had no intention of being left behind in the African hunt. Their policy hinged upon the attitude of Chancellor Otto von Bismarck, architect of German unity. Before 1871 Bismarck had no thought of acquir-ing colonies for Prussia. He saw his map of Africa as lying in Berlin. "A colonial policy for us," he said, "would be just like the silken sables of Polish families who have no shirts."[4] He was skeptical about the necessity for colonies: in his estimation they provided only sinecures for officials and they were a luxury for Germany.[5]

Even in the middle 1870s, after the African hunt had started, the Chan-cellor adopted a course of watchful waiting. He felt that there still were obstacles to a successful German colonial policy, namely, the *Kultur-kampf,* the struggle with the Catholic Church which kept Bismarck occu-pied on the domestic scene; the jealous *revanche* policy of France, which seemed to refuse to accept the defeat of 1870-71; the acute irritableness of Britain, which wanted no successful rivals on the imperial scene; and Germany's own insecure position in world affairs.[6] In Bismarck's view, all these factors, in combination, worked against a strong German colonial policy.

But both the times and Bismarck's views were changing. In the early 1880s the *Kulturkampf* was nearing its end, France was softening in her calls for revenge, and Germany's status in Europe was strengthened in 1882 by formation of the Triple Alliance. Bismarck's eyes – and those of his son – turned to Africa. Germany would create her own colonial policy and would join in the spoliation of the Dark Continent.

There was an annoying problem. Britain, master of the seas and fore-runner in the colonial drive, stood squarely in the way of Bismarck's goal. There began a long series of negotiations by which the German Chancellor managed to challenge the British and obtain a foothold in Africa. Impatient at the British delaying and holding trump cards, he assumed a bullying attitude. He hinted at a *quid pro quo* – he let it be understood that his own support for British claims in Egypt could be won only at a price – colonies for Germany.[7]

The British were wary of the German Chancellor and his bullish diplo-macy. As early as 1863 Prime Minister Lord Palmerston called Bismarck "that crazy Minister at Berlin."[8] Later on, British diplomats who clashed with the Bismarcks over the African scene became even more convinced of the eccentricities of the belligerent Chancellor and his sarcastic son. Germany's acquisition of her first colony on the continent, in South-West Africa, was a story of a successful drive by the Bismarcks, aided by ineffective British resistance. Differences between the two powers eventually contributed to the blood bath of World War I.

The clash between the Bismarcks and the British Foreign Office was an important incident in the growth of nineteenth-century imperialism. It revealed the problems of conducting negotiations between a democratic state and one not quite so democratic. It showed the conflict inside England between different systems of colonial thought. Above all, it revealed the diplomatic skill of Bismarck and the role Herbert played in the negotiations.[9]

It was a classic case of confrontation diplomacy.[10] In the end, Bismarck got what he wanted. But the battle of wits was won only by a mixture of guile, arrogance, and skillful diplomacy practiced by both Bismarcks – father and son. In the delicate negotiations, Herbert became the good right arm of his illustrious father. Both understood the type of behavior that would be necessary to humble the British.

For the Bismarcks, the "Open sesame!" lay in the Bay of Angra Pequena along the South-West African coast in a region that had not yet attracted the attention of other European powers. In 1486 King John of Portugal gave Bartholomeu Dias command of an expedition to investigate the Congo and then proceed southward. Before rounding the "Cape of Storm" (later called the Cape of Good Hope), Dias discovered numerous bays, capes, and inlets, including the Bay of Angra Pequena. In accordance with his instructions, he erected in conspicuous places stone columns (*padrões*) bearing the Royal Arms and the Cross. In the middle of the sixteenth century, the Portuguese sent Paulo Dias to set up a colony in Angola to the north of what later became South-West Africa.[11] The Portuguese had prior claim to the area.

The British were not altogether convinced by Portuguese claims. In 1796 a British ship under command of a Captain Alexander sailed into Angra Pequena Bay and took possession of the surrounding land in the name of Great Britain. In 1805 several German missionaries in the service of the London Missionary Society landed at a small village on the coast, and in 1814 founded a settlement at Bethany, 125 miles east of the bay.[12] In 1842 a German missionary named Knudsen, representing the Rhine Missionary Society, moved into Bethany. Other Germans established settlements in the Walfisch Bay area on the coast line to the north.[13] In this way Angra Pequena took on a German coloration and later became a source of contention between Germany and Britain.

British authorities at nearby Cape Colony, including its governor, Sir Henry Bartle Edward Frere, were annoyed by Germans settling in the Angra Pequena and Walfisch Bay region. According to the British, German missionaries were involved in angry relations with the natives. In 1877 Frere urged London to take over all of South-West Africa, but no decision was made. The next year the British Government placed under British protection Walfisch Bay and the surrounding territory, extending for fifteen miles.[14]

Portugal still claimed sovereign rights in the area. The British, however, countered with the principle of "effective occupation," which recognized sovereignty only of the occupying power. Britain was the ally and patron of Portugal, but she had no compunction about disposing of the territory of an allied nation behind its back. To London, possession was nine points of diplomatic law.

German missionaries protested to Berlin.[15] The German Ambassador in London, Count Georg zu Münster, asked the British to explain the extent of their sovereignty in South-West Africa.[16] Lord Granville, Foreign Secretary, replied on November 29, 1880: "Her Majesty's Government cannot be responsible for what may take place outside British territory, which only includes Walfisch Bay and very small portions of the country immediately surrounding it."[17] A month later, on December 30, 1880, a note from the Colonial Office to the Cape Government defined British claims: "Her Majesty's Government are of the opinion that the Orange River should be maintained as the northwestern limit of the Cape Colony, and they will give no countenance to schemes for the extension of British jurisdiction over Great Namaqualand and Damarsland."[18]

But there were complicating factors. As early as 1876, F.A.E. Lüderitz, head of a large mercantile house in Bremen, and spokesman for a German Hansa merchants' group, had proposed to Chancellor Bismarck a scheme for founding a German colony in South Africa. For the moment his plan was rejected as impractical.[19] Undiscouraged, in 1881 he founded a factory at Lagos on the African Guinean coast as the nucleus for a future German colony.[20] Later, on November 16, 1882, Lüderitz was to ask his own Foreign Office whether or not he would receive imperial protection for his contracts with native chieftains.[21] At this time he managed to win from Bismarck a secret agreement for imperial protection of his factory provided that he could acquire a harbor for which no other nation could assert a claim.

By this time the German Chancellor was ready to open negotiations with London. For quite too long the British had dominated the African scene. There was no reason why he should not do the same thing for the Second German

Reich. What was the best way to approach the gentlemen of Whitehall? Bismarck had little faith in those he viewed as incompetents crowding the German Foreign Office. His mind turned to his son Herbert. Here was a splendid chance to heal the wounds his son had received in the unfortunate Elizabeth Carolath affair. The elder Bismarck was well aware of the situation: his grievously disappointed son, the scathing criticism, the renewed attacks by the anti-Bismarck clique. It was a tragic business, but Otto von Bismarck was certain that Herbert's marriage to Elizabeth Carolath would have destroyed the entire family.

For Bismarck, the events in Africa and the growing hostility of the British provided an opportunity to smooth over differences with his son. He would keep Herbert occupied with the important business of facing the British in the confrontation over Angra Pequena. Let others cry "Nepotism!" They would be damned as far as he was concerned! Herbert would act as the extension of his father's personality in the coming clash with the British.

On February 4, 1883, Bismarck sent a note to the British through Herbert, then *chargé d'affaires* in London, asking bluntly if Britain exercised any authority over the Angra Pequena region.[22] Nearly three weeks later came the response from London: "The Cape Colony Government has certain establishments along the coast, but without more precise information as to the exact location of Lüderitz's factory, it is impossible for the British Government to say whether it could afford this protection in case it was required.[23]

It was an evasive reply. The British had already declared this part of the coast as outside their jurisdiction. In April 1883, Lüderitz, emboldened by his secret promise of protection from Bismarck, sent his agent, Heinrich Vogelsang, to Angra Pequena. After signing a treaty with the natives, Vogelsang hoisted the German flag on May 2.[24]

The news of Vogelsang's coup was greeted in Berlin with joy, in London with ridicule.[25] Officials in the Cape Colony reacted with indignation and disbelief.

The issue was getting hot. On August 18, 1883, Berlin notified the German consul at the Cape that if rights of other nations were not thereby interfered with, it would be prepared to give protection to Lüderitz's settlement. A German corvette, the *Carola,* was dispatched to the Bay. Its captain gave notice to the commander of the British gunboat *Boadicea,* which had arrived from the Cape, that he was in *German* territorial waters. It was almost comic opera – the British Navy and the German Navy, each with a small gunboat, face-to-face in African waters.[26]

Meanwhile, the British had long delayed giving a definite reply to Bismarck's inquiry. This may be explained partly by the necessity for the British Colonial Office under Lord Derby to consult the Cape Government. It is more probable that the British failed to recognize Bismarck's colonial designs and attributed his new colonial policy to "election maneuvers."[27] When the reply finally came, it stated that, although British sovereignty had been proclaimed at Walfisch Bay and the lands off Angra Pequena, any claim to sovereignty or jurisdiction by a foreign power between Angola and Cape Colony would infringe on Britain's legitimate rights.[28]

On December 31, 1883, Bismarck sent a harsh note to the British demanding by what right or title Britain claimed sovereignty over a territory formerly considered independent.[29] London did not reply.

By now the story of Angra Pequena began to be featured by the press in both countries. German editors expressed indignation about the way they were being treated in Africa. Responding to public pressure, Bismarck on April 24, 1884, sent a telegram to the German consul at Capetown declaring officially that Lüderitz's settlement was under Imperial protection.[30] The old Emperor William I was delighted: "Now I can look the Great Elector in the face when I cross the long bridge in Berlin."[31]

The Chancellor, using all his diplomatic skill, was working cautiously and shrewdly. For a time he had been successful in not arousing British suspicions. Now that the British had a good idea about what he intended to do in Africa, he knew that he had to continue his inquiries at London. Thus far he had taken advantage of British indifference, pusillanimity, and procrastination, but the issue was becoming more complicated and he had to proceed carefully. Already there were embarrassing inquiries in the House of Lords about rumors that "Germany intends to steal Angra Pequena from Great Britain."[32] The British press was mentioning "insults to the Home Country."[33] Bismarck's diplomacy was put to a hard test. It was important for him to complete the negotiations without losing his main objective and without goading the British too far.

For both Bismarcks the matter of negotiating with the British was complicated by what they regarded as an annoying obstacle. To them the German Ambassador at London seemed untrustworthy – he was "more English than German." Count Georg zu Münster-Ladeburg (1830-1902) had been born in England and was married to the sister of the Earl of Roslyn – both facts convinced the Bismarcks that he was far too much of an Anglophile. Eccentric both physically and mentally, with a disproportionately large head that reminded Bülow of "a pumpkin on a long stalk,"[34] Münster had been envoy to London since 1873. The Bismarcks believed that he was deliberately allowing the decision on the matter of Angra Pequena to be delayed.[35] The German Ambassador, they felt, was far too courteous and considerate in dealing with the British. In their view, those qualities were of doubtful value in dealing with

British diplomats. Again and again he tended to interpret unpleasant communications, which he had to pass along, in the most conciliatory method possible.[36] He softened Bismarck's tough notes in order to maintain cordial relations between the two countries. Officials at the German Foreign Office in Berlin often complained about Münster's propensity for toning down their dispatches.

On his part Münster was well aware of what the Bismarcks thought of him. For him the Chancellor was the "Central Ox" in charge of the Foreign Office, for which he (Münster) had only contempt.[37] When Münster received a written censure from "the great Otto," he said indifferently in the presence of Herbert Bismarck: "How annoyed he must have been when he wrote this!"[38] Münster was sure that Germany had nothing whatever to fear from British statesmen, who impressed him as "wealthy amateurs who live from hand to mouth, without really understanding the situation."[39]

The Chancellor felt otherwise. He felt that he was not understood by the British because of Münster's dilatory tactics. He wanted the British to know that on the Angra Pequena matter Germany would deal only with the British Government directly and not with the Colonial Office or Cape Colony. Moreover, in Bismarck's view, his ambassador at London failed utterly to realize Bismarck's intention of founding a colony at Angra Pequena.[40] In addition, and most important of all, Münster had not informed the British emphatically enough that Germany might change her mind about Egypt if she was not satisfied on the Angra Pequena question. Bismarck saw his support of British claims in Egypt as a contingent upon British recognition of German claims in Angra Pequena. He was certain that the complexities of Egyptian finance could not be unraveled without his help.

Apparently, Münster either did not understand Bismarck's attitude or was unwilling to make the Chancellor's feelings known to Britain. The Chancellor severely reprimanded his envoy.[41]

The wily Bismarck believed that delicate negotiations were necessary in London and that Münster clearly was unsatisfactory for the job. Herbert could do far better. As one means of making his son forget the painful marriage tragedy, the Chancellor had sent him on special missions. Herbert kept in close touch with his father, sending him careful reports and letters.[42] The son acted as an instrument of his father, almost as an extension of his personality.[43]

In the process Herbert took on more and more the qualities of his distinguished father. On occasion, he could be gracious, charming, and witty. But, again like the old man, he could switch to rough and overbearing behavior if he felt it to be in his own interest. The senior Bismarck was suspicious of British gentlemanly behavior, which he saw as a cloak for harsh realistic goals. He believed that toughness and even arrogance were necessary to counter exterior courtesy and graciousness hiding British perfidy. Herbert would know far better than the Anglophile Münster how to handle the situation. He could project the Bismarckian determination to go ahead in Africa. It was high time to match British diplomacy with strong German resolve.

As early as 1881 Bismarck sent Herbert to London on a special mission. On November 20, 1881, he sent a message through Gerson von Blei-chröder,[44] his personal banker and secret agent, to Lord Odo Ampthill, British Ambassador in Berlin, informing him that he had decided to send his eldest son as Second Secretary to London, and that he personally hoped and flattered himself that it might be regarded as a compliment. Moreover, Bismarck said, he had an earnest desire to wipe out the painful impression made by a scandal that had taken place the previous summer at the German Embassy in London.[45] A few days later Bismarck wrote Ampthill directly, asking him as a personal favor to recommend his son Herbert "to Lord Granville's benevolence."[46]

Lord Ampthill reported to London: "Bismarck adores this son, who is a remarkably clever youth, and hopes to make a great statesman of him. He has often told me in confidence that Herbert, young as he is [*Herbert at this time was 32*], would already make an abler ambassador than all the members of the German diplomatic body taken together."[47] Sensing that he and his family were not in the "odor of sanctity" in high quarters, Bismarck decided to keep Herbert's mission to England a secret at the Palace from all except the Kaiser, until the press revealed his arrival.[48]

British Foreign Secretary Lord George Leveson Gower Granville, anxious to maintain good relations with the German Chancellor, received the young Bismarck warmly. He gave Herbert a flattering reception, despite a "Berlin letter" sent him by the Queen, painting Herbert in shades of black. [49] He found Herbert "clever, well-informed, bright, and easy to please."[50] Granville was convinced that the visit would "do much to dispel the want of knowledge of each other which some politicians display."[51]

It was a curious situation. The British Foreign Secretary was almost pathetically eager to lionize the young German cub as a means of appeasing the stern father. English aristocrats were equally impressed: they saw the visitor as the political and personal heir of the "Bismarck dynasty,"[52] and by treating him as such they would cater to the vanity of the great man in Berlin. They gave Herbert a hearty welcome and vied with one another in paying attention to him.

Herbert himself was astonished by the cordiality of his welcome both by governmental officials and by English society. He allowed that he had never been made so much of before![53] But he made it clear that he was the representative of his father, even if not officially credited.[54]

Herbert's nominal chief in London was Ambassador Münster, but he had no intention of working through channels. Herbert saw himself as the Chancellor's personal envoy and therefore, without consulting Münster, sent to his father, Count Kuno von Rantzau (Bismarck's amanuensis and son-in-law), and Friedrich von Holstein in the Foreign Office, reports of gossip he had picked up in the London clubs. These tidbits were then forwarded to the Kaiser and occasionally made use of in the press.[55]

Bismarck and his wife Johanna were delighted by the reception accorded their son in London. They made it a point to thank Lord and Lady Granville through Ambassador Ampthill for the cordiality of the treatment of their beloved Herbert. Ampthill reported to London: "He [*Bismarck*] said that he could never be sufficiently grateful for the reception his son had received in England."[56] And again: "Princess Bismarck never ceases to talk in grateful and eloquent language" about Granville's kindnesses to her son.[57]

The Bismarck's were sure that Herbert was doing a magnificent job in smoothing relations between the two countries. For the Chancellor it was an especially good omen: Herbert was serving his country well.

The cordial reception in London did not last long, especially after the shadow cast by Angra Pequena. Herbert had done his work beautifully in London, but differences over German policy in Africa had begun to disturb Anglo-German relations. Bismarck now seriously considered using his trump card – the threat of withdrawing his support for Britain in Egypt. On June 14, 1884, he informed Ampthill that he deplored "the delay in answering his question which had been respectfully and loyally put," but feared that "public opinion in Germany would resent the fact that after six months' delay the Cape Government had been wedged in between German aspirations and interests and Angra Pequena."[58] The Central Ox was running true to form – he was blandly utilizing the weapon of German public opinion, for which he had seldom shown much consideration.

The crisis was growing. Again Bismarck turned to his son for a special mission to London to deal with the Angra Pequena problem. On the same day that the Chancellor spoke to Ampthill (June 14, 1884), Herbert was having his first long conversation with Granville in London.[59] The young envoy complained about the long delay in responding to his father's inquiries. Replies, he said, could have been made in a few days. He brusquely informed Granville that Berlin would negotiate only with the British Foreign Office and not with the Colonial Office. He accused Lord Edward Henry Stanley Derby, the Colonial Secretary, of taking advantage of the delay to press the government of Cape Colony to take actions anticipating those of the German Government.

Granville meekly laid the blame for delay on Britian's "peculiar" form of governmental machinery. He defended Derby: "It was a complete misunderstanding of Lord Derby's action to suppose that his action in consulting the Government of the Cape Colony was intended in any sense to be hostile to the German Government. On the contrary, he had acted in the belief derived from some of the questions which had been asked by the German Government that it was their desire that the German settlers should receive British protection."[60]

Herbert was not appeased. He told Granville that his father placed great importance on the matter of Angra Pequena. The Chancellor, he said, intended to set up an arrangement at Angra Pequena which would preclude the possibility of annexation of the area by any other power.

Herbert then, on his father's instructions, carefully presented the trump card. Prince Bismarck, he said, still entertained the same friendly feeling toward His Majesty's Government and desired to support British policy in Egypt. However, Herbert thought it right that Granville should be warned that sentiment in Germany on these colonial matters was so strong that, with the best of intentions, the Chancellor would be unable to give Britain the same friendly assistance as hitherto, unless Granville could give some satisfaction to German public opinion.

Granville was not inclined to be intimidated. He replied that he "objected to anything in the nature of a bargain between us. Each question ought to be discussed on its own merits." Herbert then said that he did not raise any question of a bargain, but "the German Government expected its rights to be respected." "We have the painful impression that you will evade the question and are awaiting reports, whether you can want the thing." Granville denied any evasion: "If it is your *right* you will see England at your feet at once."[61]

The interview did not go well. There was another one between Herbert and Granville three days later. The two gave different accounts of what happened. Herbert reported to Berlin that Granville had said that it was the opinion in England that national possessions were already too great and that Britain did not have the slightest intention of opposing German efforts at colonization.[62] Granville, on the other hand, wrote to Ampthill that he had asked Herbert Bismarck to give him some definite idea of what Germany wanted: "Did they wish," I said, "to protect the German settlers only, or were they desirous of undertaking the protection of both the German and the British settlers, or thirdly – did they claim to extend protection to all settlers of whatever nationality who might obtain concessions?"[63]

Both interviews were unhappy affairs. In the first one Granville said that because the problem of Angra Pequena affected his colleagues more than it did him, he would be pleased if Herbert Bismarck would confer, in his presence, with Lord Derby and Lord Kimberley. Herbert curtly refused. [64] In the second interview, Granville brought up the question of sovereignty at Angra Pequena. Herbert expected the proposal, for he had been prepared for this very matter in an exchange of telegrams with his father; he retorted, not over-politely, that he thought it "a question of mere curiosity if you ask about sovereignty: it can be all the same to you, what another power does in a country not belonging to you." "Moreover," Herbert added coldly, "my Government will decline to give an answer in a matter that is of no concern to you." [65]

This was an extraordinary way for a thirty-five-year-old diplomat to speak to the seventy-year-old minister of a great power. But the elder Bismarck was delighted by his son's behavior. When he received Herbert's report on the incident, the Chancellor showed the letter to the journalist Moritz Busch with the remark that he was pleased by his son's toughness.[66]

Both Bismarcks were noted for their rudeness, but this was a coldly calculated procedure designed to strike at British sensitiveness. Herbert, in fact, seemed to be carried away by his role of tough negotiator. He had little pleasant to say about British officials: again and again he sent home scornful reports on almost all the British ministers.[67] By adopting a harsh and critical attitude, he believed he would be able to win the battle of wits with his diplomatic opponents in London.

The British were not unaware of the ill-mannered and discourteous stance adopted by both Bismarcks, but there was little they could do about it. Radical statesman Sir Charles Dilke commented after attending a Cabinet meeting at Lord Granville's home: "Herbert Bismarck was rude to Lord Granville about Angra Pequena, which was mentioned to the Cabinet, which could do nothing."[68] Dilke was annoyed.[69] The offspring of the German Chancellor was obviously getting too big for his *Lederhosen:* by now he was interfering full scale in the domestic affairs of a foreign power. Britons were not amused.

The Bismarcks believed they had the British in a tight corner and proposed to take advantage of it. Hence, they employed the policy of calculated rudeness, which they regarded as the proper reply to British delay, indifference, expressions of ignorance, and the hope that somehow South-West Africa could be saved either for Britain or for Cape Colony. British officialdom must be pushed and pushed hard. It must learn that Germany intended to go ahead with her plans for colonization and that she would not be thwarted by temporizing delays made by British ministers. For the Central Ox in Berlin, polite inquiries by the Anglophile Ambassador Münster were clearly unsatisfactory. What was needed was harsh diplomacy, and in that matter Herbert was a proper chip off the old block.

The climactic confrontation came on June 22, 1884, when Granville received Herbert again. This time Granville said that the Cabinet, after a thorough examination of the Angra Pequena question, had come to the conclusion that Britain was not in a position to afford protection to its own citizens who had settled there.[70]

Victory! The Bismarcks had gotten exactly what they wanted, and their persistence had won the diplomatic battle. The Second Reich had successfully embarked upon a colonial program. The German press happily applauded "the clever manipulating and use of great patience by both Bismarcks."

For the Central Ox the venture into Africa had turned out to be another great triumph. Earlier, Bismarck had asserted repeatedly that he was not a colonialist, but once he entered the African sweepstakes he intended not to emerge a loser. Always suspicious of British pretensions, he suspected that the British intended to set up their own Monroe Doctrine for the whole of south Africa. Biding his time, he presented Whitehall with a *fait accompli* by ordering that Angra Pequena, and specifically Lüderitz, be placed under imperial protection. The colonial question became his triumph and placed him on a still higher pedestal.

Moreover, the Chancellor was delighted by the fact that, in his estimation, he had won an additional victory over his enemies, the Carolath-Schleinitz-Loë cabal which, with the approval of Empress Augusta, had attempted to draw his son away from him with the weapon of marriage. He had kept Herbert occupied in London, where he had performed with extraordinary brilliance. He had control of his adored son again and looked to him to carry on in his prospective Bismarck political line.

For the British it was a clear-cut defeat. The London press reacted with bitterness regarding "this ignominious chapter in the colonial history of England."[71] But, in fact, the British position was a weak one. Eighty-eight years previously, British troops had landed on the coast of South-West Africa, but Britian had never claimed the area or set up a government there. Now they were forced to admit that German protection over that area acquired by Lüderitz was justified. Had they not done the same thing on scores of occasions? Reluctantly, they had to withdraw their claim to South-West Africa, with the exception of Walfisch Bay.

Although annoyed and disgusted with Herbert's behavior, the British were being realistic. There was little sensitive sentiment in the Foreign Office: had the occasion warranted it, British diplomats could easily have matched Herbert's stiff-necked rudeness. But they were aware of the weakness of their own position. Moreover, in their view Bismarck's support in Egypt was well worth the loss of Angra Pequena.

Historian Fritz Stern sees it otherwise: "The British procrastinated for months; in their almost incredible bungling, born of complacency and arrogance, Lord Granville at the Foreign Office and Lord Derby at the Colonial Office must be regarded as patron saints of the German Empire."[72]

And what about Herbert Bismarck? He was well satisfied with what he saw as a job well done. He had met the British on their own turf and he had conquered them. It was all very simple: he had deliberately adopted an aggressive rudeness, so often the gambit of English aristocrats, and it meant dividends for his country. He had matched British inscrutability and arrogance with perfectly timed obstinacy of his own, and it had worked.

Also, the everday details of his London negotiations did much to keep Herbert's mind busy and distracted from the awful marriage tragedy. He still felt remorse and guilt. Underneath the hard enamel of his exterior behavior there was a residue of insecurity. His diplomatic triumph could not altogether blot out the picture of the deserted woman in Venice whom he had loved passionately, but not enough to break with his father.

The matter was settled, but there was one more flare-up. In July 1884, the government of Cape Colony suddenly declared that, with Lord Derby's sanction, it was annexing South-West Africa. There was consternation in Berlin. Bismarck immediately dispatched three warships. In early August German troops ostentatiously raised the German flag on land. London had no desire to go to war. Knowledgeable men at the time judged South-West Africa unfit even for a penal colony.[73] The Foreign Office explained lamely that the annexation order referred only to such lands as were not occupied by the Germans.[74]

The Bismarcks could drink another toast to victory!

Most German officials and most of the German public welcomed the success of Bismarck's new colonial policy and many applauded its anti-British character. But there were some who deplored it and saw it as a possible source of friction between the two countries. Anglophile German Ambassador Münster, who had opposed German expansionism from the very beginning, spoke of the colonial fanaticism in Germany which dominated those who knew nothing about it. Because of his years of friendly contact with British officials, he resented the behavior of Herbert in London. On Christmas Eve, 1884 he complained of "all the cheap nastiness [*Pöbeleien*]" which Germany exhibited toward England, causing problems for him. He obviously meant Herbert Bismarck. That nastiness, Münster believed, was gratuitous: the British were not really opposed to German colonialism; it was strongly possible that they welcomed it as a counterweight to French and American imperialism. "Why our colonial fever has suddenly become mixed with wild chauvinism I would not be able to grasp if I did not know what the theory-mongers [*Theoretiker*], what silver-tongued orators, and – in place remote from us – what idealists we Germans are."[75] For the perverse Münster all this was "colonial nonsense" and the German Michel had wrongfully stuck his finger in the dark mush [*Brei*].*

The Bismarcks had no way of knowing that the colonial policy they were pursuing would contribute critically to Anglo-German hostility – culminating in World War I. For the moment they could applaud as African natives were marched down the streets of Berlin – exactly as in London.

For Herbert, the reconciliation with his father and his successful work in London on the Angra Pequena matter meant that a fine political career was under way. Perhaps he could win the approval of the German public and continue to make the name of Bismarck respected not only in Germany but in the entire world. Why not a Bismarck the Elder and Bismarck the Younger, comparable to the two Pitts who had strengthed the office of Prime Minister in Britain?

---

*Ambassador Münster meant that the German Michel, a stock character equivalent to Britain's John Bull and America's Uncle Sam, had become mixed in a pulpy affair with which he really should not have been concerned.

6

SECRETARY OF STATE

After the triumphs of Angra Pequena, Herbert Bismarck decided that he could continue a political career that would justify his father's confidence in him. As a good son he would carry on the work of his illustrious *père* and stand up to their enemies like a true Bismarck.

Like his father, Herbert was attracted by the aura of political life. There was nothing to equal the sense of power at the top of the surging heap. To be at the core of critical events, to guide his country's destiny, this was the life he wanted. Most of all, the interplay of political struggle would do much to blot out the memory of his love for Elizabeth Carolath. Also, like thousands of other victims of an unhappy love affair, Herbert found comfort in alcohol. He was as certain that he could handle his liquor as the many others who have been conquered by drink.

Herbert had not altered his cantankerous personality. As he made ready for a career in the upper bracket of German administrative life, there was no dramatic change in his lifestyle. He deliberately used his brashness as a weapon to defend himself against the hostility he always engendered in other people. "Sheer cussedness" characterized his performance as a state official.

Promotion came rapidly. On March 4, 1885, after Germany's colonial policy was well under way, Herbert was sent once more to London as a special minister of the Foreign Office to conciliate British-German differences.[1] On his return to Berlin he was made Under Secretary of State for Foreign Affairs.

In October 1885, when Secretary of State Count Hatzfeldt was sent as envoy to London, Herbert took over his duties in the Foreign Office. By now it was clear that the Chancellor was grooming his son for the secretaryship. One newspaper reported that "the public is getting more and more used to the thought that the elder Bismarck is training a very capable successor in his son."[2]

On April 1, 1885, Prince Bismarck's birthday, Herbert was decorated by the Emperor with the title Knight of the Red Eagle, a portent of agreeable things to come.[3] The two gossiping journalists in public service, Lothar Bucher and Moritz Busch, were certain that Herbert was being groomed for higher office.[4]

They were, of course, right: on May 18, 1886, Herbert became Secretary of State for Foreign Affairs (*Staatssekretär des Auswärtigen*). He was not yet thirty-seven. The nomination was not altogether unexpected to Friedrich (Fritz) von Holstein, reputed to be the evil genius of the Foreign Office, who had declared to Prince Radolin as early as 1885: "Bismarck is a Wallenstein. His ambition is to found a Bismarck dynasty."[5]

Once again there came the familiar cries of nepotism and *Hausmeiertum* from all levels of German society, not excluding the old Emperor himself. The latter spoke aloud, concealing nothing from those who were listening, at a "punch" (party) given by his grandson to officers of all arms. He was reported to have said: "It must be admitted that this young Count Herbert has got on prodigiously fast under the rule of his father. It is the greatest act of nepotism ever recorded....I should readily have made this remark [*to Prince Bismarck*], but I reflected that, as he does not feel the impropriety of these extraordinary promotions, he could not take the remark coolly, and that, if I had made it [*to him*], it might have more serious consequences than I intended."[6] The Emperor said nothing to Bismarck.

To any such criticism of Herbert the elder Bismarck merely raised a condescending eyebrow. Besides he was tired, and in contrast with earlier times, he had little interest in private affairs. Already he had turned over many details to Herbert.[7] He was now ready to entrust his political work to his son, on the ground that it was but natural that he turn to his closest relative to help him in the practice of his heavy and responsible duties.

When Herbert made his debut before the *Reichstag* as Secretary of State for Foreign Affairs, Progressive Socialists and members of the Center tried to bring him to confusion by interruptions and laughter.[8] They were not successful. Having been through a rigid training under his father, the son thought and acted politically in Bismarckian fashion.[9] He conducted the affairs of the Foreign Office with the strictest discipline. "He trained his messengers," reported Bülow "to jump in....He had kept them in such a permanent state of tension and fear that when he rang the bell they would dash into his room like a trout when it leaps over an obstruction."[10] The old boorishness and arrogance were still there. William II later wrote: "Count Herbert's rudeness to his subordinates particularly struck me. The members of the staff simply flew when they were summoned or dismissed by the Count, so much so that a jocular saying arose at the time that 'their coattails stood straight out behind them.' The foreign policy was conducted and dictated by Prince Bismarck alone, after consultations with Count Herbert, who passed on the decisions of the Chancellor and then transformed them into instructions. Hence, *the Foreign Office was nothing but an office of the great Chancellor.*"[11]

This estimate of Herbert was written by William II long after his bitter quarrel with both Bismarcks which led to their resignations. But at the time when the younger Bismarck became Secretary of State there was an effort on both sides to maintain a relationship of sorts. The then Crown Prince regarded Herbert Bismarck as an important man in the government.[12] "I was on good terms with him," William wrote. "He could be a very gay companion and knew how to assemble interesting men around his table, partly from the Foreign Office, partly from other circles. True friendship, however, never ripened between us."[13] Freiherr von Wilmowski, Chief of the Civil Cabinet of William I, noted at that time that the Crown Prince was under the influence of Waldersee and Herbert Bismarck, "both of whom were working for war."[14] This kind of malicious backbiting was traditional in German official circles.

The poisonous atmosphere continued after Herbert became Secretary of State. He tried to forget his troubles by plunging into more and more work. His father, sometimes jokingly but often earnestly, warned him against overwork. Herbert was not inclined to take his advice.

Within five months Herbert broke down. Concerned, his father wrote to him on October 29, 1886: "Don't work too hard....Take care of yourself for my sake, if you will not do so for yourself. I cannot get along without you....There is no one able to take your place....I will gladly give the rest of my years to my country, but I do not feel as did Brutus, who sacrificed his sons and their youth on the altar of the State....Take care of yourself, and you can serve the country well and make my tasks easier. If you destroy yourself you do not destroy yourself alone."[15]

Herbert soon recovered. By early December 1886 he was back in the office working harder than ever and again displaying the fiery Bismarckian temperament on public occasions. When the Bavarian Ambassador, Count

Lerchenfeld, gave a dinner to Prince Luitpold, Herbert excused himself on the ground that the seating arrangements were unsatisfactory: the Chancellor demanded, he said, that at diplomatic dinners the Secretary of State should always have the first place at table.[16] In relating this incident Waldersee added: "If Herbert were a smart man he would have done nothing, for he has the whole reasonable world against him."[17]

For Herbert it was not a case of smartness. He was a Bismarck, and nobody must ever be allowed to upstage the Bismarcks.

In late December 1887, after Herbert had served as Secretary of State for a year and a half, he was given the title of Acting Privy Councillor *(Wirklicher Geheimer Rat)*. The announcement was made by William I in a letter to Prince Bismarck:

> Enclosed I send you the appointment of your son to be an Acting Privy Councillor with the title of Excellency, that you may give it to your son − a pleasure of which I did not wish to deprive you. The pleasure will, I think be threefold − for you, for your son, and for me.[18]

To this letter Bismarck replied from Friedrichsruh on December 20, 1887:

> I am, above all, happy about the appointment of my son to Acting Privy Councillor, because I can see that Your Majesty is pleased with my services, and that the aim for which I called my son into my work has been fulfilled. I beg Your Majesty for your further indulgence for him, in the knowledge that he will serve you loyally even if he still lacks experience.[19]

It was a moment of joy for the old man. Herbert had gone through a difficult childhood and adolescence, and had weathered the crisis of a marriage fiasco. Now, at last, he had justified the faith his father had in him. The elder Bismarck was gratified: now his good name would be carried on by a distinguished son, who was obediently following in his footsteps. This was the way it was supposed to be, excellent news in the maelstrom of petty backbiting and jealousy aroused by the very name of Bismarck.

Herbert, on his part, believed that as Secretary of State it was important to maintain good relations with Prince William, heir to the throne, as insurance for the future. He depended upon Philipp Eulenburg, at that time his close friend, to act as a kind of friendly broker between him and the young Hohenzollern. Herbert wrote often to Eulenberg about Prince William: "Our Crown Prince will arrange things with the *Bundesfürsten* [*Federal Princes*], he is smart enough for that. Besides, he possesses quick perception and cleverness, and if he wishes, so dominating a charm that the princes will soon see their protector in him. With his great goals he will certainly grow in stature, and his innate dignity will prepare him for the great position to which he may be called in a few weeks."[20]

And again in another letter: "My dear Phili: That you have looked up Prince William is most helpful. He thinks a great deal of you and has sung your praises to me in many tones. You must use that and speak to him again in Reichenhall and work on him. The thunder of many of his views must be toned down more and more, so that the Potsdam lieutenant's ideas can be changed gradually into more statesmanlike reflections. Otherwise the Prince is a pearl."[21]

The Crown Prince was a favorite subject: "My dear Phili: Tomorrow you shall be in Bayreuth with Prince William. I have just had a letter from this gracious gentleman. I hope that you make a good impression on him....I always fear that the Prince tires himself with his furious energy; we must avoid that because his health is invaluable for the German Fatherland."[22]

At this time Herbert was obviously enthusiastic about the Crown Prince, an attitude he was to change drastically later on. He did not have an equal regard for the old Emperor, though he tried to remain on his good side. In the summer of 1885, when Eulenburg accompanied the Emperor on the first of his Nordland cruises, and Eulenberg was not certain as to whether or not he should go along, Herbert wrote to him: "Concerning the cruise of His Majesty on the Norwegian coast, it would be very pleasing to me if you went along, and do not quite see why you have any doubts about it. Your influence on His Majesty is splendid and very dear to me. In the weeks of musing on board you can do much good."[23] But once he became Secretary of State, Herbert began to treat the old monarch with the same overbearing and dominating attitude he used toward his inferiors. Shortly before the death of William I, his adjutant, Lt. Col. von Plessen, entered the royal apartment just after Herbert had been received in audience. He found the Emperor exhausted, almost in a state of collapse. The old man said to Plessen: "These audiences with young Bismarck always take it out of me. He's so stormy – worse even than his father. He has not a grain of tact."[24] The old Emperor was unaware that "tact" was not a word in the Bismarckian vocabulary.

Herbert had little use for the third Hohenzollern, Frederick III, who ruled but ninety-nine days from March 9 to June 15, 1888. Tragically, Frederick was a victim of throat cancer. Herbert, who saw him as an ineffectual visionary, confided to Bülow: "I understand that you and your wife are overcome by the dreadful disease of the Emperor, which also touches my father so nearly. But I disagree with my father. I think the Emperor's political departure a good thing.

Considering the influence his wife has had on him and her very English attitude of mind, a long reign of the Emperor Frederick would make us dependent
on England, and that would be our greatest misfortune."[25] To the Prince of
Wales, who had come to Berlin for the funeral, Herbert said that an Emperor
who could not talk was not fit to reign.[26] Frederick III had been aware of
Herbert's antipathy towards him: Lucius von Ballhausen reported that at Leipzig,
on March 12, 1888, three days after he had become Emperor, Frederick, while
receiving ministers at the railway station, "at first looked at Count Herbert, who
accompanied his father, somewhat unfriendly, but then gave him his hand."[27]

In the early years of his secretaryship, Herbert had wide scope for his
energy and diplomatic talents. Despite his touchy personality, he was a conscientious and versatile worker in his new post. He directly supervised German colonial policy in east and west Africa, and was the leading German figure
in the difficult negotiations with England and the United States on the Samoan
question.[28] He accompanied William II on his travels to various European
courts. His performance gave great satisfaction to his father. When Moritz
Busch, the new Under Secretary of State, praised Herbert's industry, Prince
Bismarck replied: "You need not praise him to me. I would have made him
Secretary of State even if he had not possessed all those qualities for which
you praise him, since I wanted at my side a man in whom I can have complete
confidence, and whom it is easy for me to deal with. At my great age, when I
have used up all my energies in the royal service, I think I have a right to ask
that."[29]

Despite his father's confidence, Herbert had to work in what he saw as a
nest of vipers. Among the legion of Bismarck critics was Count Alfred Waldersee, Quartermaster General of the Army, with whom Herbert clashed again
and again. Waldersee saw Herbert as "ruthless," "coarse," and "tactless."
"Herbert Bismarck has gotten used to the idea that he can act as if he were
his father. The Chancellor can be utterly charming, so that no one can withstand him. Because of his powerful services and his unusual personality he
can get away with this, but no one gives the son a similar break, and many
who toady to him do so only out of regard or fear of his father. That the son
does not see this is no great evidence of his cleverness. If in his present
position he would use more tact and exert his influence to calm matters instead
of stirring them up, as he does now, he would, indeed, have a great future."[30]

Waldersee denounced both Bismarcks: "The Bismarcks, father and son,
want to reign alone, and convince themselves that they can lead the Crown
Prince. They make the mistake of making enemies of all those people who
must hang together."[31] And again on Herbert: "The resentment against him is
growing; there is no minister who does not complain about him."[32] On one

occasion, at a dinner held on December 8, 1887, and attended by Prince William, Waldersee and Herbert nearly came to blows.[33]

Waldersee's grudge against Herbert was compounded of a combination of resentments. He accused the younger Bismarck of attacking him in the press and then hiding behind the cloak of his father. "What will become of the good Herbert, if he cannot crawl behind his father?"[34] In late March 1888 Waldersee complained angrily to the Crown Prince that Herbert was the inspiration for newspaper attacks on him (Waldersee). "The Crown Prince," reported Waldersee, "called Herbert Bismarck to him and told him that if he placed any value on their friendship, he would see to it that the newspapers would leave me in peace."[35]

More important was Waldersee's accusation that Herbert was interfering in purely military matters. In March 1885 the *Reichstag* deputy and sub-prefect Prince Carolath voted along with the Progressives and Social Democrats against a bill which the Emperor considered to be essential for the Army and officer corps. Enraged because of what he regarded as disloyalty (Prince Carolath was a *Rittmeister* – captain of cavalry), the Minister of War recommended to the Emperor that Carolath's officer's uniform, which he wore at the Emperor's courtesy, be taken away from him. The Emperor had Carolath's name stricken from the list of active officers. All the less important princes, who wore the uniform at the Emperor's courtesy, were most concerned.

Herbert, who had just become Under Secretary of State, came forward as champion of the less powerful princes. "In my view," wrote Waldersee, "he plays an unfortunate role, for he compromises his father. I think that Herbert Bismarck went ahead without asking his father, and that his father found himself in a most inconvenient position in allowing his son to suffer such a defeat....Herbert insisted that the incident would become an embarrassing scandal in the *Reichstag,* since all inimical elements would make capital out of it....The most interesting thing about the case is that Herbert Bismarck begins to play a role and to have a certain influence over his father. He plays a dangerous game and in this matter he has not covered himself with glory."[36]

When he became Secretary of State, Herbert did not shrink from fighting Waldersee and all his many other enemies. For him political struggle was a way of life. Witness his role in the Stoecker affair.

Adolf Stoecker (1835-1909) had been a field chaplain in the Franco-Prussian War when one of his sermons on the battlefield attracted the attention of William I who later, as Emperor, called the comparatively young man to Berlin as the court chaplain (1874). In 1878 Stoecker founded the Christian-Social Workers' Party, through which he hoped to win the workingman to "national and Christian thought," to better the workingman's position, and to conquer the Social Democrats for the "spirit of nationalism." From 1879 to 1898 he was a member of the Prussian *Landtag;* from 1881-1893 and again from 1898-1908 he held a seat in the *Reichstag.* Ambitious, impulsive, energetic, and a spellbinding orator, Stoecker was continually in the limelight, always keyed for battle, the object of a sensational press. He was revered by a passionate group of followers, and just as profoundly hated by enemies. Stoecker was most happy when being heckled at mass meetings, which gave him the opportunity for withering rebuttals. He was enthusiastic when denouncing foes in the courtroom, accusing newspapers of cowardly attacks, or addressing the *Reichstag* as delegates applauded, cheered, or hissed him down. Stoecker eagerly invited investigation into his own financial affairs.[37]

Thrust as a young minister into the circles of Berlin aristocracy, Stoecker sought to prove that belief in God went hand-in-hand with a nationalistic spirit and hatred of internationalism. He was appalled by the rise of the Social Democratic Party, which he regarded as anti-religious, immoral, and un-Christian. He plunged into the thick of the fight against Social Democracy, urging the Socialists to think in a more Christian manner and to cease working for "national destruction."[38] He was the patriot *par excellence,* often speaking of German honesty, loquacity, and conscientiousness,[39] and elaborating on the Germanic-Christian *Kultur* ideal.[40] The German people, he said, were richly endowed by nature to be industrious, pious, honest, and loyal.[41] He was intrigued by the word *"Vaterland":* "The German Fatherland is where the German tongue is spoken; *ubi bene ibi patria,* my Fatherland is there where I feel at home."[42] The word almost became an obsession in his mind: "Ten years ago much blood was spilled to win freedom and unity for the Fatherland; one cannot think enough of the Fatherland and it is inspiring when young men give their Fatherland more than themselves and give their blood and lives for the Fatherland. But when one makes a repulsive idol of the earthly Fatherland, when there is no heavenly Fatherland above the earthly Fatherland, then the spirit of the Fatherland remains dark; in many souls today a wrong idea of the Fatherland exists.[43]

Stoecker was the foremost anti-Semite of his time. The Jews, he said, could not understand the high Christian *Weltanschauung* or the deep spirit of German ideas. [44] To him, Judaism was a great danger for German life. "Modern Judaism is a foreign drop of blood in our national body; it is a destructive power....We must nurse again the peculiarities of our national genius – German spirit, industriousness, and piety, our heritages."[45] It was altogether impossible to have a Christian, national life as long as Judaism played an important role in Germany.[46] The Germans would be fools to let the Jews cripple their national life.[47] When in February 1888 a statue of Heinrich Heine was to be erected, Stoecker worked feverishly against the proposal. "It alienates the healthy patriotism of the people. It ought to be made of mud....Heine- the Jew – was a rascal [*Lump*]!"[48]

Stoecker addressed a mass meeting: "Ladies and Gentlemen: Recently a body was found in the vicinity. It was examined: present were the Jewish town- physician, a Jewish doctor, a Jewish coroner, a Jewish lawyer – only the body was German! We don't want this to be the fate of Berlin. We want to keep our people alive through the real powers of life [*Lebenskräfte*]."[49]

To wean workers away from socialism, Stoecker founded the Berlin City Mission and worked among his aristocratic friends to obtain funds for it. Count Waldersee and other members of the anti-Bismarck fronde supported the bigoted man of God. Stoecker and Waldersee persuaded the young Emperor that the best way to combat socialism was by gentle treatment of the workers and by benefactions. William II was impressed by the fawning flattery of his court chaplain, who called the Emperor's word "sacred"[50] and sang praises to the patriotic-monarchistic principle.[51]

The Bismarcks were appalled, not so much by these amateurish activities as by this kind of effort to solve a social problem which they had attacked with law and sword. Although irked by the militant court chaplain, the elder Bismarck was inclined at first to let matters slide, but Herbert was infuriated by Stoecker's political activities. He initiated a campaign against Stoecker which finally bore fruit after the resignations of the Bismarcks.

On November 28, 1887, a meeting on behalf of the Berlin City Mission was held at the home of Waldersee and attended by Prince William, the Princess, and Stoecker. In his opening remarks, Waldersee stated that the *Stadtmission* had no political significance and that its only characteristics were loyalty to the Crown, patriotic spirit, and opposition to anarchistic tendencies.[52] Prince William spoke in agreement, using the term "Christian-Social ideas."[53] Afterward, Prince William called on Herbert and described the meeting that had taken place at Waldersee's home. The Prince said: "I am inclined to think that Stoecker has something of Luther in him."[54] Herbert replied that Stoecker had his merits and might be a good preacher, but that he was a vehement person and his memory was not always to be relied upon. William said that Stoecker nevertheless had won many thousands of votes for the Emperor, which he had wrested from Social Democracy. Herbert then told the Prince that since the elections of 1878 the Social Democratic vote had steadily increased; if Stoecker had really won any votes there should be a demonstrable diminution.[55]

Shortly afterward, at a hunting dinner, Prince William and Herbert again discussed the Stoecker matter. This time Herbert regarded it as his duty to speak more bluntly to William: he said that Stoecker was to be regarded not as a preacher but as a politician, and that as such he was so acrid that one could not recommend to Prince William that he allow himself to be identified with him. The elder Bismarck approved of his son's attitude, but remarked that for once the matter did not concern him.

In the meantime the clamor in the press increased. Prince William reacted violently, denouncing Herbert before witnesses as the instigator of newspaper attacks. In December 1887 there appeared a violent article in the *Norddeutsche Allgemeine Zeitung,* which became a signal for the Liberal press to turn against Prince William and his *"Stoeckerei."* "As a matter of fact," wrote the elder Bismarck, "this article orginated with Rottenberg, head of the Imperial Chancellery; my son had never read it, nor had I."[56] "My son noted the effect of this baiting of the Prince at the next and all subsequent Court banquets, where the Princess William, who had hitherto been well-disposed toward him, ignored him so persistently that her next recognition of him did not take place until he was on the eve of departing for St. Petersburg, when the Cabinet was received in a body."[57]

On December 21, 1887, Prince William sent to the elder Bismarck a long explanatory letter telling how he had acted only in the interests of poor workers. The Committee for the Berlin City Mission included such distinguished names as Count Stolberg, Minister von Puttkamer, Minister von Gossler, Count Waldersee, and Count Hochberg, with their wives. The Prince wrote: "I would rather let myself be chopped into little pieces than do anything that would make matters difficult for you."[58]

To this and a subsequent letter the elder Bismarck replied with a long communication urging the young Prince to follow in the footsteps of his ancestor, Frederick the Great, not only as military figure but as statesman. He strongly supported Herbert's position on the court chaplain: "I have nothing against Stoecker; for me he has only one failing – as a preacher he plays politics....He stands at the head of those elements who are in direct opposition to the traditions of Frederick the Great....Among the distinguished names you mention to me [*as supporting the* Stadtmission] I can find not one I would be willing to entrust with responsibility for the future."[59]

The Bismarck-Stoecker feud continued for the remaining two and one-half years the Bismarcks held office. During this period the activities of the fiery court chaplain had become so obnoxious that William, now Emperor, decided to get rid of him. His method consisted merely in ignoring Stoecker at the marriage of Princess Victoria, the Emperor's sister. Stoecker interpreted the slight correctly and resigned on November 5, 1891. The Emperor accepted his resignation without the courtesy of a reply. The Bismarcks had won a belated victory.

Meanwhile, *die Politik über alles!* For the Bismarcks, political consider-ations were always paramount and took precedence over virtually everything else. Herbert's differences with the bizarre Stoecker remained on a political level. Neither he nor his father wanted a lukewarm Christian Socialism to take credit for the social reforms they were instituting in Germany and which they saw as among the greatest of their contributions to the well-being of their country.

The Stoecker episode brought to light a difference in the attitude of father and son on Jews. Stoecker was the extremist anti-Semite. The two Bismarcks had differing attitudes toward Jews. Here father and son parted intellectual company – a rare circumstance in their lives.

Otto von Bismarck had ambivalent feelings about Jews, but he was not a confirmed anti-Semite, despite the claims of Adolf Hitler, who was fond of including Prince Bismarck in his personal pantheon of Jew-haters. Early in his career, Bismarck had no special ideology about Jews, although he often spoke of their "accounting nature." Anti-Semitism was not a part of his own nature: he regarded Jews as useful to the state and to himself. He saw virtues in them – respect for parents, faithfulness in marriage, and a sense of charity. He regretted that they had no proper home and he saw something cosmopolitan about them. They were nomads, their Fatherland was Zion. Rather than have Jewish males marrying into Junker families, he thought it might be best if one brought together "a conjunction of a Christian stallion of German breed with a Jewish mare." In his mind there was no such thing as an evil "race."

At the same time, Prince Bismarck admitted that he was full of prejudices: "I have sucked them in with my mother's milk. If I think of a Jew face to face with a representative of a king's sacred majesty, and I have to obey him, I must confess that I feel myself deeply broken and depressed."[60] But he saw himself as no enemy of the Jews, and should they be foes, he forgave them. "I would accord to them every right, except that of holding authoritative office in a Christian realm."[61]

Prince Bismarck, the classic hater, numbered among his political opponents three Jews – Ludwig Bamberger, Eduard Lasker, and Eugen Richter. His con-tempt was tempered by political rivalry, but on occasion he expressed for them a modicum of anti-Semitic sentiment. He once wrote to his Boswell, Moritz Busch, about "Bambergé, Laskère and Rickèrt," the carefully placed accents indicating something foreign about the Jews.[62] But he added that "these Jews are not dangerous: they don't go to the barricades and they pay their taxes conscientiously."[63] For him they were dangerous political foes, very much like the Catholic Ludwig Windhorst.

They were a strangely assorted lot of opponents for the Chancellor. Ludwig

Bamberger (1823-1899), an economist and publicist, had been condemned to death *in absentia* after the revolution of 1848. He went on to become the leader of the National Liberal Party. He was the man behind standardization of German coinage, adoption of the gold standard, and establishment of the *Reichsbank.* While he supported Bismarck's outlawing the Socialist Party, he opposed the Chancellor on protective tariffs, state socialism, and colonial expansion. To Bismarck he was always "the red Jew." The Iron Chancellor was an all-or-nothing leader – and the Jew Bamberger was only partially loyal to the Bismarck dynasty.

Eduard Lasker (1829-1884), leader of the left wing of the National Liberal Party, the second strongest political party during the first period of the Second Reich, was thoroughly imbued with the liberty, equality, and fraternity ideology of the French Revolution. A gifted orator and an expert on fiscal matters, he sought to maintain the rights of freedom, and excoriated the government in sarcastic tones. Bismarck hated "the little Jew, Lasker,"[64] and called him "the sickness of Germany."[65] So great was Bismarck's contempt that when Lasker died while on a visit to the United States, and the American House of Representatives sent a message of condolence to the *Reichstag,* Bismarck angrily refused to transmit the message to Germany's governing body through the Chancellor's office.[66]

The third of the triumvirate of Jews who aroused the Chancellor's ire was Eugen Richter (1838-1906), leader of the Progressives. Maximilian Harden described Richter as a "middle-sized burly man...in an ill-fitting coat with a pair of too-short trousers, who had his figures and his quotations from former parliamentary speeches at his finger tips, and who shot arrow after arrow from the string of his bow up to the Federal Council's table."[67] Bismarck sat at that table. According to the Chancellor, Richter wanted everything in direct opposition to what the government wanted. Bismarck would ostentatiously leave the *Reichstag* chamber whenever Richter rose to speak.

These three, however, were all political opponents, and Bismarck roundly hated political critics no matter what their religion. On the other hand, he entrusted both his health and his property to Jews, even though the traditional prejudices of his class persisted. Dr. Eduard Cohen remained his personal physician and friend. Throughout much of his life he entrusted his financial affairs to Jewish banker Gerson von Bleichröder. The two men, as described by Fritz Stern,[68] came from two different worlds. The great Bismarck was the adventurous Junker who circumvented the Prussian constitution and united Germany under a conservative monarch. Bleichröder was the ingenious capitalist who managed to outwit the social hierarchy of his day, and in the process won aristocratic respectability. For three decades Bleichröder was not only Bismarck's private banker but also his secret agent and confidant in politics and diplomacy. As adviser to the misanthropic and moody Chancellor, he worked within a society which regarded Jews as foreign and inferior. In the end Bismarck showed his ingratitude to the man he had trusted for decades, but he never joined the ranks of the rigid Jew-haters in their bitter denunciations of Jewry.

Like father, *unlike* son. Where his father "strongly disapproved of this fight against Jews, be it on the basis of religion or race, or worse, on the basis of racial descent,"[69] Herbert remained the "refined anti-Semite," in tune with courtiers and officials of his day who rejected the company of Jews and saw to it that they remained out of positions of political power. He was convinced that Jews were corrupting the character of the German people, a central theme of Stoecker's brand of anti-Semitism.

Herbert's attitude toward Jews was governed by his relations to Bleichröder, who handled the finances of both father and son. In the *Reichstag* elections of July 17, 1878, when Herbert was a Conservative candidate for Lauenberg, Bleichröder made it a point to help young Bismarck. As we have seen, Herbert's campaign was singularly inept, characterized by overconfidence and a tactless disregard for the voting public. The overconfident Herbert was defeated by a close vote.[70] Bleichröder had helped, but Herbert had lost the election.

In the past the financier had overwhelmed the Bismarck family with gifts – caviar, pheasants, and cigars for the father. Dutch delicacies for Johanna, fine sherry for father and son. But gradually Herbert turned against Bleichröder, especially after the marriage fiasco, because he suspected the financier of playing a part in thwarting his liaison with Elizabeth Carolath. The old banker bore the full rage of Herbert's anger. Herbert denounced "the distinguishing BL – that fellow gets more impudent all the time. Hang him!" To Holstein, he wrote: "I look upon this filthy Jew as an evil in himself.... [That] stinking Bleichröder."[71]

In 1884, when Emperor William's cousin, Louis of Bavaria, got into financial trouble, the Chancellor suggested to the monarch that Bleichröder be called upon to bail out Louis. Herbert's reaction: "I regret that the Bavarian financial affair has gone into Bleichröder's hands because...I am sorry for anyone who is or will be forced to enter into relations with him."[72]

This was no controlled, benign anti-Semitism. Herbert hated the "evil of Jewry" and extended his hatred against Jews in general. His accentuated anti-Semitism was revealed soon after he became Secretary of State when he attempted to thwart the admission of a Jewish official to the Foreign Office. He knew nothing of the man's ability or record, only that he was a Jew. Jews, he said, became pushy when given high places in government. He would have none of it. The rest of the staff, he said, would resent it if a "Jew boor" *(Juden-bengel)* be added just because his father had "jobbered together" a great deal of money.[73]

Throughout the rest of his career Herbert retained this abhorrence, not only for Bleichröder but for all the Jews of Germany. He had considerably more feeling for African slaves than for German Jews. In this area Herbert performed his most useful service as Secretary of State. His father left the issue of suppressing the slave trade in Africa to his trusted son. The scion of the great man was grateful for the opportunity of doing something on his own rather than acting as a human rubber stamp for his father's policies. He resolved to strike a blow for mankind by fighting against the deadly peril that had shocked civilized humanity.

The situation was ripe for exploitation. In the early nineteenth century the trade in slaves to America and the West Indies from West Africa had been declared illegal, and slavery was abolished in the United States after the Civil War. Yet, the traffic persisted from the northeastern and eastern coasts of Africa to Muslim countries. The surreptitious export of West African slaves to Arabia, Persia, and the Red Sea littoral was designed to satisfy the demands of minor Muslim states which had not as yet declared the illegality of the slave trade. East Africa became a vast hunting ground for the dreadful traffic in human flesh, with thousands of blacks succumbing under inhuman conditions. The major outlet for the slave trade was Zanzibar, East African seaport, capital of the island and sultanate of the same name, described by Henry Drummond in *Tropical Africa* (1888) as "a cesspool of wickedness oriental in its appearance, Mohammedan in its religion, Arabian in its morals."

Britain took the lead in the struggle to end the slave trade in its nest.[74] Germany, too, was interested in killing the traffic, especially because slaves were smuggled from German East Africa to Zanzibar. The Berlin Conference of 1885, which had been concerned mainly with the interests of the Great Powers in the spoliation of Africa, paid comparatively little attention to the slave trade; only two of its articles (six and nine) pledged "to help in suppressing slavery and the slave trade." In the meantime, reformers turned their attention to the east African and Red Sea slave trade, denouncing it as repugnant to Western morals and religious codes.

On December 14, 1888, Herbert appeared before the *Reichstag* and delivered an impassioned address on the slave trade. It was an eloquent speech, marking the high point of Herbert's career as a statesman, and a proud moment for his father, the Titan of Germany.

Herbert began by stating that suppression of the slave trade in Africa was exacting toil for German pioneers of civilization. He described it as a disgusting but lucrative business for Arabian slave traders, and it was also outrageous for mankind and the century. Natives had been torn from their villages, chased, or killed. The slave hunters, greedy and without conscience, had penetrated numerous miles into the interior, stimulating fear and terror, and killing those natives they could not take away with them. The unhappy people of Africa knew nothing of firearms, or learned about them only when they were struck by the bullets of the Arabs.

Herbert stated that it was a matter of honor for the Reich to continue its efforts to end the slave trade. Germany would be certain to have the support of England, which, true to her honorable tradition, had always been in the front of the anti-slavery movement. German officials were in constant touch with the English Government on the subject, and there was a spirit of great loyalty and cooperation between the two countries on this matter.

Warming to this thesis, Herbert placed his reaction on a high moral plane:

So long as the abomination of the slave trade remains it will not be possible to bring to Africa the morality, the Christianity, and the civilization of the Western World....

We have contributed our share, along with England, Italy, and Portugal, to the sea blockade.... The public announcement of the engagements of our naval ships indicates that as always they have held high the flag and interests of Germany with their prudence, courage, and determination.... Many slave ships have been attacked by our warships.... Unfortunately, France did not sign the treaty of 1841 directed against the slave trade,...and opposes the idea of British cruisers examining her ships, even when these are manned by Arabs and have slaves aboard.

We need the encouragement and support of the *Reichstag [to fight the slave trade]*.... Our ships have a difficult task: they must guard a coastline of some 8 degrees of latitude, and it is not always possible to catch a slave ship which without lights in the dark tropic night and helped by the favoarble winds can cross from the mainland to the island of Zanzibar in five hours....

Gentlemen! I have come here in the hope that you will not only give us encouragement in our task but also take a leading role *[in this struggle]*.... It will make for an honorable reputation for both the German Government and the German *Reichstag.*[75]

On November 18, 1889, an Anti-Slavery Conference of eighteen nations met at Brussels for the sole purpose of "putting an end to the crimes and devastations engendered by the traffic in African slaves, protecting effectively the aboriginal populations of Africa, and insuring for that vast continent the benefits of peace and civilization." It was a decisive move in the outlawry of such traffic. Ten days after the opening of the conference, Herbert again appeared before the *Reichstag* and spoke of his unqualified support for its work:

> To bring so many states together in peaceful and friendly consultation for a noble, humanitarian goal is a great and elevating work. It is all the more important because, since the year 1841 when English initiative took the first steps to destroy the slave trade at sea, there has been no effective international force against the slave traffic and slave hunting. Slave trade exists no more on the western coast of Africa. The main reason for this is that the countries on the other side of the Atlantic have abolished slavery.

> We are happy that Ottoman Porte and the Persian Government are taking part in the Brussels Conference, for it is a fact that the slave trade and slave hunting could exist only because the slaves were brought via Arabia and Persia to inner Asia. It is within the province of His Majesty the Sultan and His Majesty the Shah, by taking measures in their own lands, to cripple the slave trade of East Africa as it has been destroyed on the West African coast.

> Much will be done at Brussels, but it will go slowly. I trust that there will be binding agreements and that the international rights of man as far as they concern the Negro will be codified.[76]

The Brussels Conference lasted until July 2, 1890, by which time the Bismarcks had fallen from power. Herbert's role in its success was not an unimportant one. Representing one of the major Western Powers concerned by the East African slave trade, he threw the weight of his prestige and that of his Government on the side of the reformers. The General Act of Brussels, prefaced by the words "In the name of Almighty God," contained 100 articles designed to suppress the slave trade by land and sea, including regulations on the right to search. A new era began in the international suppression of the trade. By the end of the first decade of the twentieth century, slave-dealing was under control throughout Africa.

Herbert's performance as Secretary of State on the slave trade delighted his father. Here was his intimate collaborator and heir apparent! Herbert had proven himself a worthy successor in the Bismarck dynasty. Let the political enemies who denounced Herbert take notice. Herbert *was* a Bismarck.

When William II decided to honor his Secretary of State, he, characteristically, promoted him to the military rank of lieutenant-colonel[77] at a ministerial dinner on Februray 28, 1889. The sudden announcement, apparently the young monarch's idea of a joke, was greeted with derision by the anti-Bismarck circle. General of Cavalry von Loë, in a letter to Count Waldersee, wrote sarcastically: "This promotion of Herbert Bismarck to lieutenant-colonel means an essential strengthening of our military power, and Boulanger[78] will now think twice before starting anything."[79] This was the typical sort of sniping criticism which the anti-Bismarck crowd used with pleasure against the Bismarcks.

Herbert himself saw his duty and sense of mission in his high office as indispensable for the welfare of his father. The obedient son was always solicitous for the welfare of "Papa." At the same time, as throughout his life, he remained torn psychologically between veneration for his great father's genius and a gnawing resentment against the parent's domination.

It was a psychic malady from which he never recovered.

7

DIPLOMACY BY IRRITATION

Herbert Bismarck's success in the Angra Pequena negotiations and his performance as Secretary of State for Foreign Affairs provided some balm for his shattered ego after the marriage tragedy. He had worried a great deal about his idolized father, and he was shaken by the old man's determination to kill himself if the marriage went through. Added to that shock was the unexpected threat of disinheritance. He still felt a sense of longing for Elizabeth. But that strong woman, after denouncing him as a weakling and cad, was busy entertaining her peers in the soothing atmosphere of Venice.

By keeping busy with affairs of state Herbert had managed, also, to assuage the hurt. In negotiations with British diplomats he learned what he regarded as a valuable lesson: behind the charming gentility of his hosts was an inner hardness which to a large extent was responsible for creation of a great empire. He considered it essential to get behind that ingratiating exterior.

Herbert was well-prepared for the psychological task of penetrating the English veneer. He had absorbed much of his father's personality – toughness of mind, hatred and contempt for political enemies, and the ability to gauge success and failure. Above all, he shared a curt and biting sarcasm. A confirmed misanthrope, he respected nothing and expected nothing. In political behavior he was definitely his father's clone.

With this background Herbert was well-equipped for "diplomacy by irritation." He believed that there was more to be gained by harshness than by charm and warmth. Besides, it amused him to throw his ample Bis-marckian weight around and display his power.

Herbert's attitude was not calculated to win friends and influence Englishmen. Outwardly, the men of Whitehall gave him the usual attention accorded a successful diplomat; inwardly, though impressed by the Blood and Iron Chancellor, they dismissed Herbert as a bloody ironic German nuisance, the lowest category of the British pantheon of undesirables. Herbert knew it – and did not care. The bottom line in his diplomacy was profit for father and country.

Herbert's success in negotiating the Angra Pequena settlement with England, which marked the beginning of Germany's penetration into Africa,[1] did not mean the end of Anglo-German friction in the colonial field. There were still conflicting claims in the South Sea Islands and in Africa – in Togo, the Cameroons, and Zanzibar, which caused serious differences between the two countries.[2] To Herbert, Germany's transoceanic aims were modest and insignificant in comparison to English colonial enterprise, but he felt that they were meeting with an unfriendly reception in England. To Lord Granville he wrote on August 30, 1884: "The national agitation, which is going on in Germany on account of the colonial question...will, I am afraid, make it very difficult for my Government to pursue as friendly a policy toward England as they hitherto have done, as long as the German nation remains under the impression to be treated by England in an unfriendly and jealous manner on colonial questions."[3] Again the persistent suspicion was evident.

Annoyed by continual German prodding, Lord Granville, in an address before the House of Lords on February 27, 1885, committed what one historian described as a "blazing indiscretion."[4] Germany's colonial policies, he said, hindered England's freedom of movement in transoceanic affairs. Perhaps, he continued with angry irony, the Liberal error had been to disregard the advice of Prince Bismarck with regard to Egypt, which was to "take it."[5] Granville's outburst, though probably unpremeditated, cleared the air. Bismarck replied in an infuriated address before the *Reichstag* on March 2, 1885, in which he publicly denied that he had ever given England the advice to take Egypt and in which he whipped the *Reichstag* into frenzy with a denunciation of English policy toward German expansion.[6]

Within a week Herbert was in London for urgent conferences. His behavior now was a calculated mixture of exaggerated modesty and courtesy with sarcasm and contempt. Of this visit Sir Charles Dilke wrote: "Count Herbert Bismarck came over again. If at his former visit he had only tried to get us to dismiss Lord Derby, on this occasion he wanted us to dismiss

Lord Granville and Lord Derby."⁷ The negotiators were Herbert Bismarck and Count Georg zu Münster, the German Ambassador to London, on the one side, and Foreign Secretary Lord Granville, Privy Seal Lord Rosebery, and Colonial Secretary Lord Derby on the other.

When negotiating at this level, Herbert used his offensive weapons of arrogance and irritation. Sir Charles Dilke reported: "On Friday, March 6, 1885, I saw Herbert Bismarck twice....I, having expressed anxiety about Zanzibar, he told me that his father had directed him to say that 'he considered Zanzibar as independent as Turkey or Russia.' It is to my mind shameful that after this, Lord Granville should have begun and Lord Salisbury have rapidly completed arrangements by which Zanzibar mainland, the whole trade of which was in our hands, was handed over to Germany."⁸

But with Prime Minister Gladstone, at the top level, Herbert was all graciousness and modesty. To the Prime Minister he explained: "We are the youngest of the Great Powers and we wish to undertake this function of colonization, which belongs to a great Power. But we only hope to do it in a small and humble manner, and we see in doing it giving to you the strongest proof of confidence in the future friendship of the two countries. For we knew that if a continental power were to attack our little colonies, we could invade them in return. But we also know that you can assail our colonies with effect; and that we cannot get at you in return, as you are masters of the sea."⁹ It was calculated flattery by a suddenly humble Herbert.

Encouraged by this unexpected modesty, Gladstone urged his Foreign Office to "wind up at once these small colonial controversies" while the favorable mood lasted. "It is really impossible to exaggerate the importance of getting out of the way the bar to the Egyptian settlement."¹⁰ On March 12, 1885, Gladstone publicly welcomed Germany to the ranks of the great colonizing Powers: "She becomes our ally in the execution of the great purposes of Providence for the advantages of mankind."¹¹ The pious Gladstone was working hand-in-hand with Providence for the glory of Britain.

As a result of these and subsequent negotiations settlements were made, by which Britain and Germany divided the disputed colonial areas among themselves. Germany took a part of New Guinea and several other islands in the South Pacific, while Britain retained the portion of New Guinea adjacent to Australia. In Africa, Germany appropriated Togo, the Cameroons, and a still undefined share of Zanzibar on the east coast, while Britain took a share of southeast Africa and most of the island of Zanzibar.¹²

Although the settlements were made in part after his resignation, Herbert was a leading figure in these negotiations while he held office as Secretary of State. Two areas in particular attracted his attention – Zanzibar and Samoa. Zanzibar was a focal point of Anglo-German friction. In the scramble for territory in Africa in the 1870s and 1880s east Africa, north of the Portuguese possessions, attracted the attention of the Germans. Their aim conflicted head on with that of Britain. On November 15, 1884, representatives of fifteen major Powers assembled in Berlin to come to some agreement on "rules of the game" in the partitioning of Africa. By the General Act of the Berlin Conference (February 20, 1885), they agreed that any fresh act of taking possession must be made known in advance to the other signatory Powers by any nation taking any portion of the African coastline. By an exchange of notes in October-November 1886, the chief rivals in east Africa agreed on what territories were to be their respective spheres of influence there and what was to be left to the Sultan of Zanzibar. On September 3, 1888, the Imperial British East Africa Company was set up. Shortly afterward the German colony of East Africa was established."[13]

In these delicate negotiations, Herbert took a hard, adamant attitude *vis-à-vis* the British on the ground that this was the kind of language they understood. His belligerency was matched by that of his father who, however, wanted no war with the British and who always stopped short of the danger point. Herbert revealed his attitude in a letter to Count Paul von Hatzfeldt, Ambassador in London, sent on March 19, 1886, while he was Under Secretary of State and about to assume the secretaryship:

> We believe that in both the Zanzibar and Samoa questions English representatives have regarded it as their task to arouse the mistrust of native rulers in uncivilized overseas areas against us and to lay obstacles in the way of our colonial ambitions.

> England has such tremendous colonial possessions in all parts of the world that it is difficult to understand why she opposes us.... The official representatives of England stand on the forefront of anti-German agitators and engender suspicion and mistrust against the aims of Germany. We have documentary evidence about this in Zanzibar, and Consul Powell seems to be acting the same way in Samoa....

> This continued friction in colonial territories can lead in the final analysis to political enmity, and England may find that to settle the account she may have to pay in Egypt and in the Orient for what her officials have done in Zanzibar and Apia.[14]

In May 1887 Herbert, as Secretary of State, journeyed to London to achieve an understanding between England, Russia, and Germany on the acute Bulgarian question.[15] Again, on August 24-25, 1887, he returned to London, this time to urge an understanding between England, Austria, and Italy.[16] On both occasions he sought to ease colonial difficulties between Germany and England, and successfully paved the way for settlement of both the Zanzibar and Samoan questions. The understanding was facilitated considerably by Anglo-German agreement on the necessity for ending the scandalous slave-trading and slave-hunting in East Africa. Herbert declared himself delighted by the cooperative spirit of Lord Salisbury (Prime Minister from 1886 to 1892), as indicated in a private letter to Count Hatzfeldt on December 19, 1888: "I express to Your Excellency the conviction that Salisbury has gone as far as he possibly could, and that we should not expect any more of him: his attitude and his remaining in office is worth a hundred times as much to us as all of East Africa; my father feels the same way."[17]

This was typical of the personal plane on which the Bismarcks conducted their diplomacy during the involved Anglo-German colonial negotiations. Lord Salisbury was regarded as a friendly Englishman, but Gladstone was *persona non grata* with the Bismarcks. When the British banker Hucks Gibbs visited Friedrichsruh in October 1885, Prince Bismarck expressed himself scornfully on Gladstone and his "follies in the Sudan," holding him responsible for the death of General Gordon."[18] He stated further: "I don't like your Chamberlain;[19] my son Herbert has sent me a photograph of him which has strengthened my unfavorable opinion. He looks so impertinent. I wish Dilke were in his place."[20] On his visit to London in August 1887 Herbert, at his father's request, assured Prime Minister Salisbury that his battle against internal factions (Gladstone) was watched with sympathy and anxiety in Berlin.[21]

Herbert considered it fantastic that the foreign policy of a great country should be entrusted to Gladstone, "who does not have the least understanding of what it is all about."[22] When Lord and Lady Randolph Churchill visited Berlin on their way back from Russia in 1888, they dined with Herbert and reported that "he was a kindly man, and although to English ideas he may perhaps have seemed a little rough and uncouth, he was really very popular in England....He was greatly interested in English politics, and I remember that at this dinner he had an argument on the subject of Mr. Gladstone, whom he cordially hated, remarking much to our amusement that his father always said: 'Gladstone will drag England to the lowest depths of hell.'"[23] The "kindly man" was an expert on hatred.

In negotiations on colonial matters, Herbert relied heavily on friendship with

Lord Rosebery, to whom he felt he could speak frankly:

Berlin, February 28, 1885

My dear Rosebery:

I was delighted to receive your kind letter and to hear from you again and I must write you these few lines to express to you my very best thanks for it.

I quite agree with what you say about the political situation and the English-German relations: the latter ought never have come to the uneasiness in which to my great sorrow they are now, and I think it would not have been difficult to avoid every sort of ill-feeling on both sides, had your Colonial Office from the beginning shown a little good will and treated us in the same friendly way, as we always treated England on all political questions up to last summer.

I do not know who is the moving spirit of all the notes that are evidently elaborated in the Colonial Office and pour in here by dozens. If you will take the trouble to read Lord Granville's note of the 21st inst. about Cameroons you will see that it is not written in very civil form, I might say next door to rudeness. [*Sic!*]

Lord Granville used to be always civil and polite, that I hardly can believe he has read that note before he signed it.

My father is particularly vexed, that some of his most confidential conversations with Malet[24] have been published without asking him – a proceeding which never yet took place.

I am more sorry than I can tell you that you have given up the idea to come to Berlin: we would receive you '*à bras ouverts.*'

Perhaps I can manage to come to England in March or April. I trust I should see you in that case: I deeply regretted that I could not avail myself in autumn of your kind invitation to Dalmeny because of your accident, but I hope it will not be long ere we meet again.

Please remember me kindly to Lady Rosebery, and believe me

Ever yours,

H. Bismarck[25]

When, in February 1886, Lord Rosebery was made Foreign Secretary in the short-lived Gladstone Liberal ministry, Herbert was delighted and expressed the hope that "Lord Rosebery would walk in Lord Salibury's footsteps."[26] Similarly, Herbert sought with only a modicum of success, to cultivate friendship with Dilke, the British imperialist.[27] In September 1889, when Dilke visited Berlin, he sought Herbert's advice about placing his son in a German *Gymnasium.*[28] But there was no close friendship.

There was, however, a difference between Herbert's attempts to win favor with British statesmen and his understanding of *Realpolitik* as taught him by his father. No matter how attractive British life and manners were to him, he saw Britain as standing in the way of German colonial pretensions. Always his diplomacy was a combination of hard-headed bargaining plus a show of modesty and charm, which could be turned on and off at will. His real feelings were expressed at a dinner engagement when, in the company of foreign diplomats, he stated in animated mood: "If England and Russia come to a parting, then I can only say: a shame for every blow that misses!"[29] This was a far cry from the "good will" and "mutual friendship" which he emphasized in his letter to British friends.

That Herbert really preferred the nuances of diplomacy by irritation was revealed by the Morier affair, which gave him an opportunity to initiate a friendly act in his foreign policy *vis-à-vis* Britain. At the same time the incident was characteristic of his method and manners as well as his talent for touching off heated controversies.

Sir Robert Morier (1826-1893) had been attached to many courts in Germany. As Secretary of the British Legation at Darmstadt from 1866 to 1871, he became a trusted adviser to the Crown Princess, and through her became a close friend of the Crown Prince, afterward Frederick III. Prince Bismarck, disturbed by the influence of Crown Princess Victoria, the oldest daughter of Queen Victoria of England, on her husband, and suspicious of the Crown Prince's tendency toward liberalism and his anti-Prussianism, strenuously opposed the royal couple and their possible control on the course of German history. The Chancellor hated Morier and feared his influence on the royal court. When Morier became British Ambassador in St. Petersburg in 1884, Bismarck took alarm at the possible diminution of Germany's relations with Russia, and attempted to bring about Morier's downfall.

On December 15, 1888, there appeared in the *Kölnische Zeitung,* organ of the controlled press, an official article in which it was stated that, in connection with the Geffcken trial,[30] it was necessary to prove the relationship of Sir Robert Morier, the current British Ambassador in St. Petersburg, to domestic German affairs. The article charged that in 1870, during the Franco-Prussian War, when he was Secretary of Legation at Darmstadt, Morier had used his position to betray the movements of German troops to the French military leader Marshal Bazaine.[31] The latter was supposed to have revealed Morier's conduct to the German military attaché at Madrid.

Morier angrily denied what he called "the absurd accusation" that he had passed to the French military information damaging to German operations. Marshal Bazaine had died in September 1888, but previously Morier had obtained from him a written denial, which he now published in *The Times* in the form of an open letter to Herbert Bismarck. Morier appealed publicly and personally to Herbert, the German Secretary of State, officially to disavow the libel and challenged him to produce any evidence in its support.

Herbert was now in an uncomfortable dilemma: if he chose to support the British he would certainly provoke the fury of his father. Characteristically, he remained loyal to his father, and declined either to withdraw the charge or give any evidence to support it. The result was that the libel against Morier continued to be believed in Germany. In the view of one outraged British historian: "Herbert Bismarck's conduct in the controversy with Sir Robert Morier is another example of his insolence, boorishness, and dishonourable conduct."[32]

There were varying estimates inside Germany as to the success of Herbert's colonial negotiations with England. Lothar Bucher, Bismarck's secretary and foreign affairs expert, was not impressed: "Herbert has not shown particular skill in the recent African negotiations. He can be very offensive at times, which is useful, but he has not sufficiently mastered these colonial questions. He does not understand, for intance, that colonies require a coast if they are to prosper, so he made concessions which we are now trying to alter. He allows himself to be won over too easily. Rosebery has been particularly successful in that, and has quite mesmerized him."[33] And again: "Count Herbert's second mission to London has not turned out as well as the first respecting Angra Pequena and the Fiji Islands, in which he had taken up a very strong position with good results....The object [*of the second mission*] was to negotiate respecting Lucia Bay and the Benue district; and Herbert, who was not sufficiently well acquainted with the maps, etc., conceded too much to Rosebery, who was very sharp, so that the result was disadvantageous to us. We lost Lucia Bay. The English minister argued that they could not abandon it to us, as it was impossible to allow the Cape Colony to be hemmed in on both sides."[34]

Inside Germany the anti-Bismarck clique, of course, criticized Herbert unmercifully at every step he took in colonial matters, deeming him rash, imprudent, and overhasty.

But for the elder Bismarck, Herbert's success in colonial negotiations with England was obvious and a matter of paternal pride. It was the same old story – a father blind to his son's faults. On January 26, 1889, Prince Bismarck addressed the *Reichstag* in happy terms about the understanding achieved with Britain on colonial questions in East Africa and Samoa.[35] "I regard England as our oldest and traditional ally with whom we have no quarrels – when I say 'ally' that is not to be understood in diplomatic terms; we have no treaties with England; – but I should like to hold fast to the friendly sentiment for England that we have had for some hundred and fifty years, also in colonial matters. And if it were shown to me that we were about to lose this friendship, I would be very careful to guard ourselves against the loss."[36]

Alarmed by the drawing together of France and Russia, Bismarck proposed an alliance with England sanctioned by Parliament for mutual defense against an attack by France. He argued that knowledge that such a treaty existed would of itself be instrumental in preventing war. Lord Salisbury, then Foreign Secretary, seemed to be inclined to favor this suggestion. On March 21, 1889, Bismarck sent Herbert to London on a special mission to consider with his British counterparts several undecided problems, notably the acute matter of Samoa. Herbert was instructed to take the opportunity to mention the possibility of an alliance. But this time Lord Salisbury held distinctly aloof: it was his duty, Herbert reported him as saying, to recommend that nothing be done for the present. He was very thankful for the idea and he hoped some day to do something about it, but "meanwhile we leave it on the table, without saying yes or no: that is unfortunately all I can do at present."[37] Another Bismarck plan had gone astray.

While his special sphere of interest was Anglo-German relations Herbert, as Secretary of State, was called upon to maintain the system of secret treaties constructed by his father as a means of assuring German hegemony and the peace of Europe. France was to be isolated; the Triple Alliance of 1882 between Germany, Austria-Hungary, and Italy was to be maintained; and "the wires to St. Petersburg were to be kept open" by the Reinsurance Treaty of 1887. In all these aims Herbert conscientiously and explicitly followed the wishes of his father, although personally he had little use for Frenchmen, Austrians, Italians, or Russians.

In order to turn French eyes from the lost provinces of Alsace and Lorraine, Prince Bismarck had offered France a free hand "within reasonable limits" in North Africa. But the war party in France, led by General Georges Boulanger, a prospective "man-on-horseback," loudly called for *revanche*. Because of this war scare, Bismarck won the election of 1887 handily.

On April 20, 1887, there occurred an incident which in normal times would have been regarded as trivial but which, in this strained atmosphere, endangered peace for a few days. A French official of the frontier police, named Schnäbele, was lured across the border on the pretext of discussing a minor routine matter and then was arrested as a spy. The French were infuriated, regarding the arrest as a trap laid by Herbert Bismarck to provoke a war. Emperor William I was vexed with Herbert, whom he regarded as responsible for the untenable German position in the Schnäbele affair.[38] The excitement died down within a few days – fortunately for Herbert.

Herbert was aware that the problem of maintaining close relations with Russia was a delicate one, especially in view of Russian chagrin at having their ambitions checked in the Balkans at the Congress of Berlin (1878). Prince Bismarck was blamed by the Russians for his activites as "honest broker" at the Congress. Both Bismarcks tried to maintain friendly relations with Russia, despite the existence of the embarrassing "Bulgarian letters," which they claimed were either forged or falsified to indicate that they promoted an anti-Russian policy in the Balkans, contrary to their offical policy. Herbert was anxious to show that his father was not guilty of advising his allies to support the Russian proposals at Constantinople while secretly encouraging them to take the opposite course. It was widely believed that a Janus-faced approach was the usual Bismarckian technique in diplomacy. There was much to justify that belief.

The change of government with the death of Frederick III on June 15,1888, presented both Bismarcks with a problem of critical importance. Neither one was shattered by the death of Frederick III because both feared the influence of his British wife.[39] It now became necessary for the Bismarcks to prepare the young Emperor for a role as promoter of Bismarckian policies. For two years Herbert was to play the part of mentor.[40] On his journeys shortly before and after his accession, William was accompanied by Herbert. As representative of the Foreign Office, Herbert drew up the speeches and political conferences[41] and in general carefully watched his charge. In the travels of 1888-1889 in the Scandinavian countries, Italy, Greece, Turkey, England, and elsewhere, Herbert became his father's eyes and ears in the important task of winning the young Hohenzollern to the Bismarckian line. [42] In a conversation with Minister-President Crispi of Italy on August 21, 1888, Prince Bismarck said: "When recently the Emperor was about to leave for St. Petersburg, he said to me: 'I am taking Herbert with me.' With that he meant to say: 'You remain here.' That is perfectly natural: Herbert's character and taste are appreciated by His Majesty. The Emperor is 30 and Herbert is 38 – I am 74."[43]

This was unwarranted optimism. The old Prince was spending most of his time at Varzin and Friedrichsruh, and relying upon his son to step into the breach and relieve him of the greater part of his official as well as social duties.[44] "So long as Herbert is in Berlin I can be completely at ease, for he knows the Emperor intimately; they are close friends, and they will never break."[45]

But in the meantime the anti-Bismarck camarilla was busily at work straightening out lines to the young Emperor and warning him of the rivalry beween "Hohenzollern and Bismarckian dynasties." In a short time, hinted the cabal, Prussia would lie helpless at the feet of Herbert Bismarck.[46]

The campaign against the Bismarcks was unremitting – and successful. By the middle of July 1889 the Emperor and his Secretary of State were exchanging sharp words about the relations of the elder Bismarck with the banker Bleichröder.[47]

Count Waldersee, Herbert's most unrelenting enemy and victor in the struggle for the Emperor's favor, later made this somewhat uncharitable statement: "Bismarck was altogether wrong in judging the relations between the Emperor and Herbert. The fault lies with Herbert, who did not understand the Emperor and who informed his father falsely....I am completely convinced that without...Herbert, who made enemies of everyone in Berlin and who never understood that most people were civil to him because they feared his father, the whole Chancellor crisis might have taken another course."[48]

In the struggle for Hohenzollern favor, as well as in his negotiations with the British, Herbert continued his calculated behavior of stiff-necked brusqueness, sarcastic flippancies, and alienating argument. That remained his nature. Always like his father, he could adopt a tone of graciousness when necessary, usually only in the presence of higher authority. His most potent weapon was the introductory phrase: "Father thinks...." And he did, indeed, speak for the old man, whose least desire became his command. He was not likely to win any popularity contests in the procedure.

In both Berlin and London, Herbert continued to arouse resentment and ill will. In the German capital almost all who passed his shadow reacted with disdain for the Central Ox's bully boy. In London, British aristocrats were both amused and angered by Herbert's behavior. Most were inclined to dismiss him as a drunken boor.

Both Prince Bismarck and Johanna were blind to criticism of their darling boy. After all, in the eyes of his parents, Herbert was a Bismarck – the product of a superior Junker blood line.

8

FROM SAMOA TO HELIGOLAND

Samoa and Heligoland were two pinpoints on the map of German foreign policy in the Bismarck era. In both Herbert played a central role.

The Samoan Islands, "pearls of the South Seas," were the last of the Pacific archipelagoes to be partitioned among the Great Powers. During the last quarter of the nineteenth century, these highly desirable islands attracted the attention of three rival Powers – Great Britain, the United States, and Germany. The British were the first to obtain a foothold in 1830. Within a few decades British missionaries were successful in Christianizing large numbers of natives. Later, under the initiative of such imperialists as Joseph Chamberlain, J.A. Cramb, and J.R. Seeley, the British decided to stay in Samoa and use it as a base for their Pacific empire.[1]

In 1838 the United States, under pressure from whaling companies, sent a scientific expedition to Samoa. In 1839, on completion of the transcontinental railroad in the United States, Washington showed further interest in Samoa. In 1872 an American naval officer, Commander Meade, concluded a treaty with the Great Chief at Pago Pago.[2] The fine harbor of Pago Pago, in the direct path of American trade with the Far East, aroused the attention of American commercial organizations and naval strategists.

German interest in Samoa began in 1857 when the trading house of Godeffroy and Sons of Hamburg established headquarters at Apia. Throughout the controversy over Samoa the commercial interests of this firm were closely identified with the German position *vis-à-vis* Great Britain and the United States.³ Although Germans appeared on the scene relatively late, they insisted that Samoa was a logical area for German colonialism.⁴ The Bismarcks, planning German expansion, saw opportunity in Samoa. Confrontation was in the offing.

During the two decades from 1870 to 1890 there was frenzied jockeying for position among the three Powers for a dominating position in Samoa. In 1878 the six-foot-four, tattooed Prince of Samoa, La Mamea, visited the United States, where he created a sensation. He offered Americans a protectorate over the Islands, which was politely refused, but a treaty was signed on January 17, 1878, giving the United States rights to a naval station at Pago Pago. The agreement included an ambiguous Article V: "If, unhappily, any differences should have arisen between the Samoan Government and any other Government in amity with the United States, the Government of the latter will employ its good offices for the purpose of adjusting those differences upon a satisfactory and solid basis."⁵ The United States was thus placed in the delicate position of binding itself to support the weak native government against foreign Powers.⁶

The course of a true imperialism never runs smoothly. Both Germany and the United States managed to win treaty rights in Samoa, including a harbor and similar commercial privileges. Neither of these treaties contained a "good offices" clause. A general convention was drawn up, which turned over to the consuls of Germany and Great Britain the government of Apia, the center of foreign commercial interests. The United States, although asked to adhere to the convention, did not approve, but in practice American consuls took part in the administration. In common imperialist practice, each Power pronounced Samoa independent.

The resultant situation was described by Thomas A. Bailey: "The tiny islands fairly seethed with the intrigues of land-grabbers, concessionaires, naval officers, commercial agents, and consuls. The natives were bullied and browbeaten, and brother was set against brother in the blood and turmoil of civil war. Nervous consuls hoisted the flags of their governments, only to be disavowed."⁷ The nearest cable was in New Zealand, and each consul had to act on his own responsiblity, a situation which Bismarck called *"furor consularis."* ⁸

In 1885 the German consul Dr. Steubel suddenly raised his flag in the islands. Unprepared, Prince Bismarck disavowed the act. Malietoa, joint king of Samoa, appealed to the American consul, who raised the American flag. Secretary of State Thomas F. Bayard ordered him to haul it down.⁹ It was truly a comedy of errors!

More quarrels and intrigues followed. So unendurable was the situation by the summer of 1887 that Bayard called German and British ministers to Washington for a conference.[10] The meeting was foredoomed to failure. Bayard proposed a plan of Samoan independence with temporary tripartite supervision by the three Powers. The German representative deemed both native autonomy and tripartite control as impractical, and urged that the Power commercially dominant in Samoa control the islands – meaning, of course, Germany.[11] Great Britain, which had obtained concessions from Germany elsewhere, supported the German position. Bayard was adamant. The conference adjourned without agreement. The *status quo* prevailed, temporarily.

Then came even worse confusion and chaos. Not the least troublesome factor was that the total amount of land claimed by foreigners in Samoa exceeded the entire acreage of the islands by several hundred acres.[12] The German consul declared war "personally" on King Malietoa, and set up his own favorite, Tamesese, as sole monarch. With the aid of four warships, the German consul had his own way for nearly a year. Meanwhile, Samoan followers of the deposed king rebelled against Tamesese and his German "Prime Minister" and, under the leadership of Mataafa, ambushed a party of German sailors in December 1888. The Germans were humiliated by their losses. In reprisal, the Germans declared martial law and sent the warship *Adler* to shell a village that had supported the former ruler. As the commander of the German ship took position to carry out his safe mission, he was amazed to see the American cruiser *Adams* anchored in his line of fire with crew ready to use her guns. *Donnerwetter!* Unwilling to risk starting a war with the United States, the commander sailed back to Apia. The German consul now lamely decreed martial law applicable to foreigners and natives.

Public opinion in both the United States and Germany, inflamed by the jingoistic press, was now at a boiling point. Newspapers in both countries wrote about "insults" to their respective flags. Americans were already angered by Prince Bismarck's imposition of an import tax on American hogs on the ground that they were infected with trichinosis. In reality he wanted to strengthen German protectionism.[13] Congress passed an appropriation of $500,000 for the protection of American lives in Samoa, and another $100,000 for improvements of the harbor of Pago Pago.[14] In March 1889, as Benjamin Harrison assumed the presidency, the United States dispatched the warship *Trenton* to Apia harbor, where two American, one British and three German warships, were already anchored.

It was a delicate situation. Then, on March 15-16, 1889, nature intervened to cool inflamed passions. Suddenly, a terrific hurricane descended on the poorly protected harbor, tossing virtually all the shipping, including the three German and three American warships, onto the beach, with great loss of life. Only the British *Calliope* was able to move to the open sea: as the warship strained her way to safety, the American crew on the doomed *Trenton* gave the British a hearty cheer, which was returned in an outburst of good will.

Robert Louis Stevenson described the incident: "Within the duration of a single day, the sword-arm of each of the two angry powers was broken; their formidable ships reduced to junk; their disciplined hundreds to a horde of castaways, fed with difficulty, and the fear of whose misconduct marred the sleep of their commanders. Both paused aghast; both had time to recognize that not the whole archipelago was worth the loss in men and costly ships already suffered. The so-called hurricane of March 16th made thus a marking epoch in world history; directly, and at once, it brought about the Congress and the Treaty of Berlin; indirectly, and by a process still continuing, it founded the modern navy of the [*United*] States."[15]

The storm effectively ended the possibility of combat. The three Powers decided to send representatives to Berlin for a conference.

The diplomatic history of the Samoan Islands may be divided into three periods: first, that of the treaties with the three Great Powers from 1872-79; second, the period of quarrels and disturbances ending with the Samoan Conference of 1889; and third, the last decade of the nineteenth century, when an unsuccessful attempt was made to implement the decisions made at Berlin.[16]

In the second of these three periods, roughly the 1880s, Herbert Bismarck played a major role as the top German official responsible for handling Germany's affairs in the dispute. He was pledged, of course, by training and temperament, to carry out his father's wishes in the matter of Samoa. And it is clear that the elder Bismarck, while heartily wishing for the success of the German penetration of Samoa, adhered to the idea of equality of all three contending foreign Powers – in the absence of no better solution from Germany's point of view. He did not desire to antagonize the United States, whose friendship he valued.[17] He had not the slightest intention of going to war over Samoa, and his replies to official American protests were most conciliatory. As Ambassador Pendleton[18] reported to Secretary of State Bayard on February 9, 1889, "Bismarck remarked that untrue statements and intemperate comments by the press, telegraphed from America and elsewhere, which were in marked contrast with considerate official utterances, had created in the minds of many the impression – a most erroneous one – that grave difficulties existed between the German and American Governments. There existed, he said, nothing to cloud the traditionally pleasant, amicable relations between the two governments and peoples and nothing affecting them could or should arise."[19]

In a message sent to Count Emmerich Arco-Valley, German Ambassador in Washington in 1889, the elder Bismarck indicated that he was willing to abandon Samoa completely if it was necessary to avoid a major conflict: "I personally would rather that we withdraw entirely from Samoa in a decent manner if it is at all possible, for it will never be of any real worth to us, but will rather serve only to worsen our relations with America, perhaps later with Australia, and then with England."[20] It was only with reluctance that Bismarck had embarked on a colonial policy ("The British are water rats and we are land rats and the two don't mix!"), but once the process started he was anxious that Germany avoid any major friction in her drive for colonies. In his memoirs he wrote: "My ideal aim, after the unification of Germany, was to achieve confidence not only of the smaller nations of Europe but also of the Great Powers....I followed this line not without struggle against my inner convictions in such affairs as Schnäbele [*April 1887*], Boulanger, Kaufmann [*September 1887*], with Spain in the question of the Caroline Islands [*1885*], and with the United States in Samoa."[21]

This was the *Realpolitik* of a master diplomat. But Herbert, though he respected his father's views, was considerably more belligerent and showed it in his handling of the Samoan problem. In his estimation the iron policy used by his father in unifying the Germanies should be extended to foreign affairs. He saw aggressiveness in Samoa in the tripartite struggle as more advantageous to Germany than giving in to the other two Powers. He was pulled in two directions: on the one side he wanted to implement a firm, unyielding policy in Samoa, and on the other he knew that in the final analysis he had to give in to the wishes of his father. For once there was a glimmer of independence, but not enough to break the bond with the great man.

A clue to Herbert's attitude may be found as early as 1885 in the matter of the Caroline Islands, a widely scattered archipelago of some 600 islets and islands in the Pacific Ocean. In 1686 Admiral Francesco Lazeano had named the islands in honor of Charles II of Spain. Spain definitely claimed the group in 1875, but this was contested by Germany, which had considerable economic interests there and was concerned by potential American claims to the islands. The elder Bismarck concluded that the Caroline Islands were not worth the trouble and that "it was only Spain's insolence that created it."[22] Herbert, then Under Secretary of State, was ordered by his father to assure the American State Department that there was no information as to United

States claims to the Caroline Islands, and that assertions on the question had evidently been made for the purpose of creating problems between the two countries.[23] This was a task for which Herbert had little heart, for he was anxious to push German claims to the Carolines to the limit. Bülow later wrote: "All informed opinion was unanimous that in 1885 Prince Bismarck had probably done well not to take possesion of the Carolines, in face of the violent objections shown by the Spaniards at that time, as the impetuous Herbert Bismarck wanted to do."[24]

Impetuous Herbert! His view of the Samoan problem may be judged from an interview he held with Lord Salisbury in London on August 24, 1887. The Washington Conference, held in the preceding June and July, had already failed to settle Samoan difficulties. Now Secretary of State, Herbert expressed himself bitterly on American pretensions: "I told Lord Salisbury that all possible reservations must be made on the American position. The Americans seem to interpret the Monroe Doctrine in the sense that the Pacific Ocean was to be considered an American lake; not only did they want Hawaii (in which, Salisbury said, Great Britain was not at all interested) to be under their exclusive influence, but also Samoa and Tonga as stations between the future interoceanic [*Panama*] Canal and Australia. There are even some American visionaries who dream of a forthcoming fraternization and consolidation of the various Australian colonies with the United States."[25] Herbert reported that Salisbury, obviously impressed, said that the Americans would have to be watched closely (*"Man müsse den Amerikanern jedenfalls scharf auf die Finger sehen"*).

Herbert denounced Malietoa, whereupon Salisbury expressed the opinion that "whichever nigger chief became King of Samoa would be all right with the New Zealanders, so long as the political situation was not altered." Herbert then said that a German squadron would deal with Malietoa, and expressed the hope that the British Government would stand fast on the German side in Samoa, just as Germany supported Britain in Egypt. Salisbury replied: "Certainly," and added that he hoped the Germans would not carry on a war against Samoa. "No, only against Malietoa personally," replied Herbert. "In Samoa we just want to protect our interests against civil war and piracy."[26] Herbert, in classic imperialist style, pitched his argument on a high moral plane.

The Central Ox's son was not quite as innocent as he claimed. Herbert was not without blame in the struggle between German, American, and British consuls – the *furor consularis* in Samoa from December 1888 to March 1889. On January 8, 1889, when the Chancellor was absent from Berlin, Herbert sent a telegram to Knappe, then German consul in Samoa: "Repression is necessary of any insurrection which might lead to a sudden state of war."[27] It was on the basis of this vague instruction that Consul Knappe had declared martial law in Apia after Samoan natives had attacked German sailors, martial law not only for natives but also for subjects of Great Britain and the United States in Samoa. In his desire to annex the islands, Knappe reckoned that he had the support of Herbert Bismarck and the German Foreign Office.

The Central Ox, however, cancelled Knappe's action and indirectly his son's encouragement of the consul. In the German White Book on Samoa, which appeared on February 15, 1889, obviously to present the German case before the convening of the Samoa Conference, Bismarck maintained that Knappe's conduct of affairs in Samoa, in working for annexation and declaring martial law, was without authorization. In the following quotations from Bismarck's preface to the *White Book* he places the entire blame on Knappe, with no mention of Herbert:

> This [*Dr. Knappe's*] repeated statement that he had been commissioned or empowered by the Imperial Government to declare war, or even martial law, was arbitrary or due to an error difficult to explain....It seems to me that his touchiness in the matter of the respect he claimed, together with the letter of Capt. Brandeis of December 13th last, and the presence at Apia of three German ships of war deprived Herr Knappe of that *sangfroid* which alone could enable him to retain a clear view of the situation and its possible consequences.

> In his correspondence, too, with his colleagues, he seems to have written in a brusque and excited tone, which sometimes even took the form of threats against the other consuls. You are aware that the demands put forward by Consul Knappe when negotiating with Mataafa that Germany should take over the administration of the islands, including their representation abroad, were unwarrantable, and that he was telegraphed to from here to withdraw them at once. The further statements in his report that all the Samoans would prefer to see the islands annexed by Germany, but that, nevertheless, there was little hope that the rebels would give way, are partly contradictory and partly lack practical import, as without the assent of England and America the political status of Samoa cannot be aimed at.

> It is incomprehensible to me how Herr Knappe should again recur to the idea of annexation, seeing that from his experience in the Foreign Office as well as his instructions, and our recent correspondence with him he must have known that all thoughts of annexing Samoa are in direct contradiction to the policy pursued by me in accordance with the ideas of the Emperor.[28]

Obviously, the shrewd elder Bismarck was preparing the public for a change in policy with regard to Samoa.[29] Consul Knappe was the most convenient scapegoat under the circumstances. Others were not as charitable in their estimate of Herbert's role in instigating Knappe's frenzied conduct. The Secretary of State was accused of giving Knappe specific instructions and then blandly allowing the consul to take full blame for the consequences. This was Herbert's conception of Bismarckian *Realpolitik*. On March 28, 1890, two days after Herbert's resignation, and two weeks before the German ratification of the Samoan Treaty (April 12, 1890), the *Berliner Tageblatt* published a scathing attack:

> Even if one wants to excuse Herbert Bismarck's conduct in the Samoan Affair as an overflow of that colonial enthusiasm that has found so welcome an echo in many circles of the people, still the most zealous supporters of the Bismarck dynasty would have to hesitate in this situation. Count Bismarck showed a lack of chivalry in allowing Consul Knappe to do penance for him. The consul followed to the letter the instructions of the Secretary of State.[30]

Similarly, in the judgement of the journal *Germania,* Dr. Knappe "did not bear full blame," which Herbert Bismarck "had to share with him in large part."[31] Herbert, naturally, paid no attention to his critics.

In early 1889, Prince Bismarck suggested that the Samoa Conference, which had been broken off in Washington in 1887, be resumed in Berlin. On March 21, 1889, he sent Herbert on a special mission to London to help prepare the way for an Anglo-German alliance, which was unsuccessful, and to sound out the British on presenting a common front at the forthcoming Samoa Conference. Herbert reported back that "we can count absolutely on England's complete support,"[32] and that "our friendly arrangement with England will be of use against the Yankees."[33]

The Berlin Conference convened on April 29, 1889. The American commissioners were John A. Kasson, former Ambassador to Germany; William Walter Phelps, the new Ambassador to Germany; and George H. Bates, who had been on a mission to Samoa as investigator in 1886. The British representatives were Sir Edward Malet, Charles Stewart Scott, and Joseph Crowe. The German delegation, headed by Herbert Bismarck, included Baron Friedrich von Holstein, who was regarded as a specialist in the Foreign Office in American affairs, and a Dr. Krauel. Bismarck's instructions to his son were explicit: despite the jingoistic tone of the German press and despite the personal feelings of himself or of his son, a settlement *must* be reached on Samoa and the situation must not get out of hand.

These were orders Herbert could not possibly ignore. But he permitted himself one final display of irritation before showing all his charm. The American commissioner George H. Bates, after his visit to Samoa in 1886, had published in 1887 a report most unfavorable to Germany. In addition, in the April and May issues of the *Century Magazine*, two of his articles on the Samoan question appeared, in which Bates publicly attacked Germany on the ground of bad faith and insulting conduct. Bates had been appointed before the articles were published. Nevertheless, when the American commissioner reached Berlin, Herbert at first refused to meet him. But the former Ambassador, Kasson, with whom Herbert worked closely throughout the conference, arranged an interview. During the interview Bates said that he had tried to stop the publication of the articles and, furthermore, the recent appearance of the German *White Books* might have altered his opinions. Herbert, thereupon, spoke coldly to him, and then the conference was allowed to proceed.[34]

It was widely anticipated that there would be long-distance clashes between Secretary of State James Gillespie Blaine, advocate of a spirited foreign policy, and the domineering Prince Bismarck. Much publicity was given to a story that the American commissioners found Prince Bismarck overbearing and irritable. The Commission sent a cable to Blaine on June 9, 1889, saying "The President does not know of the irritability of those who believe they have yielded already in all essentials to the claims of the United States." Blaine replied: "Irritability on the part of your English and German associates is not a determining factor with the Government of the United States." That last sentence became famous. Actually Blaine's message was intended as a reproof for the American delegates. It came at the close of the negotiations and probably was never brought to the attention of Prince Bismarck.[35]

Throughout the negotiations, until June 14, 1889, in all of some nine sessions and many private meetings, Herbert made certain to keep his celebrated temper in check. He knew his father's instructions – conciliation and indifference to details – as long as German prestige was not damaged. For the unpredictable Herbert it was a strict order, considering his own attitude on German colonialism, and especially because of the "singular and undiplomatic frankness" of the American commissioners.

Herbert presented a strong argument, but the Americans adamantly opposed partition of the islands. He used his own weapon of *ersatz* charm. To Commissioner Phelps he related this story of what took place when King Malietoa was brought back from exile: "One night on the [*ship*] *Wolf* when the moon was full, the captain saw Malietoa struggling with one of his followers who overpowered him. On questioning the follower, he said Malietoa, at such periods of the moon, was always liable to attacks of frenzy, and he had simply engaged in an effort to restrain him. Later in the voyage, at 2 o'clock in the light of a still bright day, Malietoa leaped into the sea. Boats were lowered, and Malietoa was rescued. Think, Mr. Phelps, how fearful the consequences for our captain and for us, if the sea hadn't been still, so that the poor king could be saved! Would your lively papers ever have been persuaded that our captain hadn't pushed him overboard? And our enemies on this side of the water!"[36]

By final decision of the Conference, Germany relinquished her plan of absorption. It was agreed to maintain the integrity of the islands with a three-Power condominium or protectorate over Samoa, with the restored native dynasty ruling nominally. The first article of the agreement "recognized the independence of the Samoan Government and the free rights of the natives to elect their chief or king and choose their form of government according to their own laws and customs." The remaining articles provided for tripartite government by the three contracting parties.

The paper work was formidable, but there was little satisfaction with a settlement that soon proved to be unworkable.[37] The British signed more reluctantly. In the United States the pro-Administration Republican press hailed the outcome as a great triumph, while Democrats denounced it as abject surrender to the wily Bismarck. Robert Louis Stevenson, a great writer but an amateur in diplomacy, was impressed: "The example thus offered by Germany was rare in history; in the career of Prince Bismarck, so far as I am instructed, it should stand unique. On a review of these two years of blundering, bullying, and failure in a little isle of the Pacific, he seems magnanimously to have known his policy was in the wrong,"[38] A Samoan native orator reacted passionately: "Who asked the Great Powers to make laws for us; to bring strangers here to rule us? We want no white officials to bind us in the bondage of taxation."[39]

Outrage in Germany. Here the press attacked the Samoa Treaty as a humiliating surrender by the "outgoing Bismarck dynasty." The agreement became a focal point for the final drive against the Bismarcks, father and son.[40] The *Vossische Zeitung* denounced the settlement and pointed out that what the Liberals had prophesied had come true.[41] The *Frankfurter Zeitung* claimed that the Americans could not be dissatisfied with the treaty, "since they got everything they could have wished for."[42] The *Berliner Tageblatt* pronounced its decision: "In the name of Germany, Count Bismarck has done something which recalls to all friends of the Fatherland that Olmütz which even today is regarded as the nadir of the moral position of Prussia in the councils of the peoples."[43]

Arrows of dissent came hurtling at Herbert, as the author of the Samoan condominium. There was to be further censure directed to him after the East African Convention of 1890, when Germany obtained Heligoland in exchange for rights in Zanzibar. Ironically, though the agreement was made by Herbert's successors on July 1, 1890, several months after his resignation, the trade was credited to Herbert. He was denounced unmercifully by all his critics, who charged him with exchanging a button for a suit of clothes. The overrated Bismarck, they said, had allowed the British to best him in a new battle of wits.

It was the usual situation for the Bismarcks. Father and son went ahead with sublime confidence and little regard for the feelings of lesser men. Critics screamed in helpless dissent. The Bismarckian reaction – let them be damned.

The idea of obtaining Heligoland for Germany occurred to Prince Bismarck in 1884 at the time when Germany and England were quarreling over the acquisition of Angra Pequena in South-West Africa. The small island (130 acres) in the North Sea, 28 miles northwest of the mouth of the Elbe, was strategically important to Germany as it commanded the entrance of the Kiel, or Kaiser Wilhelm Canal. It had been ceded to Great Britain by Denmark in 1814.

In a dispatch to Count Georg zu Münster, the German Ambassador in London, on May 5, 1884, Bismarck stated that lasting friendly relations with England hinged on possession of the island of Heligoland. In British possession, he argued, the island was of little value other than as a jumping off point for possible attacks on German territory. But if Germany owned Heligoland she would not object to the expense of transforming it into a "harbor of safety," not only for British ships but for commercial ships of all nations. Moreover, this would gain Germany's friendship for England: "Our friendship can be of high value for English politics." Germany's attitude toward England's rivals was of far greater importance to England than all the trade rivalries in the world put together.[44] The Chancellor urged his envoy to pursue the matter further.

Münster replied on May 8, registering his great enthusiasm for the idea. He stated that the acquisition of Heligoland would be popular in Germany and most advantageous, and that there was hope that the British Government would agree to it. He quoted Lord Derby, the Colonial Minister: "If Germany would pledge herself to build a harbor of safety at Heligoland, costing at least 250,000 pounds sterling, within the next three years, then the matter can well be discussed further." Because the moment was favorable, Münster reported further, "it would not be advisable to await the presence of Count Herbert Bismarck. Count Herbert will work on this matter usefully with Lord Granville and Sir Charles Dilke."[45] Despite his kind words about Herbert, obviously included to please the old man, Münster in all probability wanted credit for the Heligoland deal.

On May 11 Prince Bismarck, not satisfied with Münster's handling of the Heligoland matter, further instructed his envoy to make it clear that Germany's support of England's political affairs were conditioned on satisfaction of her

claims in the South Seas and in Africa *and the cession of Heligoland.*[46] Münster discussed the subject with Lord Granville on May 17, 1884, emphasizing
the advantage that a harbor of safety at Heligoland would have for England,
but said nothing about Prince Bismarck's overseas claims, nor did he mention
the possibiltiy of a reversal of the British position if Bismack was not satisfied.[47]

The delicate negotiations over Heligoland broke down when the Angra
Pequena differences reached a critical stage. On May 25, 1884, Prince Bismarck sent a telegram to Münster, ordering him not to mention Heligoland any
further because of the attitude of England on Angra Pequena. "To bring up
this question might furnish England with the excuse to put Germany's African
claims on the same footing as the right to Heligoland."[48] The Chancellor was
thoroughly disgusted with Münster, who seemed to be interested only in the
acquistition of Heligoland, without following his instructions to tie it up with all
of Germany's overseas claims. To Bismarck this was plain bungling, but he
decided to await a more propitious moment.

Again the father turned to the son. In his visit to London in 1889, Herbert
managed to win an understanding with Lord Salisbury on the Samoan matter
and at the same time cautiously broached the subject of Heligoland. He reported
back to his father that Mr. Gorst, a prominent Conservative, had advocated in
a speech before the House of Commons the gratuitous cession of Heligoland
to Germany. Moreover, added Herbert, the Conservative Party now seemed
to favor the idea.[49] But he advised caution because "if we show too much zeal
the price will go up."[50] British statesmen at the upper level were still inclined
to delay the matter on the ground, Herbert thought, that they could make a
much better deal by waiting. Bismarckian analytic shrewdness was plainly in
high gear.

Herbert was hard at work preparing the way for a settlement on Heligoland.
In his March 1889 visit to London he made it a point to discuss colonial matters
with Joseph Chamberlain, whose political star was rising. Chamberlain was
friendly to Germany, Herbert reported to his father, and he wanted "to remove
all points from which difficulties might arise between the two countries in the
future." Herbert was pleased when Chamberlain took the initiative: "Naturally
we cannot expect you to *give* England any colonies, as worthless as they
might seem to be. There must be compensation: what do you think if we give
you Heligoland instead, which is useless for England and perhaps worth having for you, were it but for the prestige?" Herbert replied that these words
made him very happy, and added that it was a shame that he – Chamberlain
– was not currently a minister. Chamberlain then said that a Heligoland deal
would be most popular in England: "I shall defend it myself through thick and
thin in the House.... In a possible new Franco-German war there would be

great bitterness in Germany if the French warships lie off Heligoland and use it as a coaling station."[51] This argument was precisely the one which Herbert expected to present himself: Chamberlain expressed it perfectly.

The Bismarcks had carefully planted the seeds – which were to bear fruit. But it was their unexpected fate to observe results from the outside. On July 1, 1890, by the Anglo-German Agreement, the two governments settled the limits of their respective spheres of influence in various parts of Africa. In return for Heligoland, Britain obtained Germany's recognition of a British protectorate over the dominions of the sultan of Zanzibar, including the islands of Zanzibar and Pemba, but leasing a strip that was later ceded to Germany. Germany further agreed to withdraw her protectorate over Witu in favor of Britain. The net effect was to remove all serious causes of dispute between Britain and Germany in east Africa.

Prince Bismarck considered this settlement in east Africa so important that in the third volume of his memoirs, *Gedanken und Erinnerungen,* he devoted all of Chapter 11 to "The Treaty on Heligoland and Zanzibar." The fallen Chancellor had much to criticize, especially because the treaty had been concluded by his successors. He intimated that the cession of Heligoland was not equivalent for what Germany had relinquished in Zanzibar. He denied that he had ever advised the Zanzibar Treaty and placed all responsibility for it upon his successor Caprivi and his administration. Britain had not expected Germany would pull out of Zanzibar, Bismarck wrote, especially because German trade had been increasing in east Africa; futhermore, Englishmen in Zanzibar had been amazed by the extent of German concessions there, refusing at first to believe the news of the treaty.[52]

How Bismarck himself would have handled the matter and achieved a better deal with England will remain forever in the realm of conjecture. Certainly both he and his son were anxious to obtain Heligoland, but at a better price than that paid by the new regime. Much of this criticism may be attributed to the Bismarcks' searing bitterness because of the circumstance of their resignations.

William II, characteristically, took full credit himself for the acquisition of Heligoland. To his biographer, Joachim von Kürenberg, he related his version of the negotiations:

> Herbert Bismarck had been charged by his father to negotiate in London on our behalf for the acquisition of the island. But he did not attain his object. If you wanted to negotiate with the English, you must never let out the secret of what you are interested in, particularly not if that something belongs to them. On the contrary, you must try and explain that you know quite well that they wish to part with that particular object

because it is of no value to them. The important point is to wait for an opportune moment and then make your offer.

Before I started negotiations for Heligoland, I had obtained very useful information from consuls and experienced businessmen in East Africa regarding the value of our protectorate of Zanzibar. From that information it became clear to me that, owing to the increasing importance of the ports on the Tanganyika coast, Zanzibar was of value only as a port of reshipment....

By means of my proved tactics in dealing with the British, I achieved the exchange of the two islands.

Prince Bismarck was livid, for I had succeeded, without serious difficulties, where his son had failed. The Prince published numerous articles in the *Hamburger Nachrichten,* emphasizing the great importance of Zanzibar and exposing to criticism and ridicule the acquisition of Heligoland as senseless and useless. Today nobody has any doubts about the value of Heligoland, or the successful negotiations which regained for us this important island close to the mouth of the River Elbe.[53]

Cum grano salis! The impetuous young Kaiser, one of the truly outstanding egomaniacs of the day, was intoxicated by the exuberance of his own personality. Nearly everything he said was embellished by overuse of the pronoun "I" – in this case "*I* achieved the exchange of the two islands." The facts were: the groundwork was prepared by the Bismarcks, and the trade would not have been made unless the British wanted it. The conceited William II was highly proficient – not in diplomatic matters – but in the absurd practice of giving himself complete credit.

The Central Ox was as pleased as a Germanic Punch by his son's diplomatic activities. Admittedly, Herbert drank too much and tended to be a bit boisterous under the influence of the vine. So what? He, Prince Bismarck, enjoyed wines and liquors as much as the next man, but who dared to criticize the clearheadedness of his diplomacy? Certainly Herbert had minor faults – what man did not? The important thing to the old man was that he had a son in the Bismarckian image who would carry on his work.

What the elder Bismarck neither saw nor understood was the philosophic dictum that all things come to an end – even his proposed Junker "dynasty in being."

9

FALL OF THE TITAN

In July 1945, just after the end of World War II in Europe, a general election resulted in an unexpected defeat for Winston Churchill, brilliant leader of his people in victory. The world was stunned by this seeming ingratitude to a great wartime leader. Churchill himself, though shocked and dismayed, was a firm believer in the democratic process and soon got over the hurt. In 1951 he was again Prime Minister.

It was otherwise with the Bismarcks. They too were hit by an unexpected bolt of political lightning, but they were not destined to return to power. The mighty Bismarck, founding father of the Second German Reich, was struck down from his pedestal by a loud, egotistical young whippersnapper of a Hohenzollern, a braggart with a lame arm and swollen head. That was the end of the planned Bismarck dynasty – the Central Ox would not be succeeded by his beloved son Herbert.

The year 1890, when Bismarck resigned or, from his standpoint, was dismissed by William II, is an important boundary mark in both German and world history. Certainly, it was a tragedy that the Chancellor's lifework was left in the hands of a ruler who could neither further nor maintain it. But Bismarck himself must share the blame for this unfortunate occurrence: it was his fault that the new monarch possessed far too much power for his own good and for the good of the German people. Had the Chancellor supported parliamentarianism in the Western sense, there would have been some check on the pretensions of a reckless monarch.

Moreover, the fact that the German people remained politically immature also may be attributed in part to Bismarck's shortsighted authoritarianism. In a confessional mood the Chancellor told Count Helldorf that "in all earnestness I want to devote my last years to making good the greatest mistake of my life, which was the creation of equal suffrage."[1] The great Chancellor was somewhat out of tune with his century.

Historian Erich Eyck delivered a fair verdict. Under Bismarck's leadership, said Eyck, the German nation had become united, strong, and powerful. But the sense of freedom and individual independence, of justice and humanity, had been lamentably weakened by *Realpolitik* and *Interessenpolitik* – the politics of power and material interest, as well as by the personal regime which Bismarck had imposed on his countrymen.[2] "It is therefore no mere chance that his work did not last, and that the Prussian crown and the Hohenzollern dynasty, which had been exalted to heights never before known, ceased to exist twenty years after his death."[3]

Herbert Bismarck was to play a central role in the circumstance surrounding the final conflict between his father and William II. Both the monarch and his chief minister had the future status of the younger Bismarck in mind during the quarrel which led to the Chancellor's fall.

The Central Ox not only resented what he regarded as a sudden dismissal but was angered by having his hopes for a Bismarck dynasty shattered. He had looked forward eagerly to establishing Herbert as his successor in the chancellery. He had taught the business of statecraft to his son, and with great care he had nurtured his career. Now he was advanced in years (he was seventy-five) and more and more inclined to turn his duties over to his son. In his mind this succession was the least reward he could expect for his priceless service for the German people. Anyone who stood in the way of this ambition, even if he be a Hohenzollern, would earn his contempt and hatred.

There is evidence beyond court gossip to show that Bismarck intended his son to succeed him in the chancellorship. Journalists Moritz Busch and Lothar Bucher, who were intimate co-workers of the elder Bismarck, recorded nearly everything they heard him say. On February 24, 1890, in the midst of the difficult negotiations which led to the Chancellor's dismissal, Bucher mentioned to Busch that Bismarck was "not at all satisfied with the Rescript,[4] nor was he pleased in other respects with the intentions of the young Majesty,[5] who had become very self-confident and arbitrary, and that he had only remained in office up to the present because he had hoped that the Emperor would appoint Herbert to be his successor. He knew already, however, that this desire would not be fulfilled, as the Emperor objects to Herbert on personal grounds."[6] Prince Chlodwig of Hohenlohe, who had worked with the elder Bismarck for nearly two decades, stated in his *Memoirs* that "the old Chancellor enjoys the convenience of Friedrichsruh all the more, because he believes that his absence advanced Herbert's influence."[7]

Bismarck himself, of course, was not willing to admit openly that he wanted his son to succeed him in office. At the same time, he was infuriated by gossip among ministers, court circles, and public alike that he intended to set a dynasty of mayors of the palace, which would endanger the status of the royal household.

Three years after his resignation, Bismarck was interviewed by journalist Maximilian Harden, at a time when the younger Bismarck was running for office again in the *Reichstag* (1893). Harden reported the fallen Chancellor as saying that he had never had any intention of having his son succeed him: "He did not underestimate Herbert's talents; on the contrary he valued them very highly. But he did not think the matter of succession was a factor any longer. 'He is quite different from me. He is a child of the city.... All his life long he has worked more than I and I knew of no more able diplomat among our young people. But where I despise, he hates; it is an excellent sentiment, but it does not always retain its vigor as long as might be wished. If he is beaten in the election today, then he will probably go to England, where he will probably have nothing more to do than to dress himself three times a day. Only because of that do I wish his election....' In these hours, the Prince also said, he had never thought about supporting his eldest son as Chancellor of the Reich; he had never desired it. Only a donkey could convince himself that such an office could be inherited."[8]

The Iron Chancellor by no means regarded himself as a donkey. He had always been careful to avoid giving the impression that he believed in *inheritance* of his high office. This was not in his estimation a matter of primogeniture – it was simply a case of the best man for the position. Despite his disclaimer, he was certain that Herbert was fitted by ability and experience, far better than others, for the office. He was convinced that if Germany were to maintain her place in the European state system, it was absolutely necessary that his own policies be continued, preferably by one who understood them in their entirety. In his own mind it was a simple fact – his son was the most qualified person to safeguard the fruits of his own lifetime of work.

Herbert had a similar sentiment. Prince Pless, who was close to Bismarck, reported that Count Herbert had always spoken of *"wir,"* as if he and his father were inseparable.[9] The collaboration, indeed, was so close that at times it was difficult to ascertain where the father's thoughts broke off and those of his son began. So well trained was Herbert, however, that almost automatically he could presuppose his father's reactions upon political questions of all kinds. In military and governmental circles the practice arose of using a code in letters – N.I (the Emperor), N.II (Bismarck), and N.II-Jr. (Herbert Bismack)[10] – a conscious tribute to Herbert's important position in political and diplomatic affairs.

Just the bare possibility that Herbert might succeed his father as Chancellor infuriated the camarilla of Bismarck enemies in court and political circles. The old Hatzfeldt-Schleinitz-Loë fronde, which had opposed Bismarck at every stage of his career, now turned its concentrated venom on the son.

Moreover, the Bismarck family had been most unfortunate in its associations with the feminine side of the royal house. We have seen that for more the forty years Bismarck had to contend with the machinations of Empress Augusta, wife of William I. Now, in 1890, he was faced with the combined hatred of the wives of Frederick III and William II. The Queen Mother, the Empress Frederick, had been born Princess Victoria of England, and had always remained at heart a foreigner in Germany, which she regarded as a backward country. In particular, she regarded Bismarck as a personal enemy – a point of view which he returned with interest. It was Bismarck's biting opinion that in the whole of Germany this daughter of Queen Victoria loved only the Spa Homburg von der Höhe, beloved of her countrymen, and the Appolinaris water first made fashionable by her brother, the Prince of Wales.[11] Furthermore, she was always meddling in conferences of ministers, Bismarck said, which would not have been countenanced under similar circumstances in England.[12]

The fall of Bismarck delighted the Empress Frederick who was concerned lest Herbert carry on in his place. In a letter to her mother, Queen Victoria, on March 29, 1890, she wrote:

> The confusion to me seems extreme, and the state of things most anxious and unsatisfactory. Changes in those things which were most to be regretted in Prince Bismarck's administration are not contemplated, as I hear William wishes to have the son [Herbert Bismarck] back again soon. It would be a very great mistake. The only good I see in all that is being done, is having so honest a man as General Caprivi at the head of affairs, but I doubt very much whether he can or will remain.[13]

A week after Herbert's resignation, the Empress Frederick wrote again to Queen Victoria (April 8, 1890):

I cannot tell you much about what is going on here in the way of politics, but I look with alarm to the future! Everything must be done in a hurry and be startling! and emanate or seem to emanate from one source!...

The new Minister of Foreign Affairs has never so much as written his name down in my book, nor has Herbert Bismarck announced his *Demission* or been to take leave, which is very rude, as he was Fritz's Minister, but I am heartily glad that I shall be spared having to see him, or speak to him![14]

The Empress Frederick and her daughter-in-law, wife of William II, had little use for each other, but on one thing they were agreed – Herbert Bismarck was the nemesis of William II. Born Princess Augusta Victoria of Schleswig-Holstein-Sonderburg-Augustenburg, the wife of William II was the daughter of the Prince Frederick who in 1864 had crossed Bismarck's plans by aspiring to the throne of Schleswig-Holstein. Although Bismarck had approved her marriage as helping to bring about a reconciliation with those elements in Schleswig-Holstein that still maintained the rights of the Augustenburgs, the young Princess had continued to despise the Chancellor. She now turned her contempt on his son, for whom she had an intense hatred. According to Eulenburg, the cause of this hatred was not hard to find. More and more, during his drinking bouts, Herbert had forgotten diplomatic niceties and had expressed such views as "one must seek to provide the Emperor with a mattress, from which he could most easily and lightly rule."[15] This was the sort of language the elder Bismarck often used, but generally within the confines of his home, seldom in public. Herbert's remarks, which came often when he was intoxicated, invariably found their way to the Empress, who, as may well be understood, regarded him and the whole house of Bismarck as irreconcilable enemies. The Bismarcks, in turn, ridiculed "petticoat government."

Similarly, in court, army, and political circles there was fear that the detested Herbert would be called to the vacant desk in the Wilhelmstrasse. The attitude of the *Bundesfürsten* [federal princes] was expressed by Prince von Lippe-Schaumburg in May 1890: "That the Emperor had the courage to let Bismarck go makes him in my eyes three heads larger. He would have become three heads smaller if he had carried on this *Hausmeiertum [dynasty of mayors of the palace]*."[16] This was a pointed but obvious reference to Herbert Bismarck. Count Alfred Waldersee, Chief of the General Staff, and aspirant to Bismarck's position, charged that "evil people," namely Bismarck's son, had been working against him.[17]

Most significant of all was the attitude of Philipp Eulenburg, initmate of the Bismarck family during his youth and confidant of the distracted Herbert in 1881 during the marriage tragedy with Princess Elizabeth Carolath. In the events of 1890 Eulenburg apparently tried to please both sides. On January 9, 1890, when Eulenburg was minister to the grand ducal court at Oldenbourg and ambitious for further advancement, he called on Count Waldersee to tell him about the intrigues of both Bismarcks against him [*Waldersee*].[18] When the conflict between Bismarck and William II came to a head, Eulenburg decided that he had to remain loyal to the Emperor and that eventually he had to give up the House Bismarck.[19] With indiscretion, he wrote an open letter postcard to his friend, Baron Dörnberg: "Bismarck is gone! Things will get better now than hitherto."[20] Eulenburg also conspired to transfer Bismarck's son-in-law, Count Kuno von Rantzau, from Munich to the Hague against his will.[21]

Treachery! The Bismarcks never forgot nor condoned Eulenburg's desertion. Thereafter, when Eulenburg sent the Bismarcks letters of congratulations on happy occasions, his communications were coldly and formally answered.[22] In 1894 his letter of condolence on the death of Princess Johanna Bismarck remained unanswered.[23] At the funeral of the elder Bismarck at Friedrichsruh in 1898, Eulenburg came toward Herbert with outstretched arms; the latter ostentatiously turned his back on him.[24] The Bismarcks were always confirmed haters.

From a practical viewpoint the attitude of young Emperor William II was considerably more important than the feelings of courtiers, military men, or politicians. The new monarch was intellectually gifted, but at the age of thirty-one still immature, inexperienced, pompous, vain, and willful. Susceptible to flattery, he was impressed by self-seeking courtiers who surrounded him and urged him to remember that Frederick would hardly have become Frederick the Great if, at the opening of his reign, there had been anyone in charge of affairs as powerful and important as Bismarck. As Crown Prince, William had assured Bismarck of his undying admiration, but his attitude had changed upon ascending the throne in 1888. An extreme egoist, the young monarch could not agree for long with a minister who for a generation had conducted the government according to his own principles, and who did not for a moment intend to subordinate himself to a young and inexperienced master. Bismarck was certain that Germany's position in international affairs would suffer because of the Emperor's pomposity, arrogance, and fickle behavior, and he made it a point to confine the monarch's influence between the narrowest possible limits. Under the circumstances, a clash of wills was bound to occur.

The possibility of William II and Herbert Bismarck working together successfully as a team was remote. William I and the elder Bismarck formed a harmonious team – the monarch was eighteen years older than his chief minister. Moreover, William I had implicit faith in his servant, and allowed no critic, even within his own household, to disturb that relationship. But in the case of William II and Herbert Bismarck, the roles were reversed. There were psychological implications. At first the young Emperor was in awe of the great Bismarck, and hence took every occasion to express his admiration. But Herbert as possible successor – that was another matter.

It was a difficult situation. Herbert was a man of bizarre character, not only burdened with the fate of being son of a political genius, but even more handicapped by his father's determination, despite his denial, that he should be the next Chancellor. He might have renewed the relationship of trust which had united Otto von Bismarck with William II's grandfather. But that old master-servant combination was not to be repeated in the case of William II and Bismarck II. Here the age relationship was reversed – the servant was older than the master.

There was also an important difference in the character and personality of the two Williams. The first William, though not as intellectually gifted as the second, was intelligent enough to realize the genius of his servant and made certain to accept his guidance for the good of the Hohenzollern dynasty and the state. But the second William was different.

Biographer Emil Ludwig, though not admired by Bismarck scholars, caught the psychological overtones: "The second William, impelled by his neurotic temperament, was confronted by a second Bismarck, whose filial admiration, in conjunction with the effects of his upbringing and a secret conviction that he lacked creative energy, impelled towards the service of his father rather than towards the service of his fatherland. Whereas William had too much self-confidence and too little respect for his forefathers, Herbert lacked self-reliance and was burdened by an excess of veneration for his father, so that it became impossible for him (when occasion called) to form and act upon opinions of his own. Besides, William had been brought up unlovingly, whereas affection had been lavished upon Herbert. He had, indeed, to make the great sacrifice of his passion, and almost of his honor, but in other respects his father had shown much tenderness, nay fondness, for him."[25]

It was indeed too much to expect that two men of such contrasting backgrounds could work together in harmony. Herbert was the product of loving parents, both of whom were all too willing to forgive him for his pranks as a child and for his intemperate behavior as an adult. William II was not blessed with this kind of relationship. He develped an acute sense of discomfort in the presence of his mother, whom he subconsciously blamed for the accident of birth which left him with a withered arm. The pompous young monarch was annoyed by Herbert's harsh personality, and had no intention of reenacting the warm friendship his grandfather felt for the elder Bismarck. Enough was enough. He, the young Emperor, was now in the seat of power and he would not share it with anyone, least of all the hard-drinking son of the famous Chancellor. William II soon began to think in terms of getting rid of both Bismarcks – the stiff-necked father as well as the eccentric son. Within two years after his accession he delivered the death blow to the Bismarck dynasty.

The circumstances surrounding Bismarck's fall are well-known.[26] Herbert Bismarck was at the center of the imbroglio.

The chief cause of differences on the domestic scene between Bismarck and William II concerned the prolongation of the anti-Socialist Laws when they expired in 1890. The Chancellor proposed to make the bill permanent, but William was opposed on the ground that the disaffection of labor could be removed by remedial measures. Bismarck hoped to provoke the Socialists into violence, thus providing him with the necessary excuse to smash them ruthlessly. But the young monarch, influenced by his tutor – and at first by the Christian Social movement of anti-Semitic court-chaplain Adolf Stoecker,[27] refused to start his reign with violent suppression of the workers. He did not want to be known as another "Cartridge Prince" (the appellation given to his grandfather, later William I, who, as a young officer during the Revolution of 1848, commanded troops in Berlin which fired on the people). On January 21 and 22, 1890, William wrote two memoranda: "Remarks on the Workers' Problem" and "Proposals for the Betterment of the Position of the Worker." "The workers shall learn that I care for their welfare." He was determined to extend the earlier body of social legislation, which Bismarck had inaugurated in 1881 but was now loath to continue. "Humanitarian rubbish!" (*"Humanitäts-dusel"*) was Bismarck's verdict. In the Chancellor's eyes, the young Kaiser was being naïve.

William II was not disposed to back down. He had the backing of the *Reichstag*, which was slated to assemble on January 9. The second reading of the anti-Socialist Laws was scheduled for the 23rd of January. At this time Bismarck was at his estate in Friedrichsruh, where he was content to stay, reasoning that his son could represent him in Berlin and influence the Emperor in his interest. In a matter as pressing as the anti-Socialist Laws it would seem that the Chancellor's place was in Berlin, where he could remain in close contact with the monarch and advise him, out of the fund of his own political wisdom. But, feeling tired and ill a good part of the time, he preferred the comfort of his home. At the same time, he was anxious to give Herbert as much experience as possible in matters of state so that he would be well-prepared for his future role in German administration.

On January 9 Reich Secretary of State for the Interior Karl Heinrich von Boetticher journeyed to Friedrichsruh, being aware of the seriousness of the issue, and believing that the Chancellor would fight a losing battle if he did not come to Berlin and try to meet Emperor and *Reichstag* halfway. Bismarck brusquely turned down his advice. Erich Eyck's estimate: "The only effect of his visit was that he began to suspect Boetticher of being a secret adversary, of turning his face toward the rising sun of the young Emperor, and of coveting the mantle of Chancellor. This last, of course, was the worst possible sin in Bismarck's eyes. Such a suspicion was at any time capable of poisoning his mind. On this occasion it had a double sting; to him the appearance of a rival meant not merely a threat to his own position but a danger to his son Herbert, whom he already regarded as his successor."[28]

More bitterness. Several weeks later, Prince Bismarck saw the Emperor and complained that Boetticher had been playing politics behind his (Bismarck's) back. On the same evening, without consulting Bismarck, William II conferred the order of the Black Eagle on Boetticher. When Bismarck heard of this direct slap in the face, he said jokingly: "You have gotten your way, Octavio!" But Herbert excitedly said to his father: "That's a blow that you should not take."[29] At the Chancellery, Bismarck nevertheless extended his congratulations to Boetticher, but Herbert, the greater hater, pointedly avoided any expression of congratulations.[30]

At the January 9th meeting at Friedrichsruh, the Chief of the Chancellor's Office, Franz von Rottenburg, Bismarck's intimate collaborator, agreed with Boetticher that Bismarck's obvious and best course was to return to Berlin. But the Chancellor turned down their advice, and listened, instead, to that of Herbert, who was all for remaining in Friedrichsruh.[31] It was a serious political error. Hohenlohe believed that the final break would not have taken place and that, eventually, Herbert would have succeeded his father as Chancellor, had Bismarck been in Berlin during these critical days before the damage became irreparable. Hohenlohe's comment: "The anger mounted until the moment when the appearance of the old Chancellor became necessary. Bismarck went to the Emperor in a bad mood – and found opposition. The right tactics of Herbert would have been to keep his father in Berlin as much as possible, in almost daily contact with the Emperor. I am completely convinced that the break would not have taken place, and that Herbert, after the death of his father, would have gone to the Wilhelmstrasse. But because of Herbert's appearance, there had been assembled a mass of inflammable material, which the father could not render innocuous. That was not his temperament. He came, argumentative and in bad mood, torn from his country peace, to Berlin, angry with Herbert, angry with the whole world – and in an angry frame of mind met the Emperor."[32]

Granted that Bismarck might have been able to handle matters better had he remained in Berlin, Hohenlohe's conclusion may be viewed as exaggerated. The differences between the elderly Chancellor and the young Emperor were much too deep and, in all probability, would have led to the break whether or not Bismarck came to Berlin.

These differences extended to the field of foreign policy, and here once again Herbert Bismarck, as Secretary of State for Foreign Affairs, played a major role. After the achievement of German unification in 1871, Bismarck's policy was to preserve the peace of Europe by maintaining a new delicate balance of power. He therefore carefully formed a set of alliances, all of which were secret.[33] On the expiration of the term of the Three Emperors' League in 1887, Alexander III, vexed by Austria's politics in the Balkans refused to renew the treaty. Desiring to "keep the wires to St. Petersburg open," Bismarck, without the knowledge of Austria, negotiated the Reinsurance Treaty with Russia in 1887, by which he recognized Russian claims in the Balkans. Although allied with Austria, Bismarck did not hesitate to make a secret treaty against his partner. For the Chancellor this was standard operating procedure.

William II knew about the Triple Alliance, which he regarded as the cornerstone of Germany's diplomatic structure, but both Bismarcks kept the existence of the Reinsurance Treaty unknown to him. The treaty was to expire in June 1890, but negotiations began in January, just at the time when the differences arose between Emperor and Chancellor on the anti-Socialist Laws. As chief of the Foreign Office, Herbert carried on the negotiations, at first without the knowledge of the Emperor, and then in a desperate maneuver to compel William II to retain his father and himself in office. The Bismarck propensity for personal diplomacy was revealed in this passage from the memoirs of Baron Hermann von Eckardstein, Herbert's co-worker in the Foreign Office:[34]

> On January 16 [1890] I came to Berlin and I visited Herbert Bismarck immediately in the Foreign Office....I found him in a very depressed mood, and he spoke curtly. I thought that, perhaps, he had something personal against me, perhaps someone had intrigued against me. Several days later, however, my fears proved to be groundless...for when I met him during the evening at the Hupka, he was charm itself. We spoke for a long time, and I had to tell him much about America.

> The Russian Ambassador, Count Paul Schuwalow, was at the Hupka on

that evening....As usual we were very gay. The Ambassador finally got into so good a mood that he invited us all to come to the Embassy on Unter den Linden to dine further with him. It was nearly two o'clock in the morning when we left Hupka's in order to take advantage of the Ambassador's invitation.

Count Schuwalow took command of the march to the Embassy,...saying, 'Brother Dragoons, if you don't remain in step, you won't get any more whiskey.' There were few people in the streets, and the only people we met laughed and made way for our cavalcade.

When we got to the Embassy, Count Schuwalow had the porter awaken the head steward, and before long there was in the small dining room a wonderfully outfitted table with all kind of delicacies, with German wines and countless kinds of Russian whiskies. It was about four o'clock in the morning, and we sat there until six.

The reader might take this night or rather morning dinner as harmless, but it was not so. Count Schuwalow, who sat near Herbert Bismarck, used this opportunity to carry on a conversation with him on the renewal of the Reinsurance Treaty between Germany and Russia. They both spoke in low tones, but by stretching my ears I learned from the conversation of the two statesmen that they were talking about the extension of a secret treaty. Among other things I heard the Russian Ambassador say 'Never! Never!'"[35]

In March 1890 Russian Foreign Minister Nikolay K. Giers, with the approval of the Czar, raised the question of renewing the Reinsurance Treaty with a view to giving it a permanent character later on by a further extension.[36] Both Bismarcks were in favor of the idea, and William II, who could no longer be kept in the dark concerning the treaty, gave it his assent. Russian Ambassador Count Schuwalow, was empowered to sign the document. The latter called on Bismarck on March 17 to inform him of his readiness to sign. The Chancellor now told the Russian Ambassador that in a few hours he would no longer be in office, whereupon Schuwalow hesitated about signing a treaty with his successor, whose attitude toward Russia was not yet known. He got in touch with St. Petersburg and told Bismarck that, in the meantime, he could not sign.[37]

Enter Herbert. Young Bismarck tried to take advantage of the situation by making use of the Reinsurance Treaty and the procedure for its renewal as a means of bringing pressure to bear on the Emperor to compel him to retain his father and himself in office. He informed William II in writing that the Czar's instructions to his Ambassador in Berlin, Schuwalow, required negotiation and sealing of the renewed treaty to be exclusively in the hands of Prince Bismarck. Furthermore, now that the Prince had been dismissed, the Czar was dispensing altogether with a renewal. On this report, with its startling news, William II wrote an astonished: "Why?" The monarch had already given his assent to the renewal of the treaty, which he regarded now as a national matter, not merely a private affair with the Bismarcks.[38] The circumstances surrounding these negotiations probably made William II more than ever determined to get rid of the annoying Bismarck clan.

Herbert's brain was working overtime at this critical moment. He was attempting to use the negotiations to keep his father in office. It did not work. Count Schuwalow testified to Herbert's somewhat clumsy exaggeration: "What I actually said to Count [Herbert] Bismarck was that, in view of what had just happened, I had decided to suspend the negotiations which had begun a few days before with his father. In view of the fundamental change in the stituation, and of the change of the personnel, it was entirely natural that I should want to see first how matters stood. That was the main reason why I decided to seek fresh instructions before continuing the negotiations which had been so suddenly interrupted by events."[39]

The issuance of the Reinsurance Treaty was fast coming to a head. Actually, differences on foreign policy played only a minor part in the accelerating struggle between Emperor and Chancellor. The resignation-dismissal followed a minor domestic difference concerning the relationship of the Emperor and his ministers.

The Chancellor, who with increasing age had become more irritable, suspicious, and authoritarian, was anxious to prevent any influence on the monach other than his own. Hence, he resurrected from the archives a royal order of September 8, 1852, by Frederick William IV. According to this all ministers, save the Minister of War, were obliged to consult with the Prime Minister before they were free to discuss important matters with the King.[40] Bismarck felt that this order was necessary as a means of giving the chief minister the complete control that was necessary if he were to be responsible for the whole policy of the government. William II resented this limitation of free access to him by his ministers, and repeatedly asked Bismarck to have the order rescinded.

The final bitter conversation with William II and Bismarck took place on the morning of March 15th at Herbert's home. Through a mix-up of messages, the monarch called in the morning before nine o'clock, and then remained standing throughout their conversation. The Chancellor, who was always tired in the mornings, had to remain standing too. William began by asking Bismarck whether or not Ludwig Windhorst had visited him and whether or not he had rebuked the leader of the Catholic Center Party. The Chancellor then told the Emperor what the latter already knew through his police spies – that Windhorst, in fact, had visited him. "I hope you had him thrown out of the door!"

commented William, who then informed the Chancellor that his monarch should be consulted before interviewing important people. Thereupon, Bismarck coldly explained the nature of his duties as Chancellor, including the limitation of the King's prerogatives. He could not submit to control such as the Emperor suggested. William then asked: "Not even if your sovereign should command you?" The old war horse was astonished – never before had he heard the word "command" from the monarchs he had served.

The Emperor repeated his demand that the royal edict of 1852 be abolished. Bismarck, now in a fury, refused. He began to speak of the Emperor's intended visit to the Czar, against which he advised, because the reports he held in his hands, which, unfortunately he could not show to the monarch, were unfriendly. William, his curiosity aroused, seized the documents, in which he read that the Czar had called him *"un garçon mal levé et de mauvaise foi"* ("an ill-bred youngster and of bad faith"). The angry young German ruler was being treated like a schoolboy. He retreated in haste.

On March 17 the Emperor sent Gen. Wilhelm von Hahnke, Chief of the Military Cabinet, to Bismarck bearing an ultimatum. Either repeal the order of 1852 or resign. The next day the Emperor demanded that Bismarck step down. The old man then drew up this letter of resignation:

> At my respectful audience on the 15th of this month Your Majesty commanded me to draw up a decree annuling the All-Highest Order of September 8, 1852, which regulated the position of the Minister-President *vis-à-vis* his colleagues.
>
> May I, your humble and most obedient servant, make the following statment on the genesis and importance of this order:
>
> There was no need at that time of absolute monarchy for the position of a 'President of the State Ministry.' For the first time, in the United *Landtag* of 1847, the efforts of the liberal delegate [*Mevissen*] led to the designation, based on the constitutional needs of that day, of a 'Premier-President,' whose task it would be to supervise uniform policies of the responsible ministers and to take over the responsibility for the combined political actions of the cabinet. With the year 1848 came constitutional customs in our daily life, and a 'President of the State Ministry' was named....
>
> The relationship of the State Ministry and its individual members to the new institution of the Minister-President very quickly required a new constitutional regulation, which was effected with approval of the then State Ministry by the order of September 8, 1852. Since then this order has been decisive in regulating the relationship of the Minister-President and the State Ministry, and it alone gave the Minister-President the authority

which enabled him to take over responsiblity for the policies of the cabinet, a responsibility demanded by the *Landtag,* as well as public opinion. If each individual minister must receive instructions with his colleagues, it becomes impossible in the cabinet to sustain uniform policies, for which each member can be responsible. There remains for none of the ministers and, especially, for the Minister-President any possibility of bearing constitutional responsiblity for the whole policy of the cabinet....

To this time I have never felt the need, in my relationship with my colleagues, to draw upon the order of 1852. Its very existence and the knowledge that I possessed the confidence of their late Majesties, William and Frederick, were enough to assure my authority on my staff. This knowledge exists today neither for my colleagues nor for myself. I have been compelled, therefore, to turn back to the order of 1852, in order to assure the necessary uniformity in the service of Your Majesty.

On the aforementioned grounds, I am not in the position to carry out Your Majesty's demand, which would require me to initiate and countersign the suspension of the order of 1852 recently brought up by me, and, despite that, at the same time carry on the presidency of the Ministery of State....

Considering my attachment to service for the monarchy and for Your Majesty and the long-established relationship which I had believed would exist forever, it is very painful for me to terminate my accustomed relationship to the All Highest and to the political life of the Reich and Prussia; but, after conscientious consideration of the All Highest's intentions, and to whose implementation I must always be ready to act, if I am to remain in service, I cannot do other than most humbly request Your Majesty to grant me an honorable discharge with legal pension from the posts of Reichs-Chancellor, Minister-President, and Prussian Minister for Foreign Affairs....

In view of the impressions of the last few weeks,...I am entitled respectfully to assume that this tender of resignation accords with Your Majesty's wishes, and that I can, therefore, confidently reckon upon Your Majesty's gracious approval. I should long since have tendered my resignation to Your Majesty had I not believed that Your Majesty wishes to utilize the experience and the capacity of a faithful servant of Your Majesty's forefathers. Now that I am sure that Your Majesty has no more use for these, I can retire from political life without fearing that my determination to do so will be condemned by public opinion as untimely.

VON BISMARCK

To His Majesty the Emperor and King[41]

In this skillfully written letter the retiring Chancellor accused the young Emperor of being willing to destroy Bismarck's work, and indirectly make him responsible for any future misfortunes of the German Reich. Bismarck intended to have the letter of resignation published,[42] but William forbade it, informing the press that the Chancellor had resigned because of ill health, and issuing his own expressions of gratitude for past services. Despite Bismarck's protests, on his retirement William created him Duke of Lauenburg, He had to accept the title, but he successfully resisted all efforts by the monarch to present him with a dotation, a government endowment. To the acidulous Bismarck this was equivalent to a *pourboire* paid to efficient postal servants on their retirement. His pride would not let him accept this kind of gift.

It was incredible. The mighty Bismarck, creator of German unity, the first statesman of Europe, had been struck down in comic opera fashion by an impertinent, presumptuous young Hohenzollern, whose very throne owed its existence to the brilliant old man. And this final blow also smashed the hopes and dreams of Herbert von Bismarck to hold high office in the German Reich.

There would be no Bismarck dynasty.

10

RESIGNATION WITH FATHER

"My poor old father was dismissed like a dishonest or troublesome servant."[1]

With these plaintive words, Herbert described to his friend Bülow the resignation of his father, adding what he called "astonishing details of the ruthlessness with which his father had been personally treated by William II."

Now there began a secondary battle on the vital question of whether or not Herbert would be retained in his post as Secretary of State for Foreign Affairs. William II insisted that he urgently wanted Herbert to stay on "and help me maintain tradition in our foreign policy."[2] He expressed this point of view again and again in negotiations with Herbert, but his motives may be questioned. William, on second thought, was appalled by his own courage in dismissing the great statesman. Fearing public opinion, he reasoned that the best thing to do under the cirumstances was to retain Herbert in office for a time, at least until the furore over the Chancellor's retirement had blown away.[3] He had not changed his mind about the dangers of a possible Bismarck dynasty, but in the case of Herbert he deemed discretion the better part of political wisdom. He would play a waiting game.

The dramatic events of the past few months had affected Herbert's health. On January 30, 1890, Eulenburg wrote to him: "The Emperor relies on you and your work. He has the feeling that he cannot get along without you."[4] Herbert replied: "Thanks very much, my dear Phili, for your friendly lines. I have had many worries during the last few weeks and the constant irritations have been galling. In my life thus far I have sacrificed much more of my nerves and powers than even my well-wishing friends are apt to believe. As I grow older the pressure of work has become so great that I do not know if I can bear it any longer. I have the feeling that I, with my 40 years, have worked more and lived through more than most people of 80....As for my father, thanks be to God that until middle age, before he mounted the horrible Berlin treadmill, he led a healthier life than I."[5] Others recognized the deterioration of Herbert's morale: on March 13th Count Waldersee noted: "Count Bismarck is in the highest degree in a bad temper and disinclined to work, and several people are getting ready to desert the Chancellor's ship."[6]

On March 20, 1890, the day of the Chancellor's resignation, the Emperor sent Philipp Eulenburg to visit Herbert and inform him that the Emperor was counting on him to stay in his office as Secretary of State for Foreign Affairs. Eulenburg told the Emperor that his mission would be useless, but William insisted upon it. The interview was a very painful one. Eulenburg spoke of the feelings of his colleagues in the Foreign Office, who believed that Herbert's remaining in office was important for the future of German foreign policy. If both father and son left, he argued, it might appear that the Emperor wanted to break with the name of Bismarck and, in fact, begin a new orientation of foreign policy. Eulenburg spoke warmly: he was moved by the dilemma of his friend, but at the same time he was loyal to the Emperor.

All in vain. Herbert listened but replied that the German Reich would collapse with the retirement (*Rücktritt*) of his father and that the Triple Alliance would be dissolved. Revolutions now could be expected. The Emperor, leaning on progressive politicians, would come to grief on "the dangerous road of liberalism." Herbert warned: "The Emperor does not know what he is doing." Eulenburg could not help but recognize the logic of the situation when Herbert said: "I cannot serve under anyone else than my father. I am hated because I handled people badly. Without my father I would not have the power of opposing the will of my enemies."[7]

Eulenburg recognized that the unhappy man was reaping what he had sown – a harvest of hate. Tactfully, he avoided reminding Herbert how many times he had begged him, in his own interest and in the interest of all, to mitigate the harshess of his treatment of underlings. He left in sadness to report back to the Emperor.

William spoke plainly: "I counted on Herbert. I believed that he was clever enough to judge the matter right. He probably said bad things to you about me. In the Bismarck house there is no self-control and no gratitude. But whatever words were said, I am not interested in them. Excited people do not know themselves. For me what the Bismarcks say does not exist. There will be time for reason in the future."[8]

Eulenburg made one last desperate attempt. But this time Herbert's attitude had hardened into bitterness, and he asked his friend: "Well, my old Phili, you have decided to remain with the Emperor. Why not with us?" He added with emphasis: "I will never separate myself from my father. Never! You can hardly believe seriously that I would undertake the position of Secretary for Foreign Affairs under a Caprivi?" His voice then became passionate: "What the Emperor thinks I do not know. It would be as intelligent to give a little child a costly watch as to give the Government to the Emperor. He just does not know how to carry on the fight."[9]

William was still insistent. He sent Adjutant Count Wedel to Herbert to repeat the Emperor's wish that he should remain in office. Through his emissary the Emperor offered Herbert a long period of leave. Wedel was ordered to assure Herbert of His Majesty's absolute confidence. Herbert countered that he did not believe he possessed his monarch's confidence, because William had repeatedly sent for councillors from the Foreign Office without his knowledge for the purpose of giving them orders, or to find out about what was going on. Wedel admitted that this was true, but assured Herbert that His Majesty, without a doubt would be prepared to redress this grievance. To this Herbert replied that his health was so debilitated that, without his father, he could not assume the difficult and responsible position.[10]

Wedel remained with Herbert for one and one-half hours. But the end result of the interview was a categorical and apparently irreconcilable "No!" to which Herbert added that in the future he wanted no consideration and that he did not desire appointment to an ambassador's post.[11]

All this was puerile play acting: William had had enough of the Bismarcks – both father and son. But the next day he made another attempt, when he and Herbert were at the Lehrter Railway station to receive the Prince of Wales. The Emperor said to Herbert: "You have misunderstood Schuwalow, to judge by your letter of yesterday." Herbert replied that he could no longer deal with Schuwalow, for he was on the point of sending in his resignation. William replied that he would not hear of such a proposal. He would grant Herbert all facilities, and that afternoon or later he would discuss matters with him in detail. He must remain.[12] The game was still on.

During the eight days of negotiation there was no doubt as to the sentiment of the fallen Chancellor: he did not want his son to continue in office.

He was emphatic in making his views known to people around him. There was bitterness in his voice. On March 17 he said to his assistant Moritz Busch: "The Emperor does not want to keep the old mentor....But he would like to keep Herbert, only that would not do – that would be a sort of mixed goods train, and I should always have to bear part of the responsibility. Moreover, although Herbert doubtless would stand being lectured and censured by me, he would not stand it from Imperial Chancellor Boetticher."[13]

William was obstinate. Now he sent two emissaries, Gen. Wilhelm von Hahnke and Privy Councillor Hermann von Lucanus, with a direct order for Herbert to remain in office. Bismarck informed the visitors that they would have to deal directly with his son, but he made it clear that he did not feel Herbert was needed under the current circumstances. "If one feels and knows that a ship is sinking," he told them, "one does not leave his son on it."[14] Furthemore, he added, "I know well that Abraham, on the direct order of God, was ready to sacrifice his son, Isaac, but such a divine command does not exist here."[15]

In this delicate situation Bavarian Ambassador Count Lerchenfeld visited the elder Bismarck, and during the course of his conversation suggested that Herbert not take his leave the same time as his father. Foreign powers, he said, already had been affected by Bismarck's resignation. If Herbert remained in office, in some respects the firm would be carried on and the effects of the elder Bismarck's resignation would be somewhat mitigated. To this Bismarck replied that it was best for people to see that the son remains loyal to his father, "but it would be something else again whether or not he sits in the wagon while the son drives, or he, himself, holds the reins in his hands."[16]

On March 21st, the Emperor's Adjutant, Count Wedel, made his farewell visit to Prince Bismarck. He let it be known that he came as a private individual and not as Adjutant of the Emperor. He talked energetically to the fallen Chancellor, urging him to allow Herbert to remain at his post. "The Prince answered me," Wedel reported, "that his son was of age and knew what he was doing, hence he did not consider it right to influence him one way or another. He felt, nevertheless, that the matter of Herbert's staying after his father had been treated so shabbily was impossible. I must say that I had to agree with him from the human point of view....The Prince spoke at length of the difficulties which Herbert would meet as a subordinate of Caprivi."[17] The Titan was adamant.

On his part, Herbert was still operating in the shadow of his father. He had no intention of deserting the old man in this hour of trial. He would not play the humble underling with a portfolio under his arm before any other Chancellor. He admitted the power of parental attraction: "I am so bound up with my father at every fiber of my existence," he said dramatically, "that my one and only joy is to live and work for him with all the strength that remains at my command. I can scarcely imagine a life without him. It would be like the conditions depicted in our old northern sagas where, should the wolf Fenris ever manage to swallow the sun, there would be cold darkness, confusion and despair everywhere! I should greatly prefer not to live to see that; it would be too great a contrast after our country has for so long stood upon the heights of fame and world history!"[18]

Thus, in romantic Nordic tone the son defended the father. He had no intention of allowing the young monarch to smooth over the break with the Chancellor. William II had to retain both Bismarcks or none. For Herbert, loyalty to the Fatherland was equated with loyalty to his father.

Herbert's decision was made – he would follow his father into retirement. But he would try to salvage something from the wreckage by having a say in the selection of his successor as Secretary of State for Foreign Affairs. His choice was Count Friedrich von Alvensleben,[19] but here, again, he was frustrated. The story of Herbert's attempt to name his successor was told by the elder Bismarck in that extraordinary third volume of his memoirs:

> To a question of Caprivi's as to a suitable successor, my son mentioned on the 23rd [*March*] our representative in Brussels, von Alvensleben. Caprivi declared himself as satisfied with this and mentioned doubts about the wisdom of placing a non-Prussian at the head of the Foreign Office. His Majesty had mentioned Marschall to him. In the meantime, on the 24th, the Emperor informed my son, whom he had met at the Dragoon's mess, that Alvensleben was also acceptable to him.

> On the morning of the 26th my son showed Caprivi the ropes of the Secretariat. The latter mentioned that he found the situation too complicated, and he would have to simplify it, and mentioned, that Alvensleben had been with him that morning, but the more he tried to talk him into the position the more definite became his refusal. My son came to an understanding that he would make one more attempt with Alvensleben and report back to Caprivi on the results. In the course of the same day, Herbert received his discharge, without having had the conversation which the Emperor had given him reason to expect.

> That afternoon my son, in accordance with his promise, attempted, together with Ambassador von Schweinitz, then on leave, to convince Alvensleben to become his successor, but without any success. The latter declared that he would rather give up his career than become Secretary of State, but agreed not to make any definite decision until he had spoken to the Emperor.

On the morning of the 27th the Emperor visited my son, again and again placed his arms around Herbert's shoulders, expressed the hope that his health would soon improve, and that he might see him in service again. He asked how the situation stood with Alvensleben. After my son reported, His Majesty expressed wonder that Alvensleben had not yet come to see him, and arranged that the meeting take place at 12:30 P.M. in the Palace.

My son then went to Caprivi, apprised him of Alvenleben's attitude and his call to His Majesty, and recapitulated the arguments he had sought to prevail on Alvensleben. Thereupon Caprivi spoke somewhat as follows:

This is all too late now. He [*Caprivi*] had had an audience with His Majesty yesterday during which he had informed the monarch that Alvensleben did not want the position, and thereupon he had received the authorization to go to Marschall. The latter had immediately declared himself available and said that he already had the agreement of the Grand Duke of Baden to transfer to the Imperial service; his offical request in Karlsruhe was only a matter of form. If Alvensleben now accepted, there remained nothing for him [*Caprivi*] but to request his resignation. He was slated to see His Majesty at 12:45 P.M. and would remind the monarch at that time of his authorization yesterday for Marschall.

Alvensleben, who was received at the Palace immediately before Caprivi, could not be convinced by the Emperor either; when the latter mentioned this with expressions of disappointment to Caprivi, Caprivi said he was very happy about it because it saved him embarrassment, since he had already come to terms with Marschall. The Emperor said briefly: 'All right, it is Marschall then.' Caprivi, therefore, did not wait for the results of the interview between my son and Alvensleben, but even beforehand had won over the Ambassador of Baden.[20]

After these tortuous convolutions, once again Herbert had lost out. He was disgusted with the selection of Marschall as his successor. To Lord Rosebery he wrote: "The gentleman who is going to be my successor comes from the Grand Duchy of Baden, where he was formerly employed as a public prosecutor. His name is Herr von Marschall, and he had never been conversant with the a, b, c's of foreign affairs. I wish him good luck."[21]

On March 26, 1890, Herbert, hinging his political fate to that of his father, sent in his formal resignation. It was accepted. He made his own position clear: his father had been dismissed against his will, and he could not remain in his post at a time when "a sudden change in German foreign policy was being prepared."[22] This conviction, he said, had worried him for some time.

Several days earlier Herbert complained about his father's dismissal to Freiherr von Reischach, in the entourage of Emperor Frederick III, and uttered this prophecy: "That means the dissolution of the Empire!" Reischach exclaimed:

"That would make the work of your father a Utopia!" To this Herbert replied: "No, but even so fine a structure cannot withstand the dismissal of its creator. Most people do not understand the importance of this development, from my point of view not even the Emperor. The Empire cannot withstand this blow, and in twenty years it is going to fall apart – for that period of time the treaties which my father made with Europe will hold the structure together."[23]

Remarkable prophecy! Apparently Herbert did possess some acute political judgment. What he feared actually took place after the first decade of the twentieth century. So impressed was French historian Edmond Vermeil with Herbert Bismarck's prediction that he used it in the opening paragraph of his major work on *Germany in the 20th Century:* "On March 20, 1890, when Count Herbert von Bismarck learned that his father, the Chancellor of the German Reich, had been dismissed, he foretold the impending breakup of the regime. The defeat of 1918 was to justify his prophecy. It revealed the vulnerability of a nation which was destitute of a great political conception, and which, since its origins, had been dominated solely by anxiety concerning constant threats to its internal cohesion. This was why it could not respond to the demands of an imperialism that was boundless in its ambitions."[24]

And what about the new Chancellor, Count von Caprivi?[25] Herbert was characteristically sarcastic – a worthy soldier certainly, but successor to the great Bismarck? Laughable! Herbert told Eulenburg that the soldier Caprivi would last no longer than three months.[26]

On his part Caprivi was delighted by both resignations. As the new Chancellor he felt that he now had a chance to "receive full freedom of movement from Bismarck's foreign policy."[27]

The young Emperor had made a brave show of trying to hold on to Herbert, but actually he was relieved. He had resolved an embarrassing situation. He wrote about it later in his memoirs: "My request that he [*Herbert Bismarck*] should stay by me and help me maintain tradition in our political policy elected the sharp reply that he had been accustomed to report to his father and serve him, whereupon it was now out of the question to demand that he should come with his dispatch-case under his arm to report to anybody other than his father."[28] He, the Emperor, had done all he could to retain Herbert Bismarck.

American Ambassador in Berlin William Walter Phelps reported to Washington: "The Emperor wished Count Herbert Bismarck to stay, and made as many and as earnest efforts in that direction as became a sovereign. These went so far that nothing but the condition of the Secretary of State's health, which notoriously needs amelioration, would, in courtly convention, excuse Count Bismarck's persistent refusal to yield an assent."[29]

Herbert took his fall from power with little grace. Four days after his resignation he attended a dinner in his honor given by Bavarian Ambassador Lerchenfeld, at which he became involved in an unpleasant scene. Although his successor, Freiherr Marschall, was present, he made bitter remarks about the intrigues that had been made against his father. Marschall remained silent in the face of this passionate and extreme behavior.[30] Reaction to Herbert's outburst could have been expected. When he gave a farewell dinner for the officials of the Foreign Office, four of them – Holstein, Lindau, Kayser, and Raschdau, all of whom owed their careers to the Bismarcks, declined the invitation.[31]

When news of the resignations reached Bucharest, Bülow wrote to Herbert expressing his deep regret. The latter replied on April 7, 1890:

Many thanks for both your kind letters....My health has been worse than ever this winter. I have not yet recovered from a heavy influenza attack in December, when I could not lie up owing to pressure of work. If my father had stayed in office the doctors tell me that I should have needed a leave of four months. But now that my father had been forced to resign against his will, it has been impossible for me to take over the increased duties and responsibilites which my name causes to be thrust upon me. Even if I were in the best of health this step under a new Chancellor, quite inexpert in diplomacy, would have been a very difficult one....

I should have left Berlin already if the Emperor had not invited himself to a dinner with me tomorrow. As it is I leave the day after for Friedrichsruh, and shall probably not see Berlin again. Good-bye, dear Bülow, and do good business under the new management.[32]

Expressions of sympathy came from England. Sir Charles Dilke and Lord Rosebery, both of whom Herbert considered to be his friends, sent copies of the *Punch* cartoon., "Dropping the Pilot." The cartoon, which became famous, shows a grave Bismarck, dressed in a pilot's uniform, slowly descending the ladder of the ship Germany. William II, with his crown on his head, stares superciliously over the rail.

Lord Rosebery wrote to Herbert on March 20, 1890, between the resignations of father and son:

I can hardly trust myself to write of this stupendous news. One paper (a French one, I think) describes what I should say, 'When one had the luck to have a Bismarck, which does not happen to everyone, one does not throw him away.' Of course, I do not presume to judge the Emperor, but when I think of the weary and painful and unending toil and combination by which the fabric of your policy and the peace of Europe have been maintained, I envy his courage....

And now as to yourself. You speak of your political career as closed, but that is not so. I know it was always your wish that it should end with your father's and that you should obtain an interval of rest and enjoyment. But your experience and ability must always be at the service of your country. The holiday will have one great advantage for you, that you will know your true friends. You have been so near the seat of power that it has not been easy for you to find this out. And now I doubt not that many envious asses who fear to kick the old lion may vent their spleen on the young one....[33]

Several days after his resignation, Herbert wrote to Sir Charles Dilke:

I thank you very much for your kind note, which warmed my heart, and for the sketch you have cut out of *Punch.* It is, indeed, a fine one, and my father, to whom I showed it yesterday when your letter reached me, was pleased with its acuteness, as well as the kind messages you sent him and which he requites. He has left last night for good and I follow tonight to Friedrichsruh.

It was rather a melancholy historical event, when my father stepped out of the house in which he has lived for the benefit of the country for nearly twenty-eight years. When I wrote you last, my father thought only of leaving the offices he held in Prussia, but things went on so rapidly that he did not see his way to remain as Chancellor in Berlin after the Emperor had let him know that His Majesty wished him to resign. I had no choice what course to take after he had been dismissed. My health is so much shaken that I am not able to take upon my shoulders alone the tremendous amount of responsibility for the foreign affairs of Germany which hitherto fell upon my father.

When we drove to the station yesterday, our carriage was almost upset by the enthusiastic crowd of many thousand people who thronged the streets and cheered him in a deafening way; but it was satisfactory for my father to see that there are people left who regret his departure. I shall come to Berlin after April 1 to clear my house and to pack my things, and then I shall stay with my father till the end of April. In May I hope to come to England, and I look forward to the pleasure of seeing you.[34]

Thus encouraged, Herbert went in May 1890 for a visit to London, where he remained until early June. Here he lost no opportunity to make passionate pronouncements about the *"dismissal of my father."* Invited to the German Embassy by Count Paul von Hatzfeldt, German Ambassador in London, he referred sarcastically to the new regime in Berlin, as reported by Prince Hohenlohe: "Hatzfeldt related that during his stay in England in this summer Herbert had been at his house, that they had gone downstairs together, and that Herbert had then asked for his health, to which Hatzfeldt had replied that he was very well, but had a great deal to do; whereupon Herbert said, 'It must be a nice policy that is now carried on!'"[35] Apparently seeking sympathy from his British friends, Herbert sought to make them believe that his father and he were always opponents of a German colonial policy, and that both were in favor of giving up German East Africa.[36]

The tragedy of Herbert's life was accentuated by the stress of his father's resignation and his own. It is probable that had he succeeded his father in office and at the same time retained the confidence of the new Emperor, he might well have shown himself to be a political figure of first-rate stature. As it was, he was doomed therafter to continue his life in the shadow of his illustrious parent.

It was not in Herbert's nature either to forgive or forget. His adored father, the mighty genius of German political life, had been dealt a low blow by insufferable midgets in the seats of the mighty. The men who had shoved the old Chancellor aside would be responsible for the coming disintegration of German foreign policy. Herbert would never deign to serve those who had insulted and demeaned his father. He made up his mind to strike back at them with every means at his disposal. Above all, they must recognize that he was a Bismarck, scion of a proud family which understood the ways of vengeance.

11

THE "COMBINATION" AT FRIEDRICHSRUH

Otto von Bismarck, master of diplomacy, had unified the Germanies and made Germany a world power. But, ironically, he left a political vacuum. He never understood the fragility of the edifice he had built. As early as 1917 Max Weber saw the danger which was to culminate in the diabolical Hitler regime:

> Bismarck left behind him as his political heritage a nation without any political education, far below the level which, in this respect, it had reached twenty years earlier. Above all, he left behind a nation without any political will, accustomed to allow the great statesman at its head to look after its policy for it. Moreover, as a consequence of his misuse of the monarchy as a cover for his own interests in the struggle of political parties, he left a nation accustomed to submit, under the label of constitutional monarchy, to anything which was decided for it, without criticizing the political qualifications of those who now occupied Bismarck's empty place and who with incredible ingenuousness now took the reins of power into their hands.[1]

For both Bismarcks the pains of retirement were greater than the wounds of political battle while in power. Disgruntled and resentful of his defeat, Prince Bismarck retired to his estate at Varzin in Outer Pomerania and took up his duties as a Prussian landowner. For some years the seventy-five-year-old war horse had looked forward to his days of leisure, but now he found his enforced idleness unbearable. During the first few months, the irritable outcast summoned his foresters and shepherds and lectured to village schoolchildren. It was an unaccustomed and hardly satisfying role for the master who for three decades had handled the states of Europe as if they were pawns in a chess game.

The Titan's lasting disappointment, despite his claim to the contrary, was the destruction of his plan to have his son succeed him. He was desperately anxious for that. In his view Herbert was the only human being in whom he had implicit confidence, the only one he could rely upon to carry forward the work he had initiated. He had hoped that he would be gradually relieved of his offices – he would remain for a time as Imperial Chancellor, with Herbert as Secretary of State for Foreign Affairs, and Boetticher as President of the Prussian Ministry.[2] But this intention came to naught with the battle of 1890.

William II, his confidants, and most of the military and civil bureaucrats suspected that the Central Ox intended to make his office hereditary. They saw danger in the House of Bismarck. Most recognized grudgingly that Herbert, despite his caustic demeanor and his drinking, was conscientious and able; yet they feared this continuation of Bismarckian power. Historian C. Grant Robertson described the objectionable personality: "He [*Herbert*] endeavored to prove, not that he was a chip off the old block, but the old block itself by imitating and exaggerating with repellent fidelity all the worst defects of his father's character – his brutality, coarseness, dictatorial insolence, and unscrupulous disregard of the conventions of decent existence. His manners were insufferable and a byword. ('I never go to Paris except in wartime,' Herbert Bismarck is reputed to have replied to a French diplomatist.) Men were prepared to endure much from the Chancellor who had genius and achieved miracles. They were not prepared to endure the intolerable from one who was not a genius."[3]

It was even more difficult for Herbert than for his father to become reconciled to life in retirement. An active and enthusiastic personality who enjoyed power and was used to wielding it, he found himself in an impossible situation. Here he was at home, forty years old, and unmarried, his career smashed in the débâcle of March. Once again he had sacrificed himself for his father. He had neither liking nor aptitude for the agricultural life. For the man who had been absorbed with the fate of nations, it was galling to receive letters like this, sent by his father from Varzin on October 28, 1890:

Dear Herbert: Your letter of the 24th received with thanks. The kitchen chimney is an old landmark of Schönhausen[4] and still bears in stone the date of 1563, and our fathers have cooked in it for some 200 years. If it is in your way, however, remove it.... Concerning your question about dry wood, go to Friedrichsruh; I don't believe that you will find pine there, but there are beech and oak planks.[5]

When the Chinese Viceroy Li Hung Chang visited Bismarck a few years later, he asked about Count Herbert, whose long service in the Foreign Office he cordially recognized. Bismarck replied: "Herbert always likes to busy himself with politics, and in comparison with myself has but little liking for agriculture." Li then suggested: "With us, in China, the son always has to take over his father's work." To this the ex-Chancellor answered: "That is generally the case with us also, but one cannot do so against one's nature."[6]

The ever-observant Bülow recognized Herbert's distaste for this new tranquil life: "I kept up my old relations with him, even though he was in great disfavor with His Majesty. Humanly speaking, you will have found very little companionship at Friedrichsruh. The peaceful rustling of the old beech trees contrasts sharply with Herbert's worldly, misplaced ambition. The old man was better suited to this place, he was like a strange monster who heard all kinds of demonic noises in this rustling."[7]

Bülow spoke of Friedrichsruh, the family mansion to which Bismarck now retired. The country house at one time had been a hotel. Here the citizens of Hamburg, taking their Sunday outing in the Sachsenwald, had dined and slept in the building where, for the entire last decade of his life, the old man spent most of his days. It was a wild and romantic place, set in a beech forest. Bismarck loved the trees, which he saw as ancestors. Here he drove for hours through the forest, walked on the terraces, and gazed into the green woods "without thoughts and tedium." Here he could calm his nerves by stroking the heads of the two Great Danes waiting patiently under the table, their eyes always watching their master. The great man found his only true friends in dumb animals. He trusted their instincts implicitly and always accepted their evaluation of a stranger.

In this beautiful sylvan setting, the fallen Chancellor nursed his hurt and anger. A lifetime of service had been wasted – and all because of that impertinent Hohenzollern. That obnoxious and ungrateful monarch, plus the evil anti-Bismarck camarilla, had struck down father and son and damaged the Fatherland beyond recovery. A pox on him!

The Bismarcks, however, would not accept defeat and slink into the shadows of nonentity. They would maintain silence for a decent interval and then arm themselves for battle against their enemies. They would strike back at those who had insulted and degraded them. All was fair in politics, diplomacy, and war.

Visitors soon flocked to the mansion of exile to pay tribute to the old master. For them the Bismarcks went on the attack, excoriating and denouncing those responsible for what they called their "dismissal." At first the visiting jounalists were foreigners, but then German newspapermen coming to Friedrichsruh began to write columns about the fallen Chancellor and his son. Soon the *Hamburger Nachrichten* came to be known in Germany and the world as the voice of the Bismarcks, both of whom dictated many articles for it or inspired others to contribute pieces. The German public began to regard the *"Hamburger"* as a kind of semi-official anti-governmental press organ, in which they could find an outright blast or subtle criticism of the Emperor and his entourage. For the anti-Bismarck circle the newspaper was an organ of treason.

Typical of the battles raging around the *Hamburger Nachrichten* was a clash over colonial policy. The *Deutsche Wochenblatt,* whose editor was the Free Conservative delegate Dr. Otto Arendt, reported in its November 5, 1891, issue that it had learned from "an indubitably trustworthy source" that Lord Salisbury, upon the urging of Count Herbert Bismarck, had outfitted a British expedition to Africa to head off the Peters' expedition.[8] The article stated further that the British group was under command of a Captain Bateman and that it had the strength of six officers, 150 Sudanese, eighty Somalis, and several stranded soldiers, 1150 men in all, with two large Maxim cannons, four Armstrong guns, and a rocket battery. In its edition of November 17, 1891, the *Hamburger Nachrichten* attacked this report as "a stupid libel." The British did not need such help from Germany, said the newspaper; this rumor, obviously an attack on Herbert Bismarck, should not be dignified with refutation. What mattered was that only historical truth can be registered.[9] The Bismarcks were striking back.

Around the embittered exile of Friedrichsruh grew a clique that his enemies called the "Combination," which was supposedly devoted to the task of arousing popular enthusiasm for the return of the Bismarcks to political power. Herbert, with his fierce, almost idolatrous loyalty to his father, was the driving force behind the Combination. Many of the critical articles appearing in the *Hamburger Nachrichten* were inspired by him, but he was careful to minimize the extent of his activities when talking to friends or journalists. When he met Bülow by accident in Wildbad on August 28, 1890, the latter informed him how regrettable he found the the published interviews of his father. "I could not understand," Bülow wrote, "how the man who for half a century had held the kingly colors so high, could now act in contrary fashion to his past and give anxiety to all true patriots."[10]

Herbert attempted to justify his father's attitude by repeating the arguments that were appearing regularly in the *Hamburger Nachrichten*. Bülow reported further: "As I had insisted upon my view, he let me know confidentially that he regretted these interviews very much *(auf Aeusserste)*. He had tried to bring his father away from this sort of thing, but it was impossible to guide his father. His father could not be without something to do, therefore he reads the newspapers the whole day long, and from the newspapers he gets the desire to work on the press."[11]

Herbert's explanation may be taken with several grains of salt. That he "regretted" these interviews was unlikely, for they expressed exactly what he himself felt.

Father and son were closer than ever. They were, however, past masters in misleading their enemies. Even the old Empress Frederick, always the Bismarck-hater, was fooled into believing that there was friction between the old man and Herbert. On January 6, 1891, she wrote to Queen Victoria: "I have just seen some people who have been staying with Prince Bismarck, and they say he was never so well and strong and active, and is very cheerful and in good spirits, but that his relations with his son Herbert are not nearly so confidential, affectionate or intimate as they were, and a certain coldness has set in. Bismarck is working hard at his *Memoirs.* I have no doubt they will be strange and piquant."[12]

This was interesting court gossip, but as usual it was very much exaggerated. Herbert remained the adoring, faithful son, always ready to do battle for the honor of his father. He was certain that his father was not impressed with the rumor circulated by Waldersee and others in February, 1891 that "Bismarck now begins to see that his son contributed much to his fall."[13] Malicious gossip!

For the Bismarcks, father and son, it was a frustrating situation: both had only contempt for the young Emperor, yet a return to political power was dependent on his good will. The immature and obnoxious monarch had turned them out of office and smashed Bismarckian political power, but they would never come crawling back to him. Never! The old man's contempt for William II, expressed again and again to visitors to Friedrichsruh, culminated in the famous third volume of his *Gedanken und Erinnerungen,* a classic of subtle denunciation.

Herbert, on his part, continued to ridicule the monarch on every conceivable occasion. Waldsersee, a perennial Bismarck enemy, later recorded:

"Young people already laugh over Count Herbert Bismarck when they observe how he, in society or at dinner, attacks the Emperor. Everyone observes it who speaks with him."[14]

Herbert's arraignments seldom failed to reach the ear of the sensitive monarch, whose attitude toward the Bismarck family hardened considerably. At New Year's, 1891, both Bismarcks sent the Emperor friendly telegrams, but William wrote on them "To be answered coolly" *(kühl zu beantworten).*[15] On April 1, 1891, the seventy-sixth birthday of Bismarck, the Emperor, for the first time, did not send congratulations.[16]

Every slim bond that had existed between William II and Herbert Bismarck was eventually broken. William accused Herbert of being responsible for press stories which "were filled with lies and shameful libels of his grandparents and parents."[17] William had had enough of "Bismarckian duplicity."

On occasion, the rivalry took on an almost childish quality. Philipp Eulenburg was the Janus-faced diplomat who flattered the Bismarcks during their days of power and then switched allegiance to William II. He composed for the edification of the monarch and court circles an "Egyptian Fairy Tale," an obvious and thinly disguised attack on the Bismarck family. William was delighted with this story, which he repeated with great amusement. The theme was the rage of a bull of Apis, meant to be the fallen Chancellor. The bull had performed valuable service in the past by tearing down fences that divided the realms of the old Pharoah. Now it laid claim to divine honors and was supported by renegade priests and foolish philosophers. It worked subtly and with some success to make life intolerable for the young and inspired successor of the old Pharoah, a man of good heart who had grown senile in his later years. The gifted "new master," however, decided not to tolerate this shameful behavior. He ordered that an iron ring be placed through the nostrils of the evil Apis bull, and locked it with the two young bulls, its sons, into a stall, where it could cause no further trouble. Then all Egypt rejoiced and all the loyal subjects of the young Pharoah were jubilant.[18]

It was a vicious, vindictive "fairy tale." The "two young bulls" were obviously Herbert and William Bismarck. Now Bill, the second son, was to be included in the formalized ridicule of the Bismarcks!

A further word about Bill should be added. Born Wilhelm Albrecht Otto, Count von Bismarck, on August 1, 1852, at Frankfurt-am-Main, the Titan's second son studied political economy at Bonn. He served with Herbert during the Franco-Prussian War. After passing his second state examination in law in 1878, he was attached as assistant to Gen. Edwin von Manteuffel, Governor of Alsace-Lorraine. Bill was a *Reichstag* delegate from 1878 to 1881, representing Mühlhausen in Thuringia. Losing his seat in the autumn elections of 1881, he served thereafter only in the Prussian House of Deputies. He then became assistant to Privy Councillor von Tiedemann in the Imperial Chancellery and served as secretary to his father in the Prussian Ministry.

In his comparatively minor posts Bill was hounded by his father's enemies. He was denounced for revoking an order forbidding merry-go-rounds to be accompanied by barrel organs, a well as for another order preventing National School teachers from frequenting public houses and playing cards. Bill was showing, said his enemies, the typical Bismarckian contempt for liberty and equal rights. In 1889 Bill became president of the government of Hanover, and in 1895 governor of East Prussia. In middle age, Count Bill became enormously fat and drank heavily, as his brother did. Throughout his adult years he remained, also, a target of the anti-Bismarck crowd. He died on March 30, 1901, at the age of forty-nine.[19]

Throughout the decade from 1890 to 1900 it became increasingly obvious that the Emperor had no intention of recalling Herbert to service. The chasm between the two was widened in incident after incident. When an *Ordensfest* (a ceremony for decorations) was to be held on January 21, 1894, a clerk in the General Commission for Decorations erroneously added Herbert Bismarck's name to the list of invitations.[20] The Kaiser was infuriated when he heard the news, but seemed to intimate that he would speak to Herbert at the meeting.[21] Encouraged, Eulenburg and two court chamberlains, Blumenthal and Count von Kanitz, guided Herbert to the vicinity of the monarch so conspicuously at the ceremony that everyone present, including diplomats, Bismarckians, and anti-Bismarckians, got the impression that the Emperor had commanded it in order to speak with Herbert. But William II seemed to change his mind: he spoke to the right and to the left, but not to Herbert.[22] The monarch apparently lost his nerve at the last moment.

The incident was not without political significance. From the viewpoint of the anti-Bismarck camarilla, if the Emperor had spoken to Herbert, the enemies of Caprivi would have exploited the affair for their own purposes.[23] The Bismarck party, gravely insulted, let it be known that the Emperor had informed Herbert Bismarck that he wanted to speak with him and then had not found the courage to do it.[24] Among the Bismarckians there had been some hope of effecting a rapprochement and therewith demolishing Caprivi's influence, but this had now failed.

Molehills and mountains! Afterward, on second thought, the Emperor decided to take a step of reconciliation with the father. He sent his aide-de-camp Count

Moltke to Friedrichsruh with a gift flask of old Rhine wine, Steinberger Kabinett, and a message of congratulations to Prince Bismarck on his recovery from influenza. At first Bismarck received the emissary frostily, but later declared himself willing to go to Berlin and thank the Emperor in person.

The news, fluttering the dovecotes of Berlin, was a sensation in the Foreign Office: conspiracy in the castle against Caprivi! Return of the Bismarcks to the Wilhelmstrasse! Great revenge campaign of the old Prince and Herbert![25] Eulenburg complained to the Emperor: "Herbert has said in confidential circles that the time has come for Caprivi, Marschall, Holstein, I, Kiderlin, and so on to go."[26]

Waldersee was appalled. "The Emperor really wants to reconciliate with Bismarck. Bismarck is to ride to Berlin and live in the castle. God grant that everything will turn out all right."[27] Once in Berlin, said the anti-Bismarckians, the wily Bismarck would persuade the Emperor to choose another Chancellor – and soon Herbert would be back in the saddle again: may the good Lord prevent that catastrophe!

The alarm was unnecessary. On January 26, 1894, accompanied by Herbert, the old man came to Berlin. The Emperor was pained by Herbert's presence. Surface reconciliation: the Emperor kissed Bismarck's cheeks and the old Prince bussed the Emperor's hands. These were given and received as kisses of death. Underneath was a growing hatred.

On October 24, 1896, there appeared in the *Hamburger Nachrichten* an article said to be inspired by the Bismarcks[28] on the Russian Reinsurance Treaty. The contents of the secret treaty were given and the fault of its non-extension placed at the door of Caprivi, together with a general criticism of German foreign policy. Infuriated, William II wanted to try Bismarck for treason, but Hohenlohe talked him out of it.[29]

Early the next year William II refused to attend a wedding reception unless an invitation to Herbert was cancelled. The daughter of Count von Wedel, Minister of the Royal Household, was to be married on January 13, 1897. When Wedel showed the Emperor the list of persons to be invited, William said that he would make his own appearance at the wedding only if the invitation to Herbert was withdrawn. Distressed, Wedel ordered his future son-in-law to write to Herbert asking that he decline on account of business or health because His Majesty did not want to see him. Herbert replied that it was out of the question to do this, because he was in good health and on the day of the wedding had to appear in the *Reichstag* where everyone would see him. Wedel, faced with the dilemma of withdrawing the invitation or being guilty of disobedience to the Emperor, then cancelled the invitation.[30] So much for affairs of state in William II's Germany!

By now it was obvious that Herbert's chance of being returned to office was nil. In July 1899 the Emperor informed Philipp Eulenburg categorically that he would never, under any circumstances, re-employ Herbert. "If anyone speaks to you about the possible recall of Herbert Bismarck," he informed Eulenburg, "I beg you urgently and empower you to declare that there can never be any possibility of reinstatement."[31] This was, of course, after the death of Otto von Bismarck in 1898. To Eulenburg, who had been snubbed to his face by Herbert on the day of the elder Bismarck's funeral, the Emperor's statement was sweet music indeed! There would be no further place for Herbert in the government – either in the Foreign Office or even as Ambassador in London, St. Petersburg, or Vienna.

In his memoirs, *My Early Life,* written while in exile in Holland after World War I, William II reviewed his relations with Herbert Bismarck:

> During the meeting of the Emperor's at Gastein, in August 1886, I was entrusted with an important diplomatic commission. This incident induced Prince Bismarck to accede to my desire to be taught something of foreign politics; for this purpose I was to learn by personal experience the business and managment of the Foreign Office. My grandfather at once assented to the Chancellor's proposal, so that I was able to begin work at the end of September, with Count Herbert Bismarck, the Secretary of State for Foreign Affairs....

> Count Bismarck was my instructor with regard to diplomatic events of former times, the general questions of the day in foreign politics, as well as foreign statesmen and diplomats, particularly the Ambassadors in Berlin....

> In the matter of outward discipline the Foreign Office had been very strictly trained by Count Herbert Bismarck and I was struck by his rudeness to his subordinates....

> My relations with Count Herbert were...agreeable. Apart from our official connection, the principal bond between us was the admiration we share for his great father. Count Herbert's passion for work, his inexhaustible energy, and his political knowledge were amazing; while he did not possess his father's genius, he was undoubtedly his most gifted and important pupil. In personal intercourse, despite all his rudeness and lack of consideration for others, he could be a cheerful and entertaining companion, who knew how to gather around him a circle of interesting men, not from the Diplomatic Service alone. However, beyond a certain comradeship such as readily arises between young men, given similarity of interests and good will on both sides, our relations did not progress; we were never united by sentiments of real friendship. This was made particularly clear when, on the retirement of his father, I asked him to remain at his post and help me carry on the same tradition in our

policy. Count Herbert met this request with a curt refusal: he was accustomed to serving no one but his father, and could not come with his portfolio under his arm and make his reports to any other Chancellor. And so our ways divided for ever.[32]

The Kaiser's estimate was written after he had lost his throne and at a time when his own flamboyant boisterousness was muted. He stated the facts accurately as he saw them, but the fires of hatred existing between him and the Bismarcks had been somewhat dampened by time. When he acceded to the throne in 1888 he, like may others, was well aware of Herbert's brutish coarseness and roughness, his indelicate vulgarity, and propensity for ribald behavior. He had hoped to ease the pain of the old man's dismissal by holding on to Herbert – at least for a time. This would enable him to claim a continuity of tradition. But Herbert had declined – abruptly and rudely. If the insufferable lout wanted to remain his father's boy, then so be it.

As for Herbert, loyalty to his esteemed father came before loyalty to the Hohenzollerns. After all, his father had seen three Hohenzollern kings naked, and he was not especially impressed by what he saw. Now the frivolous William II had done the unbelievable, the inexcusable – he had turned on the Junker genius who had virtually created and stabilized his throne. In Herbert's eyes that was unforgivable stupidity. But he would drink to a better day – for the Bismarcks and for the Fatherland.

12

FEUD WITH HOLSTEIN

Herbert's quirks and oddities continued well into middle age. Like his father, he managed to win a kind of notoriety for the overabundance of enemies he made. Both peers and underlings were humiliated by his authoritarian behavior, his arrogance and insulting demeanor. He was a specialist in the business of creating and maintaining feuds.

For the Bismarcks, personal animosities were a way of life. In their eyes it merely reflected a struggle for political supremacy – and they had no intention of losing such battles. Throughout their careers they found enemy after enemy in the political arena. Friction and differences added up to a kind of gladiatorial combat out of which they must always emerge victorious. The result was rudeness for rudeness, vengeance for vengeance, coarseness for coarseness. The Bismarcks were not likely to win popularity contests among court circles and officialdom. This aversion was not shared by the general public, however, which saw them as heroic examples of the German spirit.

For years the Bismarcks had worked closely with an important man in German diplomatic life. Gradually, however, they began to suspect him of dishonorable dealings and of placing obstacles in their way. Suspicious by nature, they demanded total personal loyalty and the man was not giving it. After the Bismarcks' fall from power, they turned on this man in a celebrated feud.

This special enemy was the mysterious Baron Friedrich von Holstein (1837-1909), called Fritz, but better known as the demonical *éminence grise,* the "Gray Eminence" of the Second Reich. To Princess Bismarck he was "the man with the hyena eyes."[1] For some fifteen years Fritz Holstein was the chief agent of German foreign policy. Eccentric, unconventional, and devious, he viewed himself as responsible neither to the Emperor, the Bismarcks, nor the general public. For years he had been intriguing against "the firm of Bismarck." His hatred of the Bismarcks was masked, but in later years it had consequences of global importance.

Holstein's connection with the house of Bismarck began in the early 1870s at the time of the celebrated Arnim affair.[2] Count Harry von Arnim-Suckow and the elder Bismarck had known each other from their youth. After the Franco-Prussian War, Bismarck made his friend Ambassador to France, key post in the German diplomatic service. Bismarck intended to support Thiers and the French Republic as a means of weakening France, but he soon began to feel that Arnim was undercutting his policy by favoring the monarchists. Moreover, as we have seen, Arnim had gravitated toward the Empress Augusta camarilla, and, in common with it, had strongly opposed Bismarck's *Kulturkampf* against the Catholics. Worse still, Arnim came to be regarded in Conservative circles as a possible future Chancellor, in Bismarck's eyes the unforgivable sin. Arnim had to be dropped.

The way in which the suspicious Chancellor got rid of Arnim is a well-known classic story of career smashing. In October 1874 Arnim was suddenly arrested, thrown into a Berlin prison, and accused of refusing to return certain documents which the Foreign Office regarded as offical property. Sentenced to nine months' imprisonment, he fled to Switzerland, where he published pamphlets critical of Bismarck. He was once again brought to trial, accused of treason to the Emperor and libel against Bismarck, and sentenced *in absentia* to five years' penal servitude. He died four years later in Nice, dishonored and homeless, a victim of Bismarck's unquenchable hatred and thirst for revenge.

In his memoirs[3] Bismarck gave his own version of the Arnim affair under the heading of "Intrigues." He denounced Arnim as a man of boundless ambition, of Machiavellian and Jesuitical bent, as a shameless lady-killer, and, worst of all, as one who could not hold his liquor. Arnim, wrote Bismarck, has been brought to trial because he had refused to follow instructions and, instead, entered into a conspiracy against the Chancellor. Moreover, the man had spent official funds to libel Bismarck in the press, money that was to be used to advance the German cause in French newspapers. Bismarck disclaimed all responsibility for the verdicts against Arnim, but such was the depth of his hatred that he made even more charges. The infuriated Bismarck was convinced that Arnim had his eyes on the Chancellor's office. Anyone who wanted that was to be treated ruthlessly as a personal enemy.

Enter Fritz von Holstein. In his campaign to destroy the detested Arnim, Bismarck began to use the services of this unknown thirty-seven-year-old councillor at the Paris embassy, whom he had met at St. Petersburg. It was Holstein's mission to spy on Arnim, his superior officer, and send back secret reports to Bismarck. It was a piece of undercover business for which Holstein was qualified. He informed the suspicious Chancellor that Arnim indeed had aspirations toward the chancellorship. Bismarck forced Holstein to testify at Arnim's second trial. In the witness box, Holstein attempted to evade giving direct testimony, but it was clear to all that he had used his position to spy on his immediate chief. These revelations had a profound psychological effect on the brilliant young diplomat, who from this moment on, became a social pariah in Germany. Holstein withdrew into a shell of uncommunicativeness and never again appeared in public. Inwardly, he regarded his public degradation as having been caused by the Chancellor, for whom he retained a deep-seated hatred.

Outwardly, however, Holstein appeared to be fiercely loyal to both Bismarcks, father and son. As long as the Bismarcks were in power they could provide the road to advancement. For years Holstein remained one of the Chancellor's closest working intimates, trusted with the most secret affairs of state. Herbert, as Secretary of State for Foreign Affairs, maintained friendly relations with Holstein. The younger Bismarck was impressed at first not only by Holstein's perfect French, but also by his acute perceptions and breadth of vision. In addition, he admired Holstein's cunning.[4] "Holstein possesses uncommon flair," said Herbert to Bülow. "He can feel whether a young diplomat is a 'rising man' or not, before the fellow is clear about it himself. And this, too, makes him valuable to my father."[5] At this time Herbert regarded Holstein as "the faithful Fritz," as one who could be trusted in a politically dangerous atmosphere. Later he would change his mind.

Although Holstein was received warmly in the Bismarck household, he was by no means liked by all members of the family. Princess Bismarck used such terms as "the blind worm" when speaking of the eccentric young diplomat.[6] Bill Bismarck saw through Holstein's thin veneer: "As for me, I don't deny Holstein's great talent, nor his brilliant French and English, nor his quickness and cleverness. I will only hope that if he is ever put to the test Holstein will show himself true as steel, as Herbert thinks and expects. But he suffers from an almost pathological delusion of persecution. As he is very sensitive and suspicious, this delusion is constantly finding new fuel. And so he is always working up my father, who, in any case, is suspicious enough, and always irritable with people, today against one and tomorrow against another. On the whole I consider Holstein a disintegrating element."[7]

Bill was more observant than his brother Herbert. The latter at first refused to believe the rumor that Fritz Holstein was working secretly with Windhorst, Schleinitz, and the anti-Bismarck clique.[8] Herbert changed his mind abruptly about the rising diplomat during negotiations leading to his father's downfall. From then on, he hated Holstein with an intensity that was Olympian in its magnitude. In Herbert's eyes, the *"getreuter Fritz,"* "the faithful Fritz," became the worst kind of criminal, a man who had been the trusted confidant of the Bismarcks and who now revealed himself as a cunning traitor. Bülow reported: "Herbert Bismarck now let no opportunity pass of warning me against the trickiness and malice of this man."[9] The tension between the two grew worse and worse. Wherever he went, at parties, bachelors' dinners, and the like, Herbert gave full vent to his contempt for Holstein.

After Bismarck's resignation, the affairs of state were entrusted to two inexperienced amateurs – Gen. Leo von Caprivi had been a valiant soldier but became a slow and uncertain Chancellor; Baron Marschall von Bieberstein, the new Secretary of State, had been Public Prosecutor in Baden and was ill-equipped for his new position. Actual guidance of the government fell to Holstein, now head of the political department of the Foreign Office.[10] Historian Brandenberg described Holstein's personality: "He exercised fascination over all who came into contact with him, due partly to superior mental ability and political expediency, but partly to fear of the ruthless lust for revenge deep seated in this man, who was implacable in his personal relations. Lonely, trusting no one, he deliberately withdrew into his private room, and from there guided the manifold political threads and settled all questions with a mixture of respectful admiration and secret fear." [11]

This shy, unconventional political genius had no hesitation in crushing any political enemy, a disposition he shared in common with the Bismarcks. He may have understood the Bismarcks better than anyone else in Germany did, and his greatest anxiety was lest the old Chancellor or his son should return to power. He cleverly manipulated the strings of power to see to it that this would not happen.

Holstein had his own spies to report to him everything Herbert said about him. The diplomat Hermann von Eckardstein revealed Holstein's reactions: "One day, going to Holstein on my departure for London to say goodbye, and to get his private letter to Count Hatzfeldt, Holstein led the conversation to those dinners at the Kaiserhof [*at which Herbert Bismarck had denounced Holstein*]. I at once guessed what he was after and became very guarded in my answers. 'I heard,' he said with an obviously assumed air of indifference, 'that Herbert Bismarck in these little dinners falls pretty foul of me. If I could only get an idea of what he has against me and why he bears me so great a grudge I could protect myself more easily against certain insinuations that he is systematically circulating against me.' I replied that I wasn't aware that he had ever in my presence said anything against him – Holstein. But Holstein went on: 'You have been at every one of these Kaiserhof dinners for the last three weeks, and you must know what he said, for example, to Count Hohenthal during one of them.' And as a matter of fact I had heard Herbert say to the Count that 'it was high time the German princes stopped the Kaiser from keeping so hopeless a fool as Holstein in control of his foreign policy. Prince Hohenlohe must see to it that King Albert of Saxony took the matter in hand and got the Princes to send a collective note to the Kaiser.' I was told later by Prince Philipp Eulenburg that some of the Princes had made a half-hearted sort of move with the Kaiser against the Holstein policy. But the Kaiser had simply ruled out all intervention in foreign policy, and that was the end of the matter."[12]

In all probability it was Holstein who was primarily responsible for the first great change in German foreign policy following the fall of the Bismarcks. We have seen how, in the early months of 1890, both Bismarcks sought desperately to renew the secret Reinsurance Treaty with Russia.[13] In effect, this treaty, concluded in 1887 and renewable after a period of three years, was a partnership of Russian Czardom and Prussian Junkerdom,[14] both anti-Polish in sentiment. The treaty formed the cornerstone of the entire Bismarckian treaty system. Through it the Bismarcks hoped to maintain their Russian connections. They dreaded the possibility of losing Russia to the arms of France and the consequent dangerous encirclement *(Einkreisung)* of Germany.

Holstein was well on his way to becoming top man in the Foreign Office. In his work he was motivated by a fiendish contempt for the Bismarcks and everything they stood for. He did not understand, or deliberately ignored, their policy of wooing Russia. He wanted to break the ties. Instead of remaining close to an eastern ally, he adopted a zigzag course, balance and counterbalance, playing both ends against the middle. The inevitable result was exactly what the Bismarcks feared – the Franco-Russian alliance of January 1894. Encirclement of Germany was under way.

Using his gift of persuasion, Holstein worked on the uninspired Caprivi, the inefficient Marschall, and the impressionable Emperor, all of whom he convinced not to renew the Reinsurance Treaty. At the same time, each one was adroitly made to feel that he had arrived at the decision independently. The Russians had offered favorable conditions for renewing the agreement, but Holstein maintained that all the advantages of the pact lay on the side of Russia. Nothing tangible, he hinted, could be expected from the treaty. Moreover, if the agreement was removed from the secret category and pubicized, both the German public and the whole world would be hostile to the government.

Thus, by a complicated tangle of jealousy and ambition, sparked by Holstein's neurotic hatred of the Bismarcks, the work of decades crashed in ruins. To Herbert, the success of Holstein in smashing the Reinsurance Treaty was an augury of a tragic future for Germany. When Bülow asked him how he felt about Holstein's anti-Russian attitude, he replied: "Holstein has once and for all a jester's privilege."[15]

The feud gathered momentum, with Herbert and Fritz Holstein outdoing one another in expressions of mutual aversion. "After his fall," Bülow wrote, "Herbert never spoke of Holstein with other than boundless hatred....This hate [was] a reaction from his many years of enthusiasm for Holstein – the blind confidence he had reposed in him from childhood. He felt that Holstein had deceived and betrayed him. He felt 'taken in.'"[16] To illustrate the character "of the crazy Holstein," Herbert told Eulenburg that Holstein hated Prince Bismarck because the latter had revealed that Holstein once wanted to poison Crown Prince Frederick, the former Emperor.[17] Again and always it was the same theme – hate, hate, hate!

Holstein struck back with renewed vigor. In the years immediately following the fall of the Bismarcks, he carefully consolidated his power. For a time the foreign policy of Germany was chaotic as Under Secretaries in the Foreign Office ran wild, but Holstein soon grasped the reins of political and diplomatic power. Both minor officials and Marschall, the Secretary, were officially Holstein's superiors, but "His Gray Eminence" regarded them only as a subgovernment of which he was in control. He ruled the Political Section with a rod of iron. Often he did not allow his immediate superiors to see his secret reports and letters.[18] The observant Lothar Bucher reported as early as July 10, 1890: "Holstein, who for ten years was taken seriously by nobody, now does everything."[19]

Nearly everyone in the government recognized that Holstein was determined to block any attempt to bring the Bismarcks back to power. According to Lothar Bucher: "Holstein not only slanders the Prince [*Bismarck*], which he did twelve months since, but he also abuses Herbert, who with inconceivable blindness, had supported him to the last."[20] Holstein's fear of a revived Bismarckian house was almost pathological in its intensity. Bülow recognized this: "Ever since his apostasy from the house of Bismarck, Holstein, in sleepless nights, had terrifying visions of Herbert, with his father, like a wrathful Titan, standing behind him."[21]

The savage hostility between the two men nearly resulted in a duel, with the half-blind, crotchety, and suspicious Holstein taking the initiative. In late January 1894 a story concerning the Arnim trial appeared in newspapers supposedly favorable to the Bismarcks.[22] Although the proceedings against Arnim had taken place nearly twenty years earlier, the matter still rankled, and it appeared in the press on occasion. From the contents of the article, Holstein assumed that Herbert was the author, because the point of the story concerned something that was known only to the Bismarcks and Holstein.

The angry Holstein sent two representatives, Dönhoff-Friedrichstein and Fritz Pourtalès,[23] to Herbert to demand an explanation as to whether or not he had inspired the article. Herbert was not inclined to take the matter seriously, but he was ready to declare before the two witnesses that he had nothing to do with this article or cartoons which appeared in *Kladdaradatsch.* The visitors accepted this explanation, made a protocol, and handled the matter as a secret. Herbert suggested that the incident be taken up with his attorney, Heinrich Lehnsdorff.

Several days later at a dinner held at the home of Count Paul Schuwalow, the Russian Ambassador, Herbert, while intoxicated spoke openly about the affair. Later he referred to it again in *Reichstag* circles. Thereafter, Holstein's two representatives, Dönhoff-Friedrichstein and Pourtalès, no longer felt themselves bound by secrecy. At this time, on March 1, 1894, another story appeared in the *Neue Freie Presse,* a newspaper friendly to the Bismarcks, in which the incident was portrayed in a way that Holstein regarded as insulting:

> For some weeks there has been talk about this matter in political circles.... Today it is said in Parliamentary circles that Herr von Holstein had sent two aristocratic messengers to Count Herbert Bismarck with the demand to declare whether he was the author of that attack, with the aim of provoking a duel. Count Herbert Bismarck then declared that he had nothing to do with the matter.[24]

Holstein now sent his two emissaries to Herbert's attorney with the demand that Herbert issue a public declaration to the effect that the differences between him and Holstein had come to a satisfactory conclusion in an agreement between the two. Furthermore, Herbert was to announce his lack of responsibility for the press campaign, and this explanation, or declaration, was to appear in the *Hamburger Nachrichten*, the most pro-Bismarckian newspaper in Germany.

Eulenburg thereupon reported to the Emperor: "Now what follows can be foretold. If Herbert fails to give the declaration – because he, perhaps, cannot give it, then it comes to a duel. The duel will be the proof of Herbert's guilt, for he can as an honorable gentleman, if his conscience is clear, give the necessary demanded explanation without further ado. If he denies it on other grounds, so he must come into conflict with Dönhoff and Pourtalès, who represent the cause of a gentleman.... If it really comes to a duel, which would be somewhat energetic and unpleasant for the half-blind Holstein, and should something happen to Herbert, I beg Your Majesty, in consideration of one of the most loyal servants Your Majesty has, to remain neutral in the matter, that is, not to stand on the side of Herbert through expression of partisanship or inquiry. For that would be taken as a move against Holstein, who has come to this disagreeable enmity by way of special service to Your Majesty. I do not believe that Herbert has anything to do with this dirty business, with these personal attacks in the press. I therefore hope for a peaceful outcome."[25]

The outcome, was, in fact, peaceful. Herbert, whose courage could not have been doubted, did not consider the matter worth a duel, and he had no intention of taking advantage of a half-blind opponent. Accordingly, he published an explanation in the March 6, 1894, issue of the *Hamburger Nachrichten,* in which he stood his ground and insisted that he had known nothing of the offensive article.

In a letter to Ida von Stülpnägel, Holstein wrote: "Whether Herbert B. has told the truth, that he must square with his own conscience. As a decent man I am duty-bound to believe him." He closed his letter with a satirical remark: "With the 'half-blind' one it is not so bad now. My right eye is still ready for battle."[26]

Holsteins' fear of and ill will toward the Bismarcks persisted for the remainder of his career. During the 1890s and until Herbert's death in 1904 (Holstein survived him by five years), Holstein worked shrewdly to keep Herbert from the Emperor's presence. In February 1894, when the Emperor and his wife planned to travel to Abbazia, Holstein became agitated because it was possible for the monarch to meet Herbert, who was there.[27] In November of the same year Holstein passed on to the German Ambassador in Vienna some news that he had learned from an unimportant factory tenant in Varzin, one of Bismarck's mansions, that the "Combination" was preparing to make Herbert Secretary of State for Foreign Affairs.[28]

Eckardstein reported that Holstein was greatly excited by the "not hopeless candidacy" of Herbert: "During my presence in Berlin in the middle of October 1899, Holstein said to me one day, when I found him in a very depressed mood, that he did not believe he would be on his post for long, for he had the feeling that Herbert Bismarck would come to the rudder."[29]

During his chancellorship (1900-09), Bülow retained Holstein, although he regarded him as an "incorrigible crank." Bülow wrote that in March 1899 Holstein came to him with a telegram saying that British and American cruisers had bombarded Apia in Samoa. He commented, "With a brick like this dropping on your head, the only way out of an awkward situation is to send in your resignation." Bülow, aware of Holstein's hatred for Herbert Bismarck, knew exactly how to handle his underling: "I replied perfectly calmly that that solution had much in it that attracted me. If I did retire, I would advise the Emperor that Prince Herbert Bismarck should be my successor, if only to propitiate the shade of his great father. Holstein, who since 1890 had feared the Bismarck family as the devil fears Holy water, at once took a more sensible view of the situation."[30]

His Gray Eminence, the odd intriguer, one of the most singular personalities ever to appear on the political stage of Europe, was the victor in this extraordinary battle for power. His years of depression and worry about the possibility of Herbert Bismarck returning to power were really unnecessary – the opportunity for a Bismarck dynasty no longer existed.

In retrospect, such machinations as the Bismarck-Holstein feud in the Wilhelminian era seem bizarre, and trivial as well. But they should be judged in the milieu of the day. Holstein was working to preserve his lofty place in German government, thereby preventing the return of Herbert to the seat of power; hence, the embittered clash was inevitable. Strange and pathetic are the ways of the human animal in defense of his pedestal!

13

MARRIAGE TO COUNTESS HOYOS

Eleven years had elapsed since the marriage fiasco of 1881. Herbert had never forgotten his love affair with the Princess Elizabeth Carolath nor had he ceased to regret the circumstances under which he had jilted his beloved. But now, past the age of forty-two, he decided that it was time to settle down and marry. That would please his father, now seventy-seven, who wanted heirs on the male side of the family and a successor to Herbert for the primary Bismarckian title.

There were no important changes in Herbert's personality. The arrogance, loutishness, and crudeness were still there, coupled with the old intermittent charm. He intended to use that charm to attract a mate who would have his father's blessing.

The lady was available and met the old lion's specifications. Countess Marguerite Hoyos had an English mother and a half-Austrian, half-Hungarian father.[1] That meant a union for Herbert with a representative of the Austrian and Hungarian people who owed much to the great Bismarck. Fine! This would reinforce the old alliance between Prussia and Hungary.[2] Always consider the political implications – even in marriage!

When the engagement was announced on May 5, 1892, William II sent a telegram to Herbert:

MANY THANKS FOR YOUR FRIENDLY ANNOUNCEMENT AND

HEARTIEST WISHES FOR YOUR HAPPINESS ON THE OCCA-
SION OF YOUR ENGAGEMENT TO COUNTESS MARGUERITE
HOYOS

WILHELM, IMPERATOR REX[3]

There was actually little spontaneity or warmth in this communication.
For two years, since the resignation in 1890, the Bismarcks and the blus-
tering young Emperor had been at odds. The fallen Chancellor resented
the way he had been dismissed as well as the dashing of his hopes for
Herbert. William, despite his battle royal with the Bismarcks, considered
it good politics to pretend that he was enthusiastic about the forthcoming
wedding.

No matter in what direction the Bismarcks moved, there were nearly
always political implications. If the marriage tragedy of 1881 had such a
connotation, Herbert's actual marriage of 1892 produced an even greater
political explosion. The young Emperor would not have been so quick to
send congratulations had he known that the master of Friedrichsruh himself
intended to go to Vienna for the ceremony.

There was great excitement in Berlin as courtiers and Wilhelmstrasse
officials saw political dangers ahead. It was rumored that Prince Bismarck
had said that he would "open the eyes of Francis Joseph to the young
Kaiser."[4] Once in the Austrian capital, the still dangerous old lion and his
nasty cub would seek to mend political fences and prepare the way for a
return to power. This could be the start of an effort to arouse popular
enthusiasm for the Bismarck dynasty, embarrass the Kaiser, force him to
oust Chancellor Caprivi, and then recall the Bismarcks.[5] This must not be
permitted. The Bismarcks were shrewd manipulators and they must not
be allowed to strike at the Emperor and his entourage through what seemed
to be an innocent situation.

Prince Bismarck's own advisers cautioned him not to make the trip,
arguing that it would be interpreted as a new venture into the political
arena.[6] His confidential agent and banker, Gerson von Bleichröder, especially, urged him to stay away from Vienna.[7] But the old man would not
listen. Had not Herbert already arranged for his reception by the Austrian
royal family? Furthermore, attending a son's wedding was the privilege of
any father, and it was essential, and a matter of courtesy, to please the
family of the future daughter-in-law.[8]

When it became clear that nothing could deter Prince Bismarck from
making the trip to Vienna, the Wilhelmstrasse went into action to stigmatize
him officially as a person who was not to be received. There would also

be a social boycott of the Bismarck family. On June 9, 1892, a letter signed by Chancellor Leo von Caprivi, was dispatched to Prince Heinrich VII von Reuss, the German Ambassador in Vienna:

IMMEDIATE

After an audience with His Majesty, I inform Your Excellency of the following concerning the forthcoming marriage of Count Herbert Bismarck. The rumors of a reconciliation of Prince Bismarck and His Majesty do not take into account the indispensable presumption of a first step upon the part of the Prince. But even if this did take place, the reconciliation could never go so far that public opinion would take it that the Prince had won any kind of influence in the leadership of national affairs. His Majesty requests Your Excellency that, should the Prince or his family make any approach to Your Excellency's house, you limit yourself to the conventional forms, and avoid accepting any invitation to the wedding. His Majesty will not accept any notice of the wedding. You are instructed to inform Count Kálnoky of this fact in whatever manner may seem best to you. These indications as to behavior apply to the staff of the embassy as to yourself.[9]

With malice aforethought Caprivi arranged for the publication of this letter in the government's offical newspaper, the *Reichsanzeiger.*[10] The public must be informed about the dangerous machinations of the Bismarcks!

It is probable that "Gray Eminence" Fritz von Holstein, then *Vortragender Rat* (counsellor) in the Foreign Office, had a hand in drafting this communication. The reclusive, sensitive bureaucrat was still consumed with hatred for the Bismarcks, and here was an opportunity to strike at them. Johannes Haller put it bluntly: "This unfortunate step was wholly Holstein's work."[11] According to historian Otto Gradenwitz, Holstein had a double purpose in mind: to boycott Bismarck and at the same time make the Viennese embassy ready for Eulenburg.[12]

On June 12, 1892, three days after the official dispatch was sent to Vienna, William II sent a handwritten communication to Francis Joseph:

At the end of the month, Bismarck goes to Vienna,...in order to receive planned ovations from his admirers....You are aware that one of his masterpieces was the secret treaty *à double fonds* with Russia, which, negotiated behind your back, was annulled by me. Since his retirement, the Prince has carried on a most perfidious war against me and Caprivi, my minister....He seeks, with all the art and shrewdness he possesses, to twist matters so that the world shall believe that I am making advances to him. The main feature of his plan is that he has asked you for an audience....Therefore, I venture to beg you not to complicate this unruly subject of mine until he has come to me and said *peccavi.*[13]

It was impossible to keep such communications secret in the Berlin atmosphere of gossip, intrigue, and malice. Prince Bismarck soon learned about the contents of these two insulting letters.[14] At first he reacted as if he were still a student at Göttingen: he would challenge Caprivi to a duel. The seventy-seven-year-old Bismarck would defend his name, rank, and honor himself. "But when I turned the matter over in my mind I remembered that I am an officer, and that the affair would be submitted to a court of honor composed of elderly generals. I should never have got him to face my pistol."[15] Still, it took great effort by the family to calm down the furious old man.

Privately, Bismarck denounced the Emperor's communication, which he termed a *"Uriasbrief"* ("Uriah letter"),[16] as "a contemptible piece of effrontery."

The Bismarcks left for Vienna on June 18.[17] The *Norddeutsche All- gemeine Zeitung* announced incorrectly that the ex-Chancellor and his party would arrive at the Lehrter Station in Berlin, whereas they came in at the Anhalter Station. Nevertheless, a huge mob invaded the platform and clamored for a speech. "My duty is to be silent," said Bismarck. An onlooker countered: "When you keep silent, then will the stones speak!"[18]

Next stop Dresden. Officials met the Bismarcks. The city was in banners, the Prince's private car covered with flowers. "Our unity is unbreakable," said Bismarck in a speech. That night, from his suite at the Hotel Bellevue, he reviewed 13,000 torchbearers and 1,600 singers.[19]

At 10 P.M. on the evening of June 19 the party arrived at Vienna, where the reception was so stormy that Bismarck and Herbert were nearly tram- pled by the crowds.[20] The next day, however, it became obvious that here was an official and social boycott of the founder of the Second Reich. [21] Unimportant mayors and deputies of prominent citizens did wait upon the Bismarck family, but there were no invitations from kings and princes.[22] The nobility, "the true aristocracy," held aloof.[23]

Francis Joseph, unwilling to disturb political relations with Berlin, did not receive the Bismarcks at court.[24] Prince Reuss, German Ambassador in Vienna, found himself in an embarrassing situation. He had been instructed not only not to receive Bismarck but not even to allow the German choral groups in Vienna to take part in any demonstrations.[25] Because he felt that he could not disobey his Emperor, Prince Reuss took to his bed and became diplomatically ill. But his wife, daughter of the Grand Duke Alex- ander of Saxony, made it clear that she was not in the diplomatic service; she received the insulted ex-Chancellor with great deference in her home.[26]

On the afternoon of June 20 Bismarck left his card with Count Kálnoky at the Foreign Office. [27] That evening there was a gala party at the home of Count Palffy, a relative of the bride's family, with whom the Bismarcks were staying. The guests, politically speaking, were unimportant: Count Kálnoky; Minister Szegenyi; Baron Chlumetzki, the Russian Ambassador to Berlin and Vienna; the Ambassadors of England and Italy; and the Attaché of the German Embassy in Rome, von Below. [28] Those of higher rank stayed away.

Deliberate humiliation for the Bismarcks. Neither the ex-Chancellor nor his son was allowed to wear a military uniform, because such attire could be worn in foreign countries "only with permission."[29] The old man was infuriated by the ban. "I don't know about rules on uniforms," he wrote to his son William, "and do not believe they are in effect. Think of it, at my age, to have to ask what I should wear!"[30] According to Hans Blum, when Bismarck drove to the church on the morning of June 21, he was dressed in the uniform of a cuirassier.[31] No one, not even the Kaiser, was going to tell Otto von Bismarck how to dress at his son's wedding.

These were premeditated insults. Despite them, the wedding ceremony took place promptly at noon on June 21 at the Helvetian Reform Church.[32] There was no official representation. The irrepressible Prince in effect thumbed his nose at his tormentors by delivering a political toast at the wedding dinner: "To the political unity of the two great powers."[33] At 5 P.M. that day the happy couple, orange blossoms in hand, went off on their honeymoon.[34]

Prince Bismarck remained in Vienna for two more days. Despite his age, he visited the Prater, the Rathaus, and mounted the 158 steps of the Festsaal.[35] Aching for battle, on June 23 he carried out his carefully made plan for revenge. He had a long interview with M. Benedikt, editor of the *Neue Freie Presse,* in which he openly attacked the German Government and accused it of stupidity:

> Austria, in the commercial treaty, has, of course, turned to account the weakness and ineptitude of our negotiators. This result must be ascribed to the fact that in our country men have come to the front whom I had formerly kept in the background – the reason being that everything had to be changed....For my part, I am no longer under any obligations toward the personalities now in office, or toward my successor. All the bridges have been broken down....The tie which used to connect us with Russia has been severed. Personal authority and confidence are lacking in Berlin.[36]

Sensation in Berlin. Something had to be done to discredit the "garrulous old man." Eugen Richter, leader of the Progressives and one of Bismarck's most obstinate opponents, [37] referred to legal paragraphs which could be used against Bismarck for this interview, and even reckoned how many years the ex-Chancellor would have to serve in jail.[38]

The return journey of the Bismarcks was by way of Munich (June 24), Augsburg (June 26), Kissingen (June 27), Jena (July 30), Berlin (August 6), and Varzin (August 8).[39] The German public, aware of the shabby treatment accorded the Bismarcks in Vienna, opened their hearts to the fallen Chancellor.[40] Never before had the Junker of Friedrichsruh enjoyed such popularity. It was astonishing: "My six weeks journey was a triumphal tour, such as I had never dreamed....Everywhere the people greeted me joyfully....I shall not change, my ideas remain the same."[41] Thousands of citizens flocked to the stations to greet the Bismarcks. Torchlight parades were held and choirs serenaded the heroes. During his stay in Kissingen, Bismarck received 320 messages totaling 10,000 words.[42] After breakfast at Jena, a golden tablet was placed on the walls of the dining room: "Here lived Prince Bismarck on 30 and 31 July 1892."[43] This was extraordinary attention, and the Bismarcks loved it. Let their critics suffer public condemnation.

The old man prepared for battle against his enemies. Here was an opportunity to strike back at those responsible for his fall. He exploited the situation by delivering speeches calling upon the German people to protest against their government.[44] There were major differences, he said, between his own administration and that of the new government. In the past, he said, the "inner construction" of the Reich required a certain dictatorial activity, which he had to lead. "Now, however, one need not look upon dictatorship as a lasting institution of a great Empire."[45] The man who had worked to lessen the influence of the *Reichstag,* who had broken political parties, now began to speak admiringly in terms of majorities in the *Reichstag.*[46] What had happened to the great skeptic of the political process?

All Europe was amused by the ensuing press battle between the anti- and pro-Bismarck press. One newspaper friendly to the government attacked Prince Bismarck for his speeches and interviews, recognizing "with horror that his memory is failing him." In angry prose it accused the old man of "wounding the sentiment of monarchy and of undermining respect for the Kaiser."[47] Bismarck was unimpressed. He replied in the pages of the friendly *Hamburger Nachrichten* that the attacks on him were "tasteless absurdities."[48] The old lion could still roar. It was stupid of these nincompoops to accuse him, the great Bismarck, of senility.

In the July 7, 1892, issue of the *Reichsanzeiger,* the official government organ struck back. It reproduced an article from the *Norddeutsche Allgemeine Zeitung* attacking Bismarck and also the June 9 communication to

Prince Reuss from Chancellor Caprivi cautioning him not to receive the Bismarcks in Vienna.[49] In a valiant act of loyalty, Caprivi was doing all he could to turn the scorn of an angered public from the Kaiser to himself.[50] The German public could now see how the new Chancellor had humiliated the Titan of Friedrichsruh.

Actually, the battle was being renewed between the Bismarcks and William II. And the way the struggle was going, the Kaiser seemed to be getting the worst of it. At first the German public regarded the "dimissal" of the Bismarcks in 1890 as a harsh but necessary action, indicating that the Kaiser did what he had to do. There had been a turnabout in public opinion: now most Germans saw that William II had neither tact nor genius.[51] Some observers attributed the beginning of the estrangement between the German people and their Emperor to the "Uriah letter" and its aftermath.[52] This was no way to treat the giant who had been responsible for the creation of the Second German Reich.

The tumultuous reception given to the Bismarcks by the German public had a strange effect on the old man. Perhaps there was something after all to this British conception of democracy and parliamentarianism. The public seemed to sense the justice of his position. Heretofore, Bismarck had never been known for sympathizing with the democratic way. "I am a Junker," he was fond of saying, "and mean to profit from it." Democracy, rule of the people, had no special attraction for him: "I am no democrat and cannot be one. I was born and raised an aristrocrat." And again: "Faust complains of having two souls in his breast. I have a whole squabbling crowd. It goes on as in a republic."

Now, with the German public enthusiastically on his side, the Junker squire was beginning to have second thoughts about his lifelong anti-democratic stand. It was an uncomfortable feeling – perhaps he was leaving behind a people without political education. Should he have done more to prepare the nation for self-government? There were uneasy stirrings in the old man.

Herbert had no such scruples. He remained the eternal Junker, a superman in a society that worshipped power, and he wanted others to be obedient to that power. Let the self-satisfied British and the impulsive French have their codes of parliamentarianism and liberty, equality, and fraternity. That was not for Germans, who were most happy when they were told what to do. He, Herbert, would continue to obey these silly democratic forms, but he would always serve the aristocratic elite from which he sprang.

Most of all, Herbert was pleased by the favorable turn in his personal life. He had married the woman of his father's choice. The Elizabeth Carolath affair was now but an unpleasant memory, though it had caused him much misery and pain. The important thing was that he had remained his father's loyal son. He had not dimmed the honor of the great Bismarck clan.

14

THE *REICHSTAG* YEARS, 1893-1904

Time to retire? Certainly not.

The lion's cub was now in his mid-forties and safely married to an acceptable mate. He could easily settle on an ancestral estate and enjoy the luxuries of a rich and famous family, including his lifelong inclination to drink at leisure.

But there was something missing – the heady struggle of German politics. He and the old man were always political animals, happy in the knockdown fights that went along with their careers. Without such conflicts and confrontations there would be unbearable boredom.

Once again Herbert began to think about the *Reichstag*. Unlike the House of Commons, its British counterpart, the *Reichstag* operated as a negative body. It did not initiate laws but it could place obstacles in the way of legislation, to the embarrassment of those in power. It was primarily a forum for political discussion, a kind of concession to Western political ways by a political system which was essentially authoritarian. Both Bismarcks saw the *Reichstag* as a necessary nuisance. Otto von Bismarck, in his early days of power, deliberately planned the office of Chancellor as a counterbalance to universal suffrage. He had no use then for what he saw as the way of the mob.

Herbert was even more skeptical than his father about the whole range of parliamentary life.[1] He saw the *Reichstag* as a debating assembly in which those who discussed public affairs were decidedly inferior to his own aristocratic class. But it was a forum in which he could present his

169

views and support what he considered to be the right course for Germany.

Opportunity came on May 6, 1893, when the *Reichstag* was dissolved once again because it refused to grant increased funds for strengthening the army. In 1862 the same thing had happened, setting a precedent. There was a call for new elections. Herbert was delighted; he would stand for election as a deputy *(Abgeordneter)* and, if he won, he would reenter public life and revive the Bismarckian ideals.

Herbert announced himself a candidate for the *Reichstag* in the electoral district of Jerichow I and II in Schönhausen, the old Bismarck ancestral home. His opponent was the incumbent deputy F. Wöllmer of the *Freisinnige Volkspartei.*

Fifteen years earlier, in 1878 when he was twenty-eight years old, Herbert had stood for election to the *Reichstag.* Overconfident, certain that his father's name would win the election for him, he took the matter lightly and expected to coast in to an overwhelming victory. He made few speeches and failed to inform the voters of his platform. The result was an ignominious defeat, which had astonished and shocked him.

This time Herbert took no chances. Anxious to win and revive the Bismarck name in politics, he went to the voting public in a vigorous campaign. He made speeches in the district at Sandau, Schönhausen, Genthin, Burg, Gommern, and Milow-bei-Rathenow.[2] His platform was clear-cut: because of Germany's unfavorable geographical position and the continuous rearming of her neighbors, it was a matter of life and death to increase her military strength. Again the familiar position: "He who wants to have peace," he said, "must arm for war." Differences of opinion on the wisdom of military power were unfortunate as well as astonishing. Certainly, he admitted, there would be new taxes, but these should be placed on the shoulders of the wealthier classes, while the poor must be protected from additional tax burdens.

Herbert directed his scorn at the *Freisinnige Volkspartei:* "If we give it a free hand it will work economically to our ruin and politically for a republic."[3] In his mind the very idea of a German republic was abhorrent. He denounced the party for its support of such dangerous policies as workers' insurance for old age invalidism and accidents: social insurance of this kind, he said, took too great a bite out of the national budget. His political enemies hated him, he charged, because he bore the great name of that Prince Bismarck who had throttled the revolution, and in 1862 had saved the threatened Prussian monarchy from being drowned in a flood of parliamentarianism and democracy. "I have inherited this hatred along with a great name, but I feel more honored than depressed for there is always the old maxim: 'Many enemies, much honor.'"[4]

Here was a candidate appealing to Germans for their vote and at the same time denouncing parliamentarianism and democracy. The father was delighted when he read the news report of this speech. He sent an admiring note to Herbert: "It is with great joy and agreement that I read about your election speech in Genthin. Whether it will elect you is *cura posterior.* Your stand is correct, and that is the main thing."[5]

There were more enemies to attack. Herbert ridiculed the Berlin bureaucracy as "having more straws in its head than in its barns."[6] This was language the country folk appreciated. The candidate denounced political opponents who were absurd enough to charge that current German foreign policy was being handled better than in the time of Prince Bismarck. Germany, he warned, was now in a difficult position because of the existing clumsy foreign policy. As *Reichstag* deputy he would do what he could to prevent any fatal steps by the Government in its awkward handling of foreign affairs. While he had to condemn the Government for its foreign policy, he could not help but support it in its aim to strengthen the army. This was his simple duty. "My whole political attitude rests on the glorious traditions of Emperor William [*I*] of blessed memory."[7]

Candidate Herbert had two goals: to vindicate his father plus the Bismarckian foreign policy, and to appeal to the patriotism of the electorate. It was an appealing combination.

The result of the campaign meant euphoria for the Bismarck family. In the final count Herbert received 11,700 votes on election day, June 15, 1893, against 6,812 for Wöllmer and 4,376 for Social Democrat Glocke. Although elected as an Independent, Herbert would vote mostly with the Free Conservatives.

Herbert's maiden address as *Abgeorneter* (deputy) in the *Reichstag* was explosive – a situation to be expected of a Bismarck.[8] His talk was interrupted by boos, laughter, and catcalls from the Left, applause from the Right, and interruptions by the President to maintain order. Limiting his remarks to the matter of two-year conscription, he succeeded in arousing the hostility not only of the Left but also of the Government. In 1890, he said, he favored the idea, but at that time the Ministry of War did not have the least intention of introducing two-year conscription because no one wanted to take responsibility for such an experiment. He hoped the plan would be successful, and he would vote for it, but if it did not pass he urged that some day the *Reichstag* introduce a three-year conscription. He made it clear that he was supporting the Government on this special issue not for love of the current administration but as a patriotic duty.

Consternation on both Right and Left. Concerned, Chancellor Caprivi took the podium to refute Herbert on details. Angered, Herbert began to make "personal remarks" about the Chancellor, whereupon the President abruptly stopped him.

Herbert then turned on the Social Democrats. The scorn was typically Bismarckian: "Gentlemen: I'll let you scream and yell all you want; you have more lungs than I. But it won't do any good."[9]

Herbert's maiden speech was of interest not only to *Reichstag* delegates but also to the general public. The master diplomat of Friedrichsruh was by no means forgotten, and there was much curiosity about the son and the prospects for further Bismarckian influence. Among those who heard him speak was the Conservative Party leader Wilhelm von Kardorff, a gruff and grizzled old Junker with an artificial nose (he had lost his own nose in a student duel years earlier). Kardorff had long been opposed to Herbert on general principles. But after hearing the speech he began to change his attitude, later developing a high regard for Herbert's political and statesmanlike qualities.[10] Kardorff wrote a glowing letter to Prince Bismarck, pronouncing Herbert's maiden address a complete success: "Count Bismarck spoke under the vulgar interruptions of Eugen Richter and the Social Democrats but under friendly applause of the Right. It was the general conclusion of the Right that his entrée was very successful."[11] The old man was pleased by the fighting spirit of his son. This was what he wanted — a Bismarck scion projecting as a true Junker.

Herbert looked for every opportunity to attack Chancellor Caprivi, whom he denounced as an inefficient successor to the great Bismarck. On December 15, 1893, on the third reading before the *Reichstag* of proposed trade treaties with Spain, Rumania, and Serbia, Herbert delivered an impassioned address accusing the Chancellor of destroying the tie between industry and agriculture.[12] Following the call to order, the *Reichstag* President admonished Herbert for indulging in personal remarks in reply to what he deemed to be insults *(Beschimpfungen)*. Herbert was undaunted.

In parliamentary give-and-take Herbert preferred scathing sarcasm to well-mannered debate. He used biting words in accusing bimetallists, those advocating gold-plus-silver, of working for the economic ruin of Germany.[13] Kardorff saw Herbert as "unfortunately, a gold fanatic."[14]

Herbert's *bête noire* on the floor of the *Reichstag* was Eugen Richter, in Herbert's opinion the perfect enemy, being both the contemptible leader of the Progressives[15] — and Jewish. A hefty man, badly dressed and quarrelsome, Richter had figures, quotations, and statistics at his finger tips, and shot arrow after arrow at the Government[16] from the string of his bow. He had attacked Bismarck Sr. at every step of his career. An advocate of Manchester School economics, he fought against protective tariffs on foodstuffs, against armaments, against imperial expansion, against state intervention of any kind – in short, against about everything the Bismarcks held to be their program. Prince Bismarck was annoyed by Richter, but at the same time had a grudging respect for him – "the best speaker we ever had, highly educated and industrious, with unpleasant manners, but a man of character."[17]

But if the elder Bismarck had some respect for the ability and character of Richter, Herbert, with his greater capacity for hatred, had none. Again and again the two came to verbal blows in the *Reichstag*, especially on the question of tariffs, which Herbert advocated and Richter denounced. In a typical exchange, on January 16, 1896, Herbert spoke in favor of the Kanitz resolution fixing the price of grain,[18] whereupon Richter accused him of tying up support of the resolution with the loyalty of the monarchy *("Kein Kanitz, keine Königstreue")*.[19] In Richter's estimation this was an insult to the memory of peasants who had poured out their blood for the Fatherland in 1870-71. In impassioned terms an angry Herbert denounced Richter for twisting his meaning, and insisted that he had meant no insult to the peasants. The incident was greeted with boos and catcalls from the Left. To Herbert it was a matter of duty – in battling Richter straight down the line he was carrying on the work of his illustrious father in opposing the ever-dangerous Liberals.

Herbert reserved his most contemptuous hatred for the Social Democrats, however. Here again he followed in the footsteps of his father, who had waged unrelenting political warfare against the Socialists. The Socialist Congress at Gotha (1875), which united the followers of Ferdinand Lassalle and Karl Marx, was a warning that the elder Bismarck did not intend to ignore. The new party urged the working classes of newly industrialized Germany to demand a republican form of government and a German bill of rights, and called upon them to support the international Socialist movement.

In 1878, perceiving that the Social Democrats were increasing dangerously in numbers, Prince Bismarck, had a series of Exceptional Laws enacted forbidding freedom of the press and initiating a campaign of persecution against all advocates of "subversive doctrines."[20] The Socialists went underground, and despite all efforts to eliminate them as a political factor, they thrived and grew in numbers.[21] In the meantime, Bismarck fashioned a wide program of social legislation as a means of placating the working classes and of "taking the wind out of the sails of socialism."[22] If there was to be social improvement, it would be done the Bismarck way. Herbert, however, was skeptical of such social legislation.

Herbert was not deterred by the increasing strength of the Social Democrats. He would continue the family tradition of opposing them. When on April 23, 1896, a Social Democratic deputy denounced the administration's attitude of friendliness to workers as "platonic" in nature, Herbert replied heatedly that in the years since 1881 (meaning at a time when his father was in power), the administration had done more for the welfare of working classes than any other state.[23] The day after this speech Count Rantzau wrote to Herbert: "Your papa has just read your speech in the 'N.N.' [Berliner Neuste Nachrichten] and wants you to know that you spoke very well; he would have said much the same but in tougher form."[24]

Two weeks later, in an address to the Conservative Party in Dresden, Herbert continued his attack: "I believe it to be a mistake for the Government in inficiting disciplinary punishment on Social Democrats to handle them in terms of equality. All men are, indeed, equal before the law, but in political corporations equality belongs only to those who stand with us on the same political basis. Social Democrats, who deny the state, society, the sanctity of the oath, and the monarchy, who would just as soon cut our throats if only their knife be sharp enough – to place them in that category would be sheer irony.... With us the Government is mighty, not a mere ornament as in England."[25]

For Herbert, always his father's son, any parliamentary attack on the old man in either domestic or foreign policy was a call to scornful rebuttal. When the Social Democratic deputy August Bebel accused Prince Bismarck of calling on the services of the political police even after his retirement, Herbert denounced him on the floor of the Reichstag on February 5, 1897: "It is beneath my dignity to fight him [Bebel] with denials in the press, but I shall not remain silent in the Reichstag where I intend to stand up to any man."[26] When Eugen Richter on February 9, 1898, stated blandly that the commercial policies of Prince Bismarck had been without plan, Herbert launched into a spirited defense of his father, whose protective tariff policy he described as axiomatic for the safety of the nation.[27]

Herbert ran again for his seat in the Reichstag elections of June 16, 1898, again in the electoral district of Jerichow I and II. Out of 23,005 valid votes he received 11,769; the Freisinnige Volkspartei candidate Dr. Wöllmer 6,812; and the Social Democratic candidate Glocke 4,375, with 48 invalid votes. Herbert was re-elected on the first ballot with 267 votes over an absolute majority.

During his Reichstag service, up to 1903, Herbert followed a consistent pattern based on his father's ideas. These were expressed in such major speeches as: "Commercial Relations with the United States" (February 11, 1899); "Expulsion of the Danes" (February 18, 1899); "Samoa" (April 14, 1899); "Samoa" (June 22, 1899); "General Politics" (January 20, 1900); "Meat Imports"

(May 22, 1900); "Tariffs on Grain" (January 25, 1901); "Tariffs on Grain" (January 29, 1901); "The Polish Question" (February 27, 1901); "A Question of Life in China" (March 19, 1901); "The State of Foreign Affairs" (March 4, 1902); "The Tax on Sugar" (June 11, 1902); "Commercial Treaties on the Basis of the Most Favored Nations" (January 16, 1903); "Payment for Members of the *Reichstag*" (February 3, 1903); and "Personal Defense" (February 5, 1903).[28]

On domestic issues Herbert hewed to the Conservative line on protective tariffs and opposed the Manchester School concept of free trade. Insisting that commercial and political affairs could not be blended, he made a careful distinction between them. Here again he was moved by his father's stand, expressed as early as December 5, 1876: "Commercial battles can only be fought on commercial territory; the political territory must be separated wholly from the commercial."[29] Neither Bismarck was inclined to clarify this somewhat strange view of political economy.

During the confrontation with the United States over Samoa, Herbert had been critical of what he saw as American pretensions. Later he adopted a more friendly attitude on the floor of the *Reichstag*. He praised Americans as a "highly cultivated and commercially knowledgeable people" ["*eine so hochgebildete und geschäftskündige Nation*"] who have a sense of "fair play." He recalled that Frederick the Great was the first monarch to recognize the United States, and expressed his gratitude to Americans for taking over German interests in Paris during the Franco-Prussian War of 1870-71. His father, he said, had always shown friendly interest in the United States, an attitude which he was sure Secretary of State Bülow would emulate.[30] When difficulties over Samoa threatened to become serious again in 1899, Herbert spoke twice before the *Reichstag,* indicating his certainty that the problem would be resolved. He reviewed his own part in the settlement of 1889 and confessed that he knew that it would be difficult to govern Samoa through a condominium, but the matter was in good hands (Bülow) and undoubtedly would be handled satisfactorily.[31] "Secretary of State Bülow will warmly represent our interests in Samoa. He has been one of the most faithful and discerning co-workers of the first Reichs Chancellor. We can rely on his auspicious hand."[32]

On the Samoan question and other matters of foreign policy, Herbert's urge to criticize was tempered by his high regard for Bülow, who in the autumn of 1897 had become Secretary of State. On December 6, 1897, Herbert wrote to Bülow a few hours after the latter's maiden speech in the *Reichstag*: "You will not regard it as flattery or bad taste in an old friend if I tell you without reserve that you did brilliantly. Everything was just as good as it could be – the contents, the diction, tone, and phrasing.... A man near me shouted out:

'There is voice at last from the manly days of long ago. In his style and his striking phrases Bülow forcibly recalls Prince Bismarck.'"[33] There could be no higher praise from Herbert. Again, he wrote to Bülow on New Year's Eve, 1898: "I wish you, in addition to everything else that is good, continued satisfaction and more and more triumphs in your activity for the welfare of our country.... You have now to steer us out of the troublesome channel into which we were brought by the mistakes of naviagtion of 1890-91. I wish you 'good speed,' and only regret that in your diplomatic army you have so few able assistants, so that you do everything yourself."[34]

Sincere? Not likely. This protestation of friendship is open to question, although Herbert and Bülow had been friends for many years and the latter's career had been helped by both Bismarcks. The promotion of Bülow to Secretary of State was pleasant news to Herbert, but soon it began to become obvious that Bülow had become the natural successor to Chancellor Hohenlohe[35] who was ready to resign in 1899. Baron von Eckardstein stated that in his opinion Herbert's expressions of anti-English feeling at this time were influenced by his desire to make difficulties for Bülow, "for Herbert was bent on securing for himself the nomination of the Chancellorship."[36] Eckardstein may well have been correct in his judgment. On the *Reichstag* floor Herbert always expressed confidence in Bülow's capacity and wished him well. At the same time, however, he was convinced that the state structure laboriously fashioned by his father was headed for stormy waters because of William II's view of *Weltpolitik* and Big Navy, which Bülow was committed to support. In Herbert's mind this added up to disaster.

In his earlier years Herbert had a grudging respect for his English friends, but now his attitude toward them and toward Britain began to harden. He still maintained relations with English acquaintances and friends. On the birth of his daughter in 1894, she was named Hannah, after Lady Hannah Rosebery, wife of Lord Rosebery.[37] When on October 16, 1897, Lord Rosebery came to Schönhausen for the christening of Herbert Bismarck's eldest son, he was received most hospitably. The British aristocrat spoke frankly about Herbert: "Fond as I am of him, his energy is rather overpowering. He had no idea of the loudness of his voice, and though I lead him to desolate spots, he bellows secrets in the woods. It is like living with a hurricane. But there is no warmer heart or better friend."[38]

Such friendships, however, in Herbert's mind, were not to be confused with foreign policy. Gradually, he emerged as leader of the Anglophobes in Germany. This change was all the more noteworthy in that Herbert had once worked for an English alliance, a goal of his father's diplomacy. During the Boer War (1899-1902) he attacked England both in the *Reichstag* and in the

Bismarck press. When on October 17, 1902, three Boer generals visited the *Reichstag*, Herbert greeted them cordially, causing embarrassment in official Berlin circles and much resentment in England.[39] Holstein, as usual, was critical: "Herbert Bismarck works in all quietness, puts on a good front before the British Ambassador, visits him often, makes him suspicious of the Emperor and Bülow, who are supposed at the present time to plan war against England – and – that was a masterpiece – recently recieved the three Boer generals."[40] Eckardstein reported Herbert as saying, six months before the latter's death: "The South African question which is daily getting more acute will in my opinion give the British empire its death blow; for I believe that England is being smothered in its own fat and is no longer capable of any severe exertion."[41]

In *Reichstag* debates, Herbert often displayed his Bismarckian sensitiveness and pugnacity. When, on February 4, 1903, a deputy remarked on Herbert's absence from the floor of the *Reichstag,* the latter delivered a long, rambling, and sarcastic speech on absenteeism and its meaning. "In the final analysis we are not an assembly of butterflies who are attached to our seats by nails driven through our clothing, but we all circulate through the house."[42] As in previous sessions of the *Reichstag*, whenever anyone cast reflections on the work of his father, Herbert reacted violently and replied in passionate tones. On January 20, 1900, the Social Democratic deputy August Bebel said mildly that Prince Bismarck had won no special laurels by his anti-Socialist campaign. Herbert then launched into a denunciation of Bebel and heatedly pointed out that it took a bloody attempt at assassination of the monarch before his father inaugurated the Exceptional Laws against the Socialists.[43] In a debate on the Polish question, when a deputy quoted the elder Bismarck, from the Penzler collection of the latter's speeches, Herbert denied that the publication was authorized and insisted that the official typescript be used before his father's words were quoted.[44]

In the *Reichstag* elections of June 16, 1903, Herbert, now Prince Herbert von Bismarck,[45] was returned to office, this time as a candidate of the Conservatives, the Farmers' League, and the National Liberals. However he made no more speeches on the floor of the *Reichstag* before his untimely death.

Despite his idiosyncrasies, Herbert won the respect of his colleagues as a parliamentarian, with the perhaps understandable exception of embittered Social Democrats. Conservative leader Wilhelm von Kardorff was lavish in his praise: "In our entire current *Reichstag* there is scarcely one figure who can match the statesmanlike capacity of Prince Herbert Bismarck. There are, indeed, many oratorically gifted deputies, as well as many who possess extraordinary knowledge in special fields, but few who can compare with Prince Herbert in wisdom and self-understanding,...healthy knowledge of humanity, patriotic conviction, uprightness of character, fixity of purpose, and courage."[46]

Despite this praise Herbert was unhappy in his work as a parliamentarian. The *Reichstag,* he was certain, with its mean and petty politics and its inconclusive debates, was only a secondary place for a Bismarck, chosen by destiny to lead the German people. He missed the intoxication of real power, the satisfying work at the upper level, above all the possibility of carrying on the work of his distinguished father. In his estimation the position of a *Reichstag* deputy was a demotion for a Bismarck, to whom the German people owed their greatness.

Still, whether he liked it or not, Herbert had to adjust himself to the forms of political democracy, even if it meant encounters with the "crazy ideas" of his opponents. In his view a delegate's life was a far cry from the life he had spent sharing the power wielded by the Titan in his days of glory. These were bad times for the country, which, he was sure, was headed for disaster without the guiding hand of a Bismarck.

15

CORUSCATING ROCKET

Herbert carried everything to extremes. His father looked down on enemies with disdain, but Herbert viewed them with intense hostility. The father recognized the painful travail of the son: "Herbert is quite different from me: where I despised, he hated."[1]

Unfortunately for Herbert, he suffered the pangs of unresolved tensions. It is a medical truism that stress not only causes a miserable day-to-day existence but can also trigger a variety of physical symptoms, affecting the heart, circulation, and most major organs. In its contemporary form stress often leads to overuse of alcohol and drugs in desperate attempts to relieve nervous strain.

In Herbert's case long overuse of alcohol led to an enlarged liver, and later to medically prescribed morphine to ease the unbearable pain. Relaxation was beyond the capacity of this glittering human rocket. For years he had operated in excess – too much love for his father, too much work, too many enemies, too much alcohol. Drinking exorcised the devils in his life – for the moment. But it destroyed his constitution and left him in a private hell. There is a twentieth-century parallel in the eccentric behavior of Randolph, scion of the giant British statesman Winston Churchill. Here, again, there was similar aberrant conduct.

On the surface Herbert seemed to be in good robust health, suffused with Bismarckian energy. Like his father, he was large in stature and of ample girth, but there was a flaw in his physical make-up. From his mother Johanna he probably inherited a weak constitution which made him subject to recurring illnesses, especially colds and pneumonia. Herbert's bodily weaknesses were aggravated by a hectic lifestyle, and his parents were always concerned about the physical well-being of their eldest son. Their fears were justified – this Bismarck, like his brother Bill, was destined for an early death.

Herbert's crushing urge to satisfy his father's ambitions was so overpowering that he judged his every action in the light of his father's wishes. Driven and obsessed, he became addicted to both work and alcohol.

As the nineteenth century neared its close, the fallen Chancellor was worried about the durability of his lifework and depressed by the death of his wife Johanna. He wanted nothing more than to be left in peace. However, despite all the rebuffs he had received from the Bismarck clan, William II was still attracted by the lure of the great man's name. In early 1898 the unpredictable monarch, with a retinue of courtiers, made a surprise visit to Friedrichsruh. It was an embarrassing meeting – the old man hinted at the dangers of the New Course. The Emperor jested.

Otto von Bismarck died on July 30, 1898, at the age of eighty-three. The Kaiser tried to extend more than conventional courtesies to his dead opponent. Within two days, accompanied by the Empress and members of the court, he arrived at Friedrichsruh. Herbert met him at the railway station. The Emperor embraced Herbert, and as was customary among sovereigns on solemn occasions, kissed him three times on each cheek. It was meant as a signal honor, but Herbert was unimpressed. He curtly declined William's offer to have his father entombed in the Dom in Berlin. Emphasizing each word, he pointed out that he was bound to comply with the stipulations of the last will and testament of his father, who desired to be buried on a little hill facing the manor house at Friedrichsruh along the railway line, "where there will be life around me." Chagrined by this refusal, the Emperor did not insist further.[2] With the Empress he viewed the coffin, attended funeral services, and ordered glowing obituaries to be placed in the Army Official Gazette and in the *Reichsanzeiger*, the governmental organ. There was, however, no expression of gratitude from Herbert.

Always the devoted son, Herbert never uttered a word of forgiveness or toleration for the man he considered guilty of causing the catastrophe to which his father had been exposed.[3] After the old man's death, he conscientiously perused the great mass of literature appearing on the Bismarck epoch. He maintained an extensive correspondence with historians, newspaper editors, friends and enemies alike, always seeking to defend and justify the actions of his father. He was angered especially by the writings of the court historian Ottokar Lorenz, which he felt to be unfair to the memory of his father.

Worst of all to Herbert was the "desertion" of journalist Moritz Busch, who had worked with the elder Bismarck for many years and had done the major share of work on the Chancellor's memoirs. When shortly after Bismarck's death, Busch's work, *Bismarck, Some Secret Pages of His History,* appeared in English (New York, 1898), Herbert became nearly frantic with anger.[4] The traitor had gone so far as to accuse his father of many instances of tactlessness and bizarre behavior. The criticism was mild, but to Herbert it was a thunderclap of rebellion against his beloved father.

Herbert would never accept Busch's "secret pages" as genuine. Exasperated, he called in the journalist Paul Liman. Hour after hour the two went over the thick volumes, marking suspected passages and errors so that the publication could be deemed of doubtful historical value. Liman later wrote that in his hand copy of the Busch book there were some 600 reservations made by Herbert against individual statements by the author. "This was sufficient indication of the devoted conscientiousness of the son in the pietistic battle for the memory of his father. Thereafter, the name of Busch could not be mentioned in his presence without passionate rage causing the veins to protrude on his forehead. He was not the cool historian, who strove to find the truth, but the passionately subjective son."[5]

It was an extraordinary picture – the annoyed son searching through the Busch book for minuscule errors so that the entire publication could be condemned. In the German edition, vol. III, p. 376, Busch told how Chancellor and Emperor took a coach drive in March 15, 1890, following a conference held at Herbert's home, Königstrasse 136. A lie, said Herbert. The Emperor, following the conference, returned *alone* to the Palace. A coach drive with His Majesty, insisted Herbert, lay in the realm of fantasy. "Prince Bismarck came back to Berlin on January 24, 1890, and until his discharge [*March 18, 1890*] there was no opportunity for a coach drive with His Majesty."[6] With such picayune objections did Herbert try to smear the formerly faithful Busch.

Meanwhile, Herbert's relations with his good friend Bernhard von Bülow were undergoing a radical change. For years the rising young diplomat Bülow had looked upon the elder Bismarck as his model, and often spoke reverently of him in his speeches. Bülow and Herbert considered themselves to be close friends, the cool, imperturbable man of the world and the politically passionate young Bismarck. Then, in the autumn of 1897 Bülow was appointed to Herbert's former office of Secretary of State for Foreign Affairs. Three years later, in 1900, he became Imperial Chancellor, the post previously held by Prince Bismarck.

Herbert wrote a strange letter of congratulations: "I must express to you in two lines my satisfaction that you have finally triumphed over the old mummy Chlodwig[7] and have become Chancellor. I have said to you for the last three years that it would turn out that way." Herbert could not help but add a word of caution: "But I trust that you will get rid of all your weak colleagues and all the intriguers, otherwise you will be dragging along so much dead weight that it will tire you."[8]

Herbert was adopting an unaccustomed air of sincerity. But deep down he was mortified and chagrined despite Bülow's amiable character and charm, that he should stand first in Herbert's shoes and then in those of his father. Though he was a brilliant parliamentary speaker, this man lacked the strength to accomplish what Herbert's blessed father had done for Germany. Herbert admitted that he was a good diplomat but he was *not* a great statesman. And what would Germany be without the genius of Otto von Bismarck?

Bülow was not fooled by Herbert's expressions of sympathy. He judged the situation coolly in his *Memoirs:* "After his father's fall, in the August of 1890, Herbert visited me at Wildbad.... All that he told me of the break between the great Prince and the Kaiser could only enhance my loyalty to the former.

"For nearly a quarter of a century from 1875 to 1890 Herbert had rejoiced in each of my successes, but the sight of me in his father's chair was painful to him. He had hoped for so long to succeed to the post of his incomparable father, whose natural successor he considered himself, that he could only, naturally, be chagrined at the sight of even his best friend in the very place at the Wilhelmstrasse in which he, himself, lived as a child. He dined with us there one evening, in the second or third year of my chancellorship. My wife escorted him through the various apartments of the palace, all of which he knew so well, and took him at last into what he called the Bismarck room, where he had placed all souvenirs of the Prince, and which we consecrated entirely to his memory. He was deeply moved; he kissed my wife's hand with real emotion. Next day he described the event to a mutual friend, but added: 'All the same I still hate the thought of Bernhard's being in our shoes. I can't help it.'

"His ambition to succeed his father was both Herbert's strength and his misfortune; his strength because his goal was an inspiration to unflagging zeal in politics; his misfortune, because from the very beginning, it placed him in a false position and embittered him more and more, as he watched the non-fulfillment of his hopes."[9]

Bülow's assessment is most convincing. For many years he and Herbert considered themselves to be best friends, but now the brilliant diplomat had dared step into what Herbert called "our shoes" — the shoes of the giant and the shoes of the son who should have succeeded him. It was the unpardonable sin.

Even the slightest deviation from exaltation of his father was enough to arouse Herbert to rage. On June 16, 1901, when the Bismarck Monument in Berlin was unveiled, the Kaiser at first refused to come, then decided to attend in a "modest uniform." He commissioned Chancellor Bülow to make a speech on the occasion. In his commemoratory remarks Bülow said: "We have stood on Bismarck's shoulders in every way, but not in the sense that it is our patriotic duty to approve everything that he has said or done, for only fools and fanatics would claim that Bismarck never made a mistake."[10] Thus the experienced diplomat sought to appease both the Bismarck family and the Kaiser.

Sacrilege! This was too much for Herbert. He denounced his former good friend as a turncoat, as one for whom his father had done so much, and who had now desecrated the memory of Germany's greatest son. The man had violated and profaned the name of the great Bismarck.

Herbert carefully assessed the honors accorded his father, greeting them with almost religious zeal. When on June 21, 1903, a Bismarck Tower was dedicated by students at Hamberge, near Friedrichsruh in the Sachsenwald, Herbert paid glowing tribute to his "immortal father." The meaning of the dedicaiton, he said, lay in the fact that "it honors a man to whom we are grateful that the soil on which we stand is German." He reminded his student audience of the three words on his father's tombstone: "LOYALTY, GERMAN, EMPEROR." "These words, with which he departed from us, we shall hold high as his legacy, as long as we breathe. One of the greatest historians, the Scotsman Carlyle, formulated as the quintessence of his studies the pertinent, brief sentence: 'The history of peoples is the history of their great men.' In the present generation, unfortunately, there are many who are motivated only by their inconsequential egotistical interests and have no understanding of the hero-cult. Such sentiments, thank God, are not held by our noble academic youth." The speaker could not resist adding a warning of disaster for the Fatherland: the students before him were standing in darkness, "but they would also stand for the Fatherland in the darkness which was threatening it."[11] The allusion was clear: enemies of the great Chancellor did not understand the meaning of his work. They were leading the Fatherland to destruction. Herbert undoubtedly hoped that the misguided Kaiser and the former friend, Bülow, were listening.

For Herbert it was a continuing battle to clear his father's name. On October 11, 1903, when a Bismarck monument was unveiled in Posen, he again spoke in memory of his father. He was pleased to note that only one word was necessary on the monument: BISMARCK. That satisfied his sense of historical justice. He told the crowd that he was honored by the presence of thousands to pay tribute to his father.[12]

In one most important matter, Herbert had already served his father well. It was essential that the Bismarck lineage be extended to the next generation. To the delight of Otto von Bismarck, two children were born to Countess Herbert Bismarck before the great Chancellor's death. The first child, a daughter, Hannah, was born in 1894, a year after Herbert's marriage. It was a joyous occasion, but Junker aristocracy demanded a male heir. In time, there were three sons and two daughters. Otto, the third Prince von Bismarck, was born on September 27, 1897, ten months before the death of his grandfather. He became Counsellor of the German Embassy in London, and later, during the Nazi regime, Minister at the embassy in Rome.[13] The second son, Gottfried von Bismarck, born in 1901, became Prefect of the District of Potsdam.[14]

The years of toil and stress began to take their toll on Herbert. Disappointed by what he regarded as a failed career, surrounded by real or fancied enemies, worried about the future of his Fatherland, he could not accept a graceful retirement at his early age. In early 1904, while on a trip to London, he became ill from what was said to be oyster poisoning.[15] His health began to fail alarmingly on his return to Germany and he became increasingly irritable. At first this was considered to be nothing new: his tendency to annoyance was noted by both German and foreign visitors, whom he received as if it were an onerous task. A visiting German-American millionaire reminded Herbert that, as a leader of a deputation, he had brought across the Atlantic a silver tankard to be presented to him. Herbert said, half-aloud: "I don't remember," and turned his back on the man.[16]

Worried doctors could not seem to find the cause of Herbert's illness. The formerly robust man began losing weight, alarming family and friends by his appearance. Dr. Schweninger, who apparently had strong powers of suggestion, succeeded for a time in arousing his patient from melancholia and giving him new hope. On such occasions Herbert would rise form his bed, tell jokes, and drink happily, or go on rides with his physician through the Sachsenwald.

Then came dread news. Doctors concluded that Herbert was suffering from carcinoma hepatitis, cancer of the liver. Some skeptics and amateur diagnosticians were not satisfied with this analysis, and hinted that Herbert had developed cirrhosis of the liver as a result of his long years of drinking.

Whatever the cause, the pain became excruciating. Doctors prescribed increasing dosages of morphine. The patient sank into a coma. On September 18, 1904, death came to the second Prince Bismarck. On December 28, he would have reached the age of fifty-five.

The funeral took place in Friedrichsruh in the presence of several hundred people, including Chancellor von Bülow and three young officers of the Berliner Guard Dragoons regiment, in which Herbert had held rank.[17] As his personal representative, the Kaiser sent Gen. von Hahnke, whom Herbert had hated since the resignation days of March 1890. The oration delivered by a Berlin pastor emphasized the position of confidence held by Herbert, his work in most important matters for the government, and his labors as a true guardian of the literary legacy of his distinguished father. Sixteen costumed bearers carried the coffin, flanked by Sachsenwald foresters, to the mausoleum where his father lay buried.

Here, in the quiet peace of Friedrichsruh, surrounded by scores of wreaths from organizations, war societies, private citizens, and friendly fractions in the *Reichstag*, Herbert Bismarck was laid to rest.

De mortuis nil nisi bonum. An unknown author had words to fit the occasion – "Of the dead be nothing said but what is good."

The German press did an abrupt about-face. For years after the resignations of 1890 the media had heaped abuse upon the Bismarcks. Now they turned to praise for the son of the founder of the Second German Reich. Before his death Herbert was depicted as a willing, obedient tool of his father, as well as a temperamental, arrogant scion of an equally overbearing father. Now it was admitted that, while he stood in the shadow of the Great Titan, he was no marionette, but a diplomat of special gifts who had worked hard and conscientiously for the Fatherland. The editors were obviously influenced by public opinion which, during the last days of Herbert's illness, had been in sympathy with the defeated Bismarcks.

The young lion, once regarded as haughty, conceited, and overrated, was now described as a retiring, serious, and important personality who was attached to all the fibers of political life. Editorials praised his "robust solidity, clear understanding, energy, wide experience, and inflexible and incorruptible character." The flawed son of the great man was now – in death – described as "intelligent, conscientious, cultivated, and courageous in time of danger." The sarcastic politician was now awarded the accolade of "a clean heart."

As a young man Herbert had been entrusted not only with the mechanical aspects of diplomacy but also the secrets of his father's statecraft. With his energy and his experience to lift him above the plane of his rivals, he seemed, indeed, headed for the high office for which his father was preparing him.

But in more objective estimates Herbert remained a psychic cripple. There were the gnawing defects of character. His father had traces of the old Germanic obstinacy – Herbert had much more. He was a loner who preferred to go his own way.

Basically, Herbert was never successful in emerging from his father's tight control and becoming a free personality. Yet his father expected him to carry on in the Bismarck tradition.

Actually, Herbert had ambivalent feelings toward his father. He worshipped his parent as an idol but he unconsciously resented him as the source of his own inability to lead a normal life.

In public life Herbert turned out to be an unpopular stranger to his own people. Mercurial and sensitive, he refused to change his provocative stance to satisfy anyone. Little wonder that the general public regarded him with suspicion and mistrust, as one who bore the name but not the genius of a Bismarck.

Coruscating rocket – Herbert's life was like a glittering missile rising swiftly high into the atmosphere, then suddenly shattering into a thousand pieces. And the Bismarck dynasty was like a dream that dissolved and vanished before it ever became a reality.

NOTES

CHAPTER 1

[1] Joachim von Kürenberg, *Johanna von Bismarck* (Berlin, 1935), p. 87.

[2] Otto von Bismarck, *Die Gesammelten Werke (Friedrichsruher Ausgabe)* (Berlin, 1924 ff.), VII, 18. Hereafter referred to as *Bismarck, D.G.W.*

[3] Kürenberg, *op. cit.*, p. 87.

[4] *Bismarck, D.G.W., op cit.*, XIV-1, 153.

[5] James Wycliffe Headlam, *Bismarck and the Foundations of the German Empire* (New York and London, 1899), p. 2.

[6] *Memoirs of Prince von Bülow* (Boston, 1932), IV, 23.

[7] *Bismarck, D.G.W., op cit.*, XIV-1, 160.

[8] *The Love Letters of Bismarck, 1846-1889,* authorized by Prince Herbert von Bismarck (New York, 1901), p. 281.

[9] *Bismarck, D.G.W., op cit.*, XIV-1, 184.

[10] *The Love Letters of Bismarck, 1846-1889, op. cit.*, p. 201.

[11] *Bismarck, D.G.W., op. cit.*, XIV-1, 192.

[12] *The Love Letters of Bismarck, 1846-1889, op. cit.*, p. 208.

[13] *Bismarck, D.G.W., op. cit.*, XIV-1, 299.

[14] *Ibid.*, p. 338.

[15] *Ibid.*, p. 162.

[16] *Ibid.*, p. 248.

[17] *Ibid.*, p. 444.

[18] Bülow, *Memoirs, op. cit.*, II, 58.

[19] Heinrich von Poschinger, *Aus Grosser Zeit, Erinnerungen an den Fürsten Bismarck* (Berlin, 1905), p. 258.

[20] Moritz Busch, *Our Chancellor,* trans. by William Beatty-Kingston (New York, 1884), p. 279.

[21] Not always willingly. Ludwig von Gerlach, Herbert's godfather, reported that one night at the dinner table Herbert suddenly announced that he did not want to do any studying. "When I reminded him how important study was, he merely stared at me with his large eyes." *(Bismarck, D.G.W., op. cit.,* VII, 106.)

[22] *Ibid.*, XIV-1, 554.

[23] *Ibid.*, XIV-2, 597.

[24] Paul Zauleck, *Bismarckerinnerungen* (Daheim, 1913), Nr. 27.

[25] See Louis L. Snyder, "The Iron Chancellor as a Student," *The Baltimore Sun Magazine,* January 11, 1931, p. 7.

[26] Bismarck's carved name may still be seen on the door of the jail house.

[27] See Louis L. Snyder, *Die persoenlichen und politischen Beziehungen Bismarcks zu Amerikanern* (Darmstadt, 1932), *passim.*

[28] Kürenberg, *Johanna von Bismarck, op. cit.,* p. 28.

[29] Bismarck, suspicious of Holstein's work in the German Foreign Office, later referred to him as "the man with the hyena eyes, of whom one must beware." (See Chapter 12.)

[30] Karl von Eisendecher, son of the Oldenbourg Ambassador at Frankfurt, friend of Bismarck.

[31] Count Albrecht von Bernstorff, Prussian Ambassador at London from 1854-1861 and German Ambassador there until 1873.

[32] Helmuth Rogge, ed., *Friedrich von Holstein: Lebensbekenntnis* in *Briefen an eine Frau* (Berlin, 1932), pp. 81-82.

[33] Wolf von Schierbrand, *The Kaiser's Speeches* (New York, 1903), p. 309.

[34] Kürenberg, *Johanna von Bismarck, op. cit.,* p. 197.

[35] *The Love Letters of Bismarck, 1846-1889, op. cit.,* pp. 413-15.

[36] Fritz Stern, *Gold and Iron: Bismarck, Bleichröder and the Building of the German Empire* (New York, 1977), p. 258.

CHAPTER 2

[1] Otto von Bismarck, *Die Gesammelten Werke (Friedrichsruher Ausgabe)* (Berlin, 1924 *ff.*), XIV-I. Hereafter referred to as *Bismarck, D.G.W.*

[2] *Bismarck, D.G.W.,* VI, 136. Robert von Keudell (1824-1903) was in the German diplomatic service. This passage appeared originally in Robert von Keudell, *Fürst und Fürstin Bismarck* (Berlin and Stuttgart, 1901), p. 291.

[3] John Wycliffe Headlam, *Bismarck and the Foundations of the German Empire* (New York, 1899), p. 23.

[4] In 1838, at the age of twenty-three, Bismarck himself, although young and healthy, had attempted to avoid military service on the ground of an imaginary weakness, the sequel of a wound incurred in one of his duels at Göttingen. His reluctance to enter military service then was by no means due to lack of personal courage, of which he later gave adequate evidence, but to hatred of compulsion of any kind. He served in the Jaeger Guards, but was always in trouble with his superior officers.

[5] Headlam, *Bismarck, op. cit.,* p. 347.

[6] Moritz Busch, *Tagebuchblätter* (Berlin, 1899), I, 126 *ff.* Both Herbert and William were promoted to officers later in the war. See footnote 28 in this chapter.

[7] *The Love Letters of Bismarck, 1846-1889,* authorized by Prince Herbert von Bismarck (New York, 1901), pp. 415-16.

[8] Busch, *Tagebuchblätter, op. cit.,* I, 126.

[9] *Bismarck, D.G.W., op cit.,* XIV-2, 784.

[10] *Ibid.*

[11] *Ibid.*

[12] F.P. Stearns, *The Life of Prince Otto von Bismarck* (Philadelphia, Pa., 1899), p. 202.

[13] Headlam, *Bismarck, op. cit.,* p. 347.

[14] Joachim von Kürenberg, *Johanna von Bismarck* (Berlin, 1935), p. 200.

[15] *Tagebuchblätter, op. cit.,* I, 90.

[16] Stearns, *Life of Bismarck, op. cit.,* p. 202.

[17] Kürenberg, *Johanna von Bismarck, op. cit.,* p. 200.

18 *Bismarck, D.G.W., op. cit.,* XIV-2, 785. "Phipp" was the oldest son of the Chancellor's brother.

19 Quoted in Fritz Linde, *Bismarck, Grösse und Grenze seines Reiches* (Leipzig, 1939), p. 181.

20 Busch, *Tagebuchblätter, op. cit.,* I, 102.

21 *Bismarck, D.G.W., op. cit.,* XIV-2, 792.

22 *Ibid.,* pp. 786 *ff.*

23 *The War Diary of the Emperor Frederick III, 1870- 1871,* trans. and ed. by A.R. Allinson (London, 1927), p. 65.

24 Kürenberg, *Johanna von Bismarck, op. cit.,* p. 201.

25 *Ibid.*

26 *Memoirs of Prince von Bülow* (Boston, 1932), IV, 184.

27 Kürenberg, *Johanna von Bismarck, op. cit.,* p. 200.

28 Herbert was named officer on September 2, 1870. Apparently William's promotion did not go through at this time, for about a year later Bismarck was complaining about William's lack of promotion to *Fähnrich* (officer aspirant).

29 Count Albrecht von Roon (1803-1879), on whose advice Prussian King William I appointed Bismarck as Minister-President. Roon was Minister of War during the Franco-Prussian War. In December 1871 he succeeded Bismarck as President of the Prussian Ministry.

30 *Bismarck, D.G.W., op. cit.,* XIV-2, 791.

31 *Ibid.,* p. 793.

32 *Ibid.,* p. 794.

33 See footnote 19 in this chapter.

34 *Bismarck, D.G.W., op. cit.,* VII, 466.

35 *Ibid.,* XIV-2, 813.

36 *Ibid.*

37 Busch, *Tagebuchblätter, op. cit.,* I, 289. Bernard von Roon, Captain and battery chief in the Artillery Guard, had been wounded at Sedan, and had died on September 3, 1870. See footnote #29.

38 H. von Poschinger, *Stunden bei Bismarck* (Berlin, 1910), p. 190 *ff.* In 1867 France and Prussia had nearly gone to war over Luxembourg, which Napoleon III wanted to buy from the King of Holland (who was also Grand Duke of Luxembourg), but which was still garrisoned by Prussian troops because it had been a member of the German Confederation. After some wild language ("Our honor has in fact been violated, and action has to be taken accordingly"), Bismarck accepted the neutralization of the Grand Duchy. He regarded this as evidence of his "love for peace." In fact, however, he was not yet ready for war with France.

39 K. Keil, *Ein Besuch in Varzin, Aus dem Tagebuch des Bildhauers Prof. K. Keil. Deutsche Zeitung Beiblatt, Deutsche Welt,* 1905, No. 38.

40 Bülow, *Memoirs, op. cit.,* IV, 461.

41 Wolfgang Windelband, *Herbert Bismarck als Mitarbeiter seines Vaters* (Stuttgart und Berlin, 1921), p. 7.

[42] *Ibid.*

[43] Heinrich von Poschinger, *Conversations with Bismarck* (New York, 1900), p. 259.

[44] P. Knaplund, ed., *Letters from the Berlin Embassy, Selections from the Private Correspondence of British Representatives at Berlin and Foreign Secretary Lord Granville, 1871-1874, 1880-1885* (Washington, D.C.), p. 235.

[45] Lucius Freiherr von Ballhausen, *Bismarck-Erinnerungen* (Stuttgart and Berlin, 1921), p. 54.

[46] *Ibid.,* p. 91.

[47] *Ibid.,* p. 545.

[48] Prince Chlodwig of Hohenlohe-Schillingfürst, *Memoirs,* ed. by Friedrich Curtius, trans. by George W. Chrystal (London, 1906), p. 263.

[49] Saburov was Russian Ambassador to Berlin, 1880-1884; Giers was aide to the Russian Foreign Minister Prince Gortschakov, 1876-82, later Foreign Minister, 1882-85.

[50] J.Y. Simpson, *The Saburov Memoirs, of Bismarck and Russia* (Cambridge, Eng., 1929), p. 249.

[51] Hecuba, second wife of Priam, King of Troy, and mother of nineteen children, including Hector, Paris, etc. Busch obviously was referring to relatives and nepotism. (See Busch, *Tagebuchblätter, op. cit.,* III, 72-73.)

[52] *Cf.* Maximilian von Hagen, *Bismarcks Kolonialpolitik* (Stuttgart-Gotha, 1923), p. 169.

[53] Prince and Count Philipp zu Eulenburg-Hertefeld (1847-1921), later German Ambassador at Vienna, 1893-1902, poet, musician, architect, and able diplomat.

[54] Philipp zu Eulenburg-Hertefeld, *Aus 50 Jahren, Erinnerungen, Tagebücher und Briefe,* ed. by Johannes Haller (Berlin, 1923), p. 52.

[55] *Cf.* Erich Eyck, *Bismarck and the German Empire* (London, 1950), p. 243 *ff.*

[56] Johannes Penzler, ed., *Fürst Herbert von Bismarcks politische Reden* (Berlin and Stuttgart, 1905), p. 8.

[57] Bülow, *Memoirs, op. cit.,* IV, 457.

[58] Penzler, *Herbert von Bismarcks politischen Reden, op.cit.,* pp. 5-11.

[59] In May 1878, a disgruntled student, who had been expelled by the Social Democratic Party, fired a shot at the eighty-one-year-old Emperor, William I. Striking at once not only at the Socialists but also at the Liberals, Bismarck drafted the Exceptional Laws against them. Twenty days after the attempt on the life of the Emperor the *Reichstag,* Conservatives excepted, rejected Bismarck's proposed laws. Three weeks later, a second shot was fired at the aged monarch, and this time he was seriously wounded. Bismarck promptly dissolved the *Reichstag* as a rebuke to the Richters, Windhorsts, Laskers, and Benningsens, who had been strong enough to forbid him his struggle against "the disturbers of order." In the new elections the forces of the left were greatly weakened, and Bismarck was able to push his Exceptional Laws through the *Reichstag* to punish all activities which aimed at "overthrowing public order."

[60] Penzler, *Herbert von Bismarcks politische Reden, op. cit.,* p. 9.

[61] After expelling the Jesuits from Germany in 1872, the elder Bismarck had put the May Laws (1873-75) through the Prussian *Landtag*, giving the federal government control over education and marriage, muzzling the Catholic press, confiscating Church property, and persecuting recalcitrant priests. Bismarck abandoned this *Kulturkampf* in 1878, deeming the "red international" more dangerous than the "black international."

[62] Penzler, *Herbert von Bismarcks politische Reden, op. cit.,* pp. 10-11.

[63] *Ibid.,* p. 11.

[64] Ballhausen, *Bismarck-Errinnerungen, op. cit.,* p. 541.

[65] *Bismarck, D.G.W., op. cit.,* XIV-II, 914.

[66] Busch, *Tagebuchblätter, op. cit.,* II, 424.

[67] *Ibid.,* III, 14-15.

[68] See Chapter 14.

CHAPTER 3

[1] Joachim von Kürenberg, *Johanna von Bismarck* (Berlin, 1935), p. 261. In May 1888 Prince Eulenburg wrote to Herbert Bismarck during the illness of Johanna: "Both of us have recognized the ideal of femininity in our mothers." (Johannes Haller, *Aus dem leben des Fürsten Philipp zu Eulenburg-Hertefeld* [Berlin, 1924]. p. 6.)

[2] Otto von Bismarck, *Die gesammelten Werke (Friedrichsruher Ausgabe* (Berlin, 1924 *ff.*), VIII, 638. Hereafter referred to as *Bismarck, D.G.W.*

[3] *Bismarck, D.G.W., op. cit.,* VIII, 512.

[4] Paul Liman, "Herbert Bismarck," *Westermanns Monatshefte* 97, (1904), pp. 429-33.

[5] Lord Crewe, *Lord Rosebery* (New York, 1931), p. 449.

[6] Emil Ludwig, *Bismarck* (Boston, 1928), p. 498.

[7] *Ibid.*

[8] *Memoirs of Prince von Bülow* (Boston, 1932), IV, 370.

[9] Philipp zu Eulenburg-Hertefeld, *Aus 50 Jahren, Erinnerungen, Tagebücher, Briefe,* ed. by Johannes Haller (Berlin, 1923), p. 120.

[10] *Ibid.* p. 114.

[11] Maximilian von Hagen, *Bismarcks Kolonialpolitik* (Stuttgart, 1923), pp. 170, 365.

[12] Moritz Busch, *Bismarck, Some Secret Pages of His History* (New York, 1898), III, 118-119.

[13] Lord Edmond Fitzmaurice, *The Life of Granville, George Levesen Gower, Second Earl Granville,* 2 vols. (London, 1905), II, 258.

[14] S. Gwynn and G.M. Tuckwell., *The Life of Rt. Hon. Sir Charles W. Dilke, Bart.,* 2 vols. (London, 1917), I, 432; II, 99-100.

[15] Fitzmaurice, *Life of Granville op. cit.,* 430-31.

[16] Bülow, *Memoirs, op. cit.,* IV, 631-32.

[17] Eulenburg, *Aus 50 Jahren, op. cit.,* pp. 114, 116.

[18] Bülow, *Memoirs, op. cit.,* IV, 548.

[19] Prince Chlodwig of Hohenlohe-Schillingfürst, *Memoirs,* ed. by Friedrich Curtius (London, 1906), II, 432.

[20] Gwynn and Tuckwell, *Life of Dilke, op. cit.,* I, 432.

[21] General-Feldmarschall Alfred Grafen von Waldersee, *Denkwürdigkeiten,* ed. by Heinrich Otto Meisner, 3 vols. (Stuttgart and Berlin, 1923), I, 275-76.

[22] Hagen, *Bismarcks Kolonialpolitik, op. cit.,* pp. 485-86.

[23] Paul Knaplund, *Letters from the Berlin Embassy* (Washington, D.C., 1944), p. 185.

[24] Lucius von Ballhausen, quoted in Ludwig, *Bismarck, op. cit.,* p. 329.

[25] Prince Hohenlohe, quoted in *ibid.,* p. 487.

[26] Eulenburg, *Aus 50 Jahren, op. cit.,* p. 77.

[27] Helmuth Rogge, ed., *Friedrich von Holstein: Lebensbekenntnis in Briefen an eine Frau* (Berlin, 1932), p. 140.

[28] Hermann Freiherr von Eckardstein, *Lebenserinnerungen und politische Denkwurdigkeiten* (Leipzig, 1919), I, 88.

[29] *Ibid.,* I, 81.

[30] *Bismarck, D.G.W., op. cit.,* VIII, 583.

[31] Kürenberg, *Johanna von Bismarck, op. cit.,* p. 260.

[32] Bülow, *Memoirs, op. cit.,* 548-49.

[33] Gwynn and Tuckwell, *Life of Dilke, op. cit.,* I, 342.

[34] Bülow, *Memoirs, op. cit.,* IV, 627.

[35] Haller, *Eulenburg, op. cit.,* p. 49.

[36] Waldersee, *Denkwürdigkeiten, op. cit.,* II, 34.

CHAPTER 4

[1] On Augusta, see H. von Petersdorff, *Kaiserin Augusta* (Leipzig, 1900); *Kaiserin Augusta, Aus ihren literarischen Nachlass* (Berlin, 1912); F. Nippold, *Das Kaiser-Augusta Problem* (Leipzig, 1914); and Heinz Bosbach, *Fürst Bismarck und die Kaiserin Augusta* (Cologne, 1936).

[2] Since March 1848 Bismarck nurtured hatred for Georg von Vincke, Augusta's confidant. On March 25, 1852, Bismarck and Vincke had a duel, apparently over a parliamentary difference. The real reason, as Bismarck admitted later, was the conversation in 1848 concerning Augusta's plans. According to Erich Eyck, Bismarck detested Vincke, who was aware of his moral defeat in the Augusta meeting. (See Erich Eyck, *Bismarck and the German Empire* [London, 1950], p. 23.

[3] On the meeting at Potsdam between Augusta and Bismarck, see Leopold von Gerlach, *Denkwürdigkeiten aus seinem Leben* (Berlin, 1891-92), I, 146 *ff.; Aus den Papieren der Familie Schleinitz* (Berlin, 1905), pp. 311-14; H. von Petersdorff, *Deutsche Männer und Frauen, Biographische Skizze* (Berlin, 1913), p. 271; R. Pancke, *Die Parallelerzählungen Bismarcks zu seiner Gedanken und Erinnerungen* (Halle, 1914), pp. 22-24; G. Grundman, *Der Gegenwärtige Stand der historischen Kritik an Fürst Bismarcks Gedanken und Erinnerungen* (Berlin, 1925); Friedrich III, *Tagebücher von 1848-1866* (Leipzig, 1929); and M. Lenz, *Bismarcks Plan einer Gegenrevolution in März, 1848, Sitzungsberichte der Preuss. Akademie der Wissenschaft,* Jg. 1930, pp. 251 *ff.*

[4] Otto von Bismarck, *Gedanken und Erinnerungen* (Stuttgart, 1898), I, 51. The first two volumes of Bismarck's memoirs were published in 1898 immediately after his death. The third volume was withheld from publication by Bismarck's heirs until 1921 on the ground

that its strictures on William II were too strong. Several one-volume editions have been published since 1921.

[5] To achieve his main object of German unification, Bismarck knew that he had to goad France into action at the right moment. When King William of Prussia was taking the cure at Bad Ems in the middle of July 1870, he was approached by Count Vincent Benedetti, the French Ambassador, who requested him to abandon, once and for all time, any claims to the throne of Spain. Privy Councillor Heinrich Abeken telegraphed an account of the meeting to Bismarck, who was in Berlin. Bismarck carefully edited the dispatch, leaving out important words, and released it to the press the next day, July 14, 1870, Bastille Day, the French national holiday. The result was exactly what Bismarck intended. In its abbreviated form the telegram gave the impression of an ultimatum, "like a flourish of trumpets in answer to a challenge." France declared war immediately.

Bismarck and his admirers insisted that he was entitled to use any means possible in the international battle of wits. He gave a lame excuse: "In the presence of my guests, I reduced the telegram by deleting words, but without adding or altering a single word." (Bismarck, *Gedanken und Erinnerungen, op cit.,* II, 406-08.) His critics condemned this as an unprincipled, if shrewd, trick and certainly beyond the boundaries of political morality.

[6] Eyck, *Bismarck, op. cit.,* p. 23.

[7] See the 1951 edition of *Gedanken und Erinnerungen, op. cit.,* p. 104. See also H. Robolsky, *Die Damenpolitik am Berlin Hof, 1850-1890.* (Berlin, 1897), p. 45, a study devoted to "women's politics at the Berlin court; and M. Duncker, *Politischer Briefwechsel* (Stuttgart and Berlin, 1923).

[8] Max Lenz, *Geschichte Bismarcks* (Leipzig, 1902), p. 270.

[9] See W. von Loë, *Erinnerungen aus meinem Berufsleben* (Stuttgart and Leipzig, 1906) p. 53 *ff.* See also E. Marcks, *Kaiser Wilhelm I* (Leipzig, 1897), p. 231; A. von Waldersee. *Denkwürdigkeiten* (Stuttgart and Berlin, 1925); and J. Ziekursch, *Politische Geschichte der neuen deutschen Kaiserrreichs* (Frankfurt-am-Main, 1927), II, 413.

[10] Bismarck's assistant, Lothar Bucher, told the story of Augusta's behavior: "In spring 1871 our troops were supposed to return early. But the Queen wanted to be present at the victory parade but would not end her cure at Baden-Baden. Therefore, a pause of from four to five weeks, which cost our treasury nine millions." (M. Busch, *Tagebuchblätter* [Leipzig, 1899], II, 417. See also Lucius von Ballhausen, *Bismarckerinnerungen* [Stuttgart and Berlin, 1920], p. 31; and Waldersee *Denkwürdigkeiten op. cit.,* p. 134 *ff.*)

[11] *Die Grosse Politik der Europäischen Kabinette, 1871-1914,* ed. by J. Lepsius, A. Mendelssohn Bartholdy, and F. Thimme (Berlin, 1922), I, 281.

[12] Ludwig Windhorst (1812-1891) leader of the Catholic faction in its battle with Bismarck, was a dwarfed little man with a huge head and acid tongue. The Chancellor recognized an able political opponent in Windhorst, but was consumed with contempt and even hatred for him. "Hate," said Bismarck, "is just as great an incentive to life as love. My life is preserved and made pleasant by two things – my wife and Windhorst. One exists for love, the other for hate." (Ziekursch, *Politische Geschichte, op. cit.,* II, 229).

Count Harry von Arnim (1824-1881), whose career was in diplomacy, had been a companion of Bismarck's youth. Later, Arnim, who hoped one day to be Chancellor, broke his friendship with Bismarck. He was arrested in 1874 on a charge of embezzling State papers, but avoided prison by leaving the country. He then published attacks on Bismarck for "personal jealousy." He was eventually tried, found guilty, and condemned to prison for a term of five years for libel and treason. Allowed to return to Germany for a new trial, he died on May 18, 1881.

[13] Joachim von Kürenberg, *Johanna von Bismarck* (Berlin, 1935), p. 262.

[14] See *Bismarck, D.G.W., op. cit.,* VIII, no. 307.

[15] Prince Philipp zu Eulenburg-Hertefeld (1847-1921) had long been attached to the Bismarck household and he remained a close friend of Herbert Bismarck. Known as a poet, musician, architect, and wit, Eulenburg had a distinguished diplomatic career, which came to an untimely end when he was tried on charges of homosexuality. (See Eulenburg's biography by his friend and literary executor, Johannes Haller, *Aus dem Leben des Fürsten Philipp zu Eulenburg-Hertefeld* [Berlin, 1926], in which Haller attempted to vindicate Eulenburg's character. Herbert saw Eulenburg as the only person who could understand his love for Elizabeth Carolath and depended upon him for advice in the affair. Both the elder Bismarck and his wife Johanna regarded Eulenburg as a clever mediator who would persuade Herbert to abandon his love. Elizabeth Carolath was touched by his kind letters and hoped for his support.

In 1923 appeared Eulenburg's account of the marriage tragedy *"Herbert Bismarcks Tragödie,"* in *Deutsche Rundschau,* XLIX (1923), 225-48. The article reproduced letters between Herbert and Eulenburg bearing on the affair. Before he died, Herbert asked Eulenburg to destroy the correspondence. Eulenburg, however, who wanted to reveal the role he had played in the matter, arranged for posthumous publication. He was anxious to reveal the part he himself had played in the marriage fiasco. That same year the article was incorporated into a volume of reminiscences, *Aus 50 Jahren* (Belrin, 1923), pp. 81-107.

[16] *"Herbert Bismarcks Tragödie," op. cit.,* p. 232.

[17] *Ibid.*

[18] *Ibid.,* pp. 232-33.

[19] Bismarck was equally concerned about the marriage of his second son Bill. He was later much more satisfied when Bill married Sibylle von Arnim of the house of Krochendorf on July 6, 1895. Bismarck and Sibylle's mother were brother and sister − and this marriage remained inside the Protestant family. (See Kürenberg, *Johanna von Bismarck, op. cit.,* p. 261.)

[20] Eulenburg, *"Herbert Bismarcks Tragödie," op. cit.,* p. 235.

[21] *Ibid.,* p. 236.

[22] *Ibid.,* p. 237.

[23] *Ibid.*

[24] *Ibid.,* p. 237 *ff.*

[25] *Ibid.,* p. 245.

[26] *Memoirs of Prince von Bülow* (Berlin, 1932), II, 114.

[27] Kürenberg, *Johanna von Bismarck, op. cit.,* p. 202.

[28] *Bismarck, D.G.W., op. cit.,* XIV-2, 934.

[29] Bülow, *Memoirs, op. cit.,* II, 14.

[30] *Ibid.*

[31] *Ibid.* IV, 486.

[32] *Ibid.*

[33] *Ibid.*

CHAPTER 5

[1] On European imperialism in Africa, see Parker T. Moon, *Imperialism and World Politics* (New York, 1926); William L. Langer, *The Diplomacy of Imperialism, 1890-1902*, 2 vols. (New York, 1935); Grover Clark, *A Place in the Sun* (New York, 1936); Harry Rudin, *The Germans in the Cameroons, 1884-1914: A Case Study in Modern Imperialism* (New Haven, Ct., 1938); Mary Evelyn Townsend, *European Colonial Expansion Since 1871* (Philadelphia, Pa., 1941); Earle M. Winslow, *The Patterns of Imperialism* (New York, 1948); Louis L. Snyder, *The Imperialism Reader: Documents and Readings in Modern Expansionism* (Princeton, N.J., 1962); and John A. Hobson, *Imperialism, A Study* (Ann Arbor, Mich., 1965).

[2] On the meeting between Stanely and Livingstone, see Louis L. Snyder and Richard B. Morris (eds.), *A Treasury of Great Reporting* (New York, 1949, 1965), pp. 189-97.

[3] A typical blank treaty:
We, the undersigned chiefs of   , with a view of bettering the condition of our country and people, do this day cede to the Royal Niger Company (Chartered and Limited) forever, the whole of our territory extending from _____.

We also give to the said Royal Niger Company (Chartered and Limited) full power to settle all native disputes arising from any cause whatever, and we pledge ourselves not to enter into any war with other tribes without the sanction of the said Royal Niger Company (Chartered and Limited.).

We understand that the said Royal Niger Company (Chartered and Limited) have full power to mine, farm, and build in any portion of our country.... (From Edward R. Hertslet [ed.], *The Map of Africa by Treaty* [London, 1894], pp. 467 ff.)

[4] *"Ich will gar keine Kolonien. Das sind blos zu Versorgungsposten gut.... Diese Kolonien wäre für uns genau so, wie die seidene Zobelpelz in polnischen Adelsfamilien, die keine Hemden haben."* (Quoted in R. v. Poschinger, *Fürst Bismarck als Volkswirt*, 2 vols. [Berlin 1889], I, 63, footnote 9.) See also M. Busch, *Tagebuchblätter*, 3 vols. (London, 1898), II, 157.

[5] Parker T. Moon, *Imperialism and World Politics, op. cit.*, pp. 23-24.

[6] Mary Evelyn Townsend, *The Rise and Fall of Germany's Colonial Empire, 1884-1918* (New York, 1930), pp. 84-85.

[7] Paul Knaplund (ed.), *Letters from the Berlin Embassy, Selections from the Private Correspondence of British Representatives at Berlin and Foreign Secretary Lord Granville, 1871-1874, 1880-1885* (Washington, 1942), p. 17. Hereafter cited as *L.B.E.*

[8] H. Temperley and L.M. Penson, *Foundations of British Foreign Policy* (Cambridge, Eng., 1938), p. 251.

[9] W.O. Aydelotte, *Bismarck and British Colonial Policy* (Philadelphia, Pa., 1937), p. vi.

[10] On German colonization in Africa, see Chéradame, André, *La colonisation et les colonies allemandes* (Paris, 1905); P. Darmstaedter, *Geschichte der Aufteilung und Kolonisation Afrikas*, 2 vols. (Berlin, 1913, 1920); Alfred Zimmermann, *Geschichte der deutschen Kolonialpolitik* (Berlin, 1914); W.H. Dawson *The German Empire, 1867-1914*, 2 vols., (London, 1919), Mary Evelyn Townsend, *The Origins of Modern German Colonialism, 1871-1888* (New York, 1921), and *The Rise and Fall of Germany's Colonial Empire, 1884-1918* (New York, 1930); M. v. Hagen, *Bismarcks Kolonialpolitik* (Stuttgart, 1923); W. Stuhlmacher, *Bismarcks Kolonialpolitik nach der Aktenveröffenlichungen des Auswärtigen Amtes* (Halle, 1927); W.O. Aydelotte, *Bismarck and British Colonial Policy* (Philadelphia, Pa., 1937); Harry R. Rudin, *Germans in the Cameroons, 1884-1914: A Case Study in Modern Imperialism* (New Haven, Ct., 1938); Alan L.C. Bullock (ed.),

Germany's Colonial Demands (London, 1939); Rayford Logan, *The African Mandate in World Politics* (Washington, D.C., 1949); and Sybil E. Crowe, *The Berlin West African Conference, 1884-1885* (New York, 1942). The earliest German work was Max von Koschitzky, *Deutsche Kolonialgeschichte*, 2 vols. (Leipzig, 1887-88), which stressed the colonial movement in its relations with internal politics of the empire, as well as the acquisition of colonies and the resulting international complications.

11 A.L. Hodge, *Angra Pequena* (Munich, 1936), p. 11.

12 M. v. Koschitzky, *Deutsche Kolonialgeschichte, op. cit.*, II, sec. 3, 411.

13 *Ibid.*, p. 42.

14 M. v. Hagen, *Bismarcks Kolonialpolitik, op. cit.*, IV, 1, 295.

15 *Das Deutsche Weissbuch, Aktenstücke Nr. 61, Angra Pequena.* Hereafter cited as D.W.

16 *D.W., Angra Pequena*, A, Anlage zu IV.

17 *Ibid.*, A, Anlage zu II.

18 *Ibid.*, A, III.

19 Townsend, *Rise and Fall of Gemany's Colonial Empire, op. cit.*, p. 128.

20 Hodge, *Angra Pequena, op. cit.*, p. 15.

21 D.W., *Angra Peuqena*, B. Nr. 1. See also Townsend, *Origins of Modern German Colonialism, op. cit.*, p. 157.

22 *D.W., Angra Pequena*, Nr. 2. An important portion of this document was left out in the version published in the German White Book. Herbert Bismarck was also instructed to tell the British: "Now, as formerly, we have no thought of any overseas project." The full version of Bismarck's instructions to his son may be found in *Reichsarchiv, Vermischtes Südwestafrika* 1. See also Aydelotte, *Bismarck and British Colonial Policy, op. cit.*, pp. 28-29.

23 *D.W., Angra Pequena B.* Anlage zu Nr. 4.

24 Townsend, *Rise and Fall of Germany's Colonial Empire, op. cit.*, p. 128.

25 Hodge, *Angra Pequena, op. cit.*, p. 17.

26 *Ibid.*, p. 349.

27 Townsend, *Rise and Fall of Germany's Colonial Empire, op. cit.*, p. 94, footnote 67.

28 *Ibid.*, p. 90.

29 *D.W., Angra Pequena*, B, Nr. 9.

30 Townsend, *Rise and Fall of Germany's Colonial Empire, op. cit.*, p. 91. See also Townsend, *Origin of Modern German Colonialism, op. cit.*, p. 169. See also *D.W., Angra Pequena*, B. Nr. 12.

31 Townsend, *Rise and Fall of Germany's Colonial Empire, op. cit.*, p. 91.

32 *The Times* (London), May 12, 1884.

33 Hodge, *Angra Pequena, op. cit.*, pp. 37-38.

34 Prince von Bülow, *Memoirs*, 4 vols. (Boston, 1931-33), IV, 550.

35 Busch, *Tagebuchblätter, op. cit.*, II, 370.

36 E. Fitzmaurice, *The Life of Granville*, 2 vols. (London and Bombay, 1905), II, 348.

37 Bülow, *Memoirs, op. cit.*, IV, 550.

[38] *Ibid.*

[39] Lord Vansittart, *Lessons of My Life* (New York, 1943), p. 10.

[40] See Aydelotte, *Bismarck and British Colonial Policy, op. cit.*, 58-89.

[41] *Die Grosse Politik der Europäischen Kabinette, 1871-1914,* ed. by J. Lepsius, A. Mendelssohn Bartholdy, and F. Thimme (Berlin 1922), IV, 59-62. Reference here Bismarck to Münster, June 1, 1884.

[42] W. Windelband, *Herbert Bismarck als Mitarbeiter seines Vater* (Stuttgart, 1921), pp. 6-8.

[43] Aydelotte, *Bismarck and British Colonial Policy, op. cit.*, p. 162.

[44] On Bleichröder, see Fritz Stern, *Gold and Iron: Bismarck, Bleichröder, and the Building of the German Empire* (New York, 1977).

[45] Lord Ampthill to Lord Granville, November 26, 1881, *L.B.E.*, p. 238.

[46] *Ibid.*

[47] *Ibid.*

[48] Lord Ampthill to Lord Granville, December 17, 1881, *L.B.E.*, p. 233.

[49] Lord Granville to Lord Ampthill, December 14, 1881, *L.B.E.*, p. 238.

[50] *Ibid.*

[51] Lord Granville to Lord Ampthill, March 29, 1882, *L.B.E.*, p. 258.

[52] Fitzmaurice, *The Life of Granville, op. cit.*, II, 256.

[53] Lord Ampthill to Lord Granville, February 25, 1882, *L.B.E.*, p. 254.

[54] Fitzmaurice, *The Life of Granville, op. cit.*, II, 256.

[55] Busch, *Tagebuchblätter, op. cit.*, III, 60.

[56] Lord Ampthill to Lord Granville, March 25, 1882, *L.B.E.*, p. 257.

[57] Lord Ampthill to Lord Granville, April 1, 1882, *L.B.E.*, p. 258.

[58] Lord Ampthill to Lord Granville, June 14, 1884, *L.B.E.*, pp. 333-34.

[59] Lord Granville to Lord Ampthill, June 14, 1884, *Foreign Office Papers,* Public Records Office, London 64/1102.

[60] *Ibid.*

[61] Count Herbert Bismarck to Prince Bismarck, June 14, 1884, *Reichsarchiv, Vermischtes Südwestafrika,* III.

[62] Count Herbert Bismarck to Prince Bismarck, June 17, 1884, *Die Grosse Politik, op. cit.,* IV, no. 746.

[63] Lord Granville to Lord Ampthill, June 18, 1884, *Foreign Office Papers,* 64/1102.

[64] Aydelotte, *Bismarck and British Colonial Policy, op. cit.,* p. 94.

[65] Count Herbert Bismarck to Prince Bismarck, June 17, 1884, *Die Grosse Politik, op. cit.,* IV, no. 746.

[66] Busch, *Tagebuchblätter, op. cit.,* II, 373.

[67] Erich Eyck, *Gladstone* (Leipzig, 1838), p. 436.

[68] S. Gwynn and G.M. Tuckwell, *The Life of the Rt. Hon. Sir Charles Dilke. Bart.,* 2 vols. (London, 1917), II, 81.

[69] See Chapter 7 for further evidence of Dilke's reaction to Herbert's behavior.

[70] Count Herbert Bismarck to Prince Bismarck, June 22, 1884, *Die Grosse Politik, op. cit.,* IV, No. 747.

[71] *The Times* (London), December 13, 1884.

[72] Stern, *Gold and Iron, op. cit.,* p. 410.

[73] *Ibid.,* p. 411.

[74] E.F. Henderson, *A Short History of Germany* (New York, 1917), p. 470.

[75] Münster to Bleichröder, 17 Oct., 24 Dec., 1884, Bleichröder Archiv, Baker Library, Harvard University, quoted by Stern, *Gold and Iron, op. cit.,* p. 411.

CHAPTER 6

[1] *Die Grosse Politik der Europäischen Kabinette, 1871-1914,* ed. by J. Lepsius, A. Mendelssohn Bartholdy, and F. Thimme (Berlin, 1922), IV, 26, 36, 47, 64, 100, 123.

[2] *Rheinisch-Westfälische Zeitung,* March 13, 1885.

[3] Lucius Freiherr von Ballhausen, *Bismarck-Erinnerungen* (Stuttgart and Berlin, 1921), p. 313.

[4] Moritz Busch, *Bismarck, Some Secret Pages of His History* (New York, 1898), III, 146.

[5] Karl Friedrich Nowak, *Germany's Road to Ruin,* trans. by E.W. Dickes (London, 1932), p. 23.

[6] Henry Stephan de Blowitz, *My Memoirs* (London, 1903), p. 332. Emperor William I's remarks on Bismarck's nepotism were quoted by Count Münster, German Ambassador in Paris in 1892, to M. de Blowitz, the famed Anglo-French journalist and correspondent for the London *Times,* who repeated them in his memoirs.

[7] Otto von Bismarck, *Die Gesammelten Werke (Friedrichsruher Ausgabe)* (Berlin, 1924 *ff.*), VIII, 546.

[8] *Memoirs of Prince von Bülow* (Boston, 1932), I, 390.

[9] Hermann Oncken, *Das Deutsche Reich und die Vorgeschichte des Weltkrieges* (Leipzig, 1933), I, 329.

[10] Bülow, *Memoirs, op. cit.,* I, 8. Bülow, who had a high opinion of his own capacities, added: "During the twelve years I was in office [*as Secretary of State, 1897-1900 and Chancellor, 1900-1909*] they were able to revert to more placid movements."

[11] William II, *My Memoirs, 1878-1918* (London, 1922), p. 5. The italics are by William II.

[12] General-Feldmarschall Alfred Grafen von Waldersee, *Denkwürdigkeiten* (Stuttgart and Berlin, 1923), I, 282.

[13] William II, *Memoirs, op. cit.,* p. 12.

[14] Prince Chlodwig of Hohenlohe-Schillingfürst, *Memoirs,* ed. by Friedrich Curtius, trans. by George W. Chrystal (London, 1906), II, 400.

[15] Quoted in the *Hamburger Nachrichten,* September 18, 1907.

[16] Waldersee, *Denkwürdigkeiten, op. cit.,* I, 307.

[17] *Ibid.*

[18] Otto von Bismarck, *Gedanken und Erinnerungen* (Stuttgart and Berlin, 1898, 1919), p. 570. Busch mistakenly dated this letter November 23, 1897. *Cf.* Busch, *Bismarck,* III, 383.

[19] *Bismarck, D.G.W., op. cit.,* XIV-II, 983.

[20] Johannes Haller, *Aus dem Leben des Fürsten Philipp zu Eulenburg-Hertefeld* (Berlin, 1924), p. 34.

[21] *Ibid.,* p. 20.

[22] *Ibid.,* p. 21.

[23] *Ibid.* p. 45.

[24] Reported by Bülow, *Memoirs, op. cit.,* II, 60.

[25] Bülow, *Memoirs, op. cit.,* IV, 619.

[26] Hohenlohe, *Memoirs, op. cit.,* II, 402. Hohenlohe further reported the Prince of Wales as saying that had he not valued the good relations between England and Germany he would have thrown Herbert Bismarck out of the room. The British Prince was "exceedingly angered by the boorishness of the Bismarck family, father and son." (See *ibid.,* p. 403.)

[27] Ballhausen *Bismarck-Erinnerungen, op. cit.,* p. 432.

[28] See chapter 8.

[29] Bülow, *Memoirs, op. cit.,* II, 61.

[30] Waldersee, *Denkwürdigkeiten, op. cit.,* I, 275-276.

[31] *Ibid.,* I, 286.

[32] *Ibid.,* I, 288.

[33] Philipp zu Eulenburg-Hertefeld, *Aus 50 Jahren* (Berlin, 1923), pp. 1149-150. *Cf.* Waldersee, *Denkwürdigkeiten, op. cit.,* I, 339, 342.

[34] Waldersee, *Denkwürdigkeiten, op. cit.,* I, 342.

[35] Waldersee, *Briefwechsel, op. cit.,* I, 168.

[36] Waldersee, *Denkwürdigkeiten, op. cit.,* I, 257-258.

[37] On Stoecker's life, see Dietrich von Oertzen, *Adolf Stoecker, Lebensbild und Zeitgeschichte* (Schwerin i. Mecklenburg, 1912). On his political ideas, see Adolf Stoecker, *Christlich-Sozial, Reden und Aufsätze* (Bielefeld and Leipzig, 1885).

[38] Von Oertzen, *Adolf Stoecker op. cit.,* p. 273.

[39] Stoecker, *Christlich-Sozial, op. cit.,* p. 37.

[40] *Ibid.,* p. 86.

[41] *Ibid.,* p. 87.

[42] *Ibid.,* p. 30.

[43] *Ibid.,* p. 106.

[44] *Ibid.,* p. 96.

[45] *Ibid.,* p. 186.

[46] *Ibid.,* p. 263.

[47] *Ibid.* p. 210

[48] Von Oertzen, *Adolf Stoecker, op. cit.,* p. 159.

[49] *Ibid.,* p. 165.

[50] *Verhandlungen des deutschen Reichstages,* 1882-1883, I, 802.

51 Von Oertzen, *Adolf Stoecker, op. cit.,* p. 134.

52 Bismarck, *Gedanken und Erinnerungen, op. cit.,* pp. 584 *ff.*

53 *Ibid.,* p. 584.

54 *Ibid.*

55 *Ibid.*

56 *Ibid.* p. 585.

57 *Ibid.,* p. 586.

58 *Ibid.,* p. 589.

59 *Ibid.,* p. 594, 595.

60 See Louis L. Snyder, *The Blood and Iron Chancellor* (New York, 1967), p. 3.

61 *Ibid.*

62 Moritz Busch, *Tagebuchblätter,* 3 vols. (Leipzig, 1899 *ff.*), III, 9 *ff.*

63 *Ibid.*

64 Busch, *Tagebuchblätter, op. cit.,* II, 565 *ff.*

65 Koppel S. Pinson, *Modern Germany: Its History and Civilization (New York, 1954), p. 168.*

66 See Louis L. Snyder, *"Bismarck and the Lasker Resolution, 1884" The Review of Politics,* XXIX, no. 1 (January 1967), 41-64.

67 Gustav Mayer, *Bismarck und Lasalle* (Berlin, 1928), p. 60.

68 For a superb biography, see Fritz Stern, *Gold and Iron: Bismarck, Bleichröder, and the Building of the German Empire* (New York, 1977).

69 Otto Johlinger, *Bismarck und die Juden* (Berlin, 1921), p. 105.

70 See Johannes Penzler (ed.), *Fürst Herbert von Bismarcks politische Reden* (Berlin and Stuttgart, 1905), p. 8.

71 Quoted in Stern, *Gold and Iron, op. cit.,* p. 258.

72 *Holstein Paper,* III, 14, quoted in Stern *Gold and Iron, op. cit.,* p. 223.

73 Stern, *Gold and Iron, op. cit.,* p. 259.

74 On international efforts toward abolition of the slave trade, see T. Clarkson, *The History of the Rise, Progress and Accomplishment of the Abolition of the African Slave Trade by the British Parliament,* 2 vols. (London, 1939; reprinted 1968); R. Coupland, *Wilberforce* (London, 1923); and O.A. Sherrard, *Freedom from Fear; The Slave and His Emancipation* (London, 1959).

75 *Stenographische Berichte des deutschen Reichstages (*Berlin, 1888), I, 310-12.

76 *Ibid.* (Berlin, 1889), II, 565.

77 Ballhausen, *Bismarck-Erinnerungen, op. cit.,* p. 490.

78 General George Ernest Jean Marie Boulanger (1837-1891), the fiery demagogue who became Minister of War in France in 1886, was selected by the monarchists as a suitable "man on horseback" to lead a *coup d'état* and a possible war of revenge againt Germany.

[79] General-Feldmarschall Alfred Grafen von Waldersee, *Aus dem Briefwechsel* (Berlin and Leipzig, 1928), I, 230.

CHAPTER 7

[1] See Chapter 5.

[2] See the exchange of letters between Lord Granville, the British Foreign Secretary, and Herbert Bismarck, then Ambassador at The Hague (August 20 and 30, 1884) in *Die Grosse Politik der Europäische Kabinette, 1871-1914*, ed. by J. Lepsius, A. Mendelssohn Bartholdy, and F. Thimme (Berlin, 1922), IV, 79-83.

[3] *Ibid.,* p. 82.

[4] Raymond J. Sontag, *Germany and England, Background of Conflict, 1848-1894* (New York, 1938), p. 200.

[5] *Cf. Die Grosse Politik, op. cit.,* IV, 102.

[6] *Die politischen Reden des Fürsten von Bismarck: historische-kritische Gesamtausgabe,* ed. by Horst Kohl (Stuttgart, 1892-1904), II, 56 *ff.*

[7] Quoted in C.G. Robertson, *Bismarck* (London, 1918), p. 427. See also E. Eyck, *Gladstone* (Leipzig, 1938), p. 436, and E. Fitzmaurice, *The Life of Granville* (London and Bombay, 1905), II, 430. Lord Derby (1826-1893) at this time was the British Colonial Secretary.

[8] S. Gwynn and G.M. Tuckwell, *The Life of the Rt. Hon. Sir Charles W. Dilke, Bart.,* 2 vols. (London, 1917), II, 99.

[9] Quoted in Fitzmaurice, *Granville, op. cit.,* II, 431.

[10] Sontag, *Germany and England, op. cit.,* p. 200.

[11] *Ibid.,* p. 201.

[12] *Cf. ibid.*

[13] The final settlement did not take place until after the fall of the Bismarcks. By the Anglo-German Agreement of July 1, 1890, Britain obtained from Germany, in return for the cession of Heligoland, recognition of a British protectorate over the dominions of the Sultan of Zanzibar, including the islands of Zanzibar and Pemba.

[14] *Die Grosse Politik, op. cit.,* IV, 143-44.

[15] *Cf. ibid,* V, chap. XXXIII.

[16] *Cf. ibid.,* IV, 345-49.

[17] *Ibid.,* IV, 176.

[18] Hucks Gibbs, "Bismarck at Home," *The Cornhill Magazine* 57 (July 1924).

[19] Joseph Chamberlain (1836-1914). Radical leader.

[20] Gibbs, "Bismarck at Home," *op. cit.*

[21] Sontag, *Germany and England, op. cit.,* p. 252.

[22] Eyck, *Gladstone, op. cit.,* p. 331.

[23] Mrs. George West Cornwallis, *The Reminiscences of Lady Randolph Churchill* (London, 1908), p. 197.

[24] Sir Edward Malet (1837-1908), then British Ambassador at Berlin.

[25] Lord Crewe, *Lord Rosebery* (New York, 1931), p. 188.

[26] *Letters of Empress Frederick,* ed. by *Sir Frederick Ponsonby* (New York, 1930), pp. 195-196.

[27] Sir Charles Wentworth Dilke (1843-1911), author of *Greater Britain* (1868), a famous plea for a sane and reformed imperialism, and an active political figure until 1884 when his career was ruined by a divorce scandal.

[28] Gwynn and Tuckwell, *Dilke, op. cit.,* II, 303.

[29] Reported by Bülow and quoted in Eyck, *Gladstone, op. cit.,* p. 431.

[30] In September 1888, a few months after the death of Frederick III, a reputable German review, the *Deutsche Rundschau,* published anonymously extracts from the diary which Frederick had kept during the Franco-Prussian War. The article revealed Frederick's liberalism and was mildy critical of Bismarck. Infuriated, the Chancellor instituted criminal proceedings against the editor of the extracts, Professor Heinrich Geffcken (1830-1896), a personal friend of Frederick III, and accused Geffcken of having falsified the diary. To Bismarck, Geffcken was an anti-Prussian intriguer, who played a dangerous game in seeking to influence Federick III along the road of liberalism. (See Erich Eyck, *Bismarck and the German Empire* [London, 1950], pp. 304-05. For Bismarck's version see Otto von Bismarck, *Gedanken und Erinnerungen* [Stuttgart and Berlin, 1898, 1919], 286, 427-28.)

[31] *Kölnische Zeitung,* December 15, 1888.

[32] C. Grant Robertson, *Bismarck* (London, 1918), p. 465.

[33] Lothar Bucher to Moritz Busch, May 31, 1885, in Moritz Busch, *Bismarck, Some Secret Pages of His History* (New York, 1898), III, 135.

[34] Lothar Bucher to Moritz Busch, June 16, 1885, in *ibid.,* III, 143-44.

[35] *Cf.* H. Kohl (ed.), *Die politische Reden des Fürsten Bismarcks, op. cit., XII, 574 ff.*

[36] *Ibid.* XII, 575.

[37] Herbert Bismarck to Chancellor Bismarck, March 22, 1889, in *Die Grosse Politik, op. cit.,* IV, 405. (*Cf.* Erich Brandenburg, *From Bismarck to the World War, A History of German Foreign Policy, 1870-1914* [London, 1927], p. 9.)

[38] Prince Chlodwig of Hohenlohe-Schillingfürst, *Memoirs,* ed. by Friedrich Curtius, (London, 1906), II, 379.

[39] "When Victoria mentioned Herbert's name to me, her eyes became so inflamed that I almost shrank from her. And what accusations did she make! In Herbert she saw the material and brutal type of the new risen poor Junker from the 'hateful' Altmark." It was a mutual feeling: "Herbert said that if she comes to control of Germany, then Germany is finished." (Philipp zu Eulenburg-Hertefeld, *Aus 50 Jahren* [Berlin, 1923], pp. 174, 176.]
Apparently, Herbert had little influence on the distaff side of the royal family. William II's wife, Augusta Victoria of Schleswig-Holstein-Sonderburg-Augustenburg, also detested Herbert, of whom she had heard it said that on an occasion in the past he had offered to procure a mistress for Prince William. When she mentioned his name, she spoke of him as "that drunkard," or "that roué." (*Cf.* Joachim von Kurenberg, *The Kaiser: A Life of Wilhelm II, Last Emperor of Germany,* trans. by H.T. Russell and Herta Hagen [New York, 1955], p. 110).

[40] Empress Frederick to Queen Victoria, November 2, 1888: "Bismarck could not have had a better tool than William. He has carefully had him prepared by his son Herbert for two years. All other voices and views are excluded. W. reads only the papers prepared for him, does not understand or care for all the difficult and intricate questions of internal Government and is utterly ignorant of social, industrial, agricultural, commercial and financial

questions, etc., only occupied with military things." (*Letters of the Empress Frederick, op. cit.,* p. 358.)

41 William II, *My Memoirs, 1878-1918* (London, 1922), p. 26. William II's biographer, Joachim von Kürenberg, described a trip to St. Petersburg from May 15-28, 1888: "There was general praise for his [*William's*] conduct – even Herbert Bismarck, always ready and glad to find fault, had to admit that in 'St. Petersburg the Prince had done well in solving the by-no-means easy problem of the precarious relations between Germany and Russia.'" (Kürenberg, *The Kaiser, op. cit.,* p. 52.)

42 *Cf.* Lucius Freiherr von Ballhausen, *Bismarck-Errinnerungen* (Stuttgart and Berlin, 1921), p. 477; *Memoirs of Prince von Bülow* (Boston, 1932), IV, 348; and *Letters of the Empress Frederick, op. cit.* pp. 371-72.

43 Otto von Bismarck, *Die Gesammelten Werke (Friedrichsruher Ausgabe)* (Berlin, 1924 *ff.*), VIII, 622.

44 When Bamberger in the *Reichstag* meeting of May 23, 1889, attacked Prince Bismarck, the latter became extraordinarily excited. Herbert took the arm of his father and led him from the hall. (Siegfried von Kardorff, *Wilhelm von Kardorff* [Berlin, 1936], p. 224.)

45 General-Feldmarschall Alfred Grafen von Waldersee, *Denkwürdigkeiten* (Stuttgart and Berlin, 1923), II, 56.

46 *Ibid.* II, 37. Count Waldersee's hatred of Herbert Bismarck was almost pathological in intensity. Throughout his *Denkwürdigkeiten,* in all three volumes, the editor, Heinrich Otto Meisner, left spaces to indicate that the author's remarks about Herbert Bismarck were either unprintable or undesirable to repeat.

47 *Ibid.,* II, 55.

48 *Ibid.,* II, 55-56.

CHAPTER 8

1 See Joseph Waldo Ellison, "The Partition of Samoa: A Study in Imperialism and Diplomacy, " *The Pacific Historical Review* (VIII), September, 1939, pp. 258-59.

2 Thomas A. Bailey, *A Diplomatic History of the American People* (New York, 1946), p. 460. (See also G.H. Ryden, *The Foreign Policy of the United States in relation to Samoa* [New Haven, 1933], pp. 13 *ff.*)

3 Alice Felt Tyler, *The Foreign Policy of James G. Blaine* (Minneapolis, 1927), p. 219.

4 See M. Wertheimer, *The Pan German League* (New York, 1924), p. 27; and Mary Evelyn Townsend, *The Rise and Fall of Germany's Colonial Empire, 1884-1918* (New York, 1930), pp. 188 *ff.*

5 Quoted in Tyler, *Foreign Policy, op. cit.,* p. 220.

6 Bailey, *Diplomatic History, op. cit.,* p. 461.

7 *Ibid.,* pp. 461-62.

8 Robert Louis Stevenson, who arrived in Samoa in 1889, wrote a classic account of the tense battle, quoting one politician as saying: "I never saw so good a place as this Apia. You can be in on a new conspiracy every day!" (Robert Louis Stevenson, *A Footnote to History* [New York, 1895], p. 26.)

9 Tyler, *Foreign Policy, op. cit.,* p. 22. Thomas Francis Bayard (1828-1898), Secretary of State, 1880-1889, was the first American to bear the title of Ambassador to Great Britain. 1893-97.

¹⁰ On the Washington Conference of 1887, see Alfred Vagts, *Deutschland und die Vereinigten Staaten in der Weltpolitik* (New York, 1935), I, 638 *ff.*

¹¹ The Samoan trade in 1884: Exports from Samoa: Germany, $323,884; U.S.A, $25,000; Great Britain and colonies, $9,744. Imports: Germany, $77,047; U.S.A., $73,776; Great Britain and colonies, $49,562. (S. Masterman, *The Origins of International Rivalry in Samoa, 1845-1884* [Stanford University, 1934], pp. 180 *ff.*

¹² Of some 832,000 acres on the Samoan Islands, the British claimed 1,250,270; the Americans, 302,746 acres; and the Germans 134,419 acres. In the final settlement Germany received some 85,000 acres of the best land. (*Ibid.*)

¹³ *Cf.* Louis L. Snyder, "The American-German Pork Dispute," *The Journal of Modern History,* XVII (March, 1945). pp. 16-28.

¹⁴ Bailey, *Diplomatic History, op. cit.,* p. 463.

¹⁵ Stevenson, *Footnote to History, op. cit.,* chap. V.

¹⁶ Tyler, *Foreign Policy, op. cit.,* p. 219.

¹⁷ See Louis L. Snyder, *Die persoenlichen und politischen Beziehungen Bismarcks zu Amerikanern* (Darmstadt, 1932), *passim;* and Count Otto zu Stolberg-Wernigerode, *Germany and the United States of America during the Era of Bismarck* (Reading, Pa., 1937), pp. 258 *ff.*

¹⁸ George Hunt Pendleton (1825-1889), American Ambassador to Germany from 1885 to 1889.

¹⁹ Quoted in Tyler, *Foreign Policy, op. cit.,* p. 225. Bismarck agreed that these remarks could be sent for the information of the American Secretary of State but asked that they not be published.

²⁰ Hermann Freiherr von Eckardstein, *Lebenserinnerungen und politische Denkwürdigkeiten* (Leipzig, 1919), II, 34.

²¹ Otto von Bismarck, *Gedanken und Erinnerungen* (Stuttgart and Berlin, 1898, 1919), p. 544.

²² Stolberg-Wernigerode, *Germany and the United States, op. cit.,* p. 220.

²³ *Ibid.,* p. 223.

²⁴ *Memoirs of Prince von Bülow* (Boston, 1932), I, 330. In 1899 Germany finally purchased the Caroline Islands from Spain, and held them until after World War I, when they became a Japanese mandate.

²⁵ *Die Grosse Politik der Europäischen Kabinette, 1871-1914,* ed. by J. Lepsius, A. Mendelssohn Bartholdy, and F. Thimme (Berlin, 1922), IV, 176-77.

²⁶ *Ibid.* At the end of September 1887 Malietoa was placed aboard the German warship *Adler* and interned in New Guinea.

²⁷ *Weissbuch Samoa,* February 15, 1889, No. 37.

²⁸ Quoted in the London *Times,* March 23, 1889.

²⁹ Tyler, *Foreign Policy, op. cit.,* p. 227.

³⁰ *Berliner Tageblatt,* March 28, 1890.

³¹ *Germania,* March 24, 1889.

³² Vagts. *Deutschland und die Vereinigten Staaten, op. cit.,* I, 677.

³³ Herbert Bismarck to Prince Bismarck, March 27, 1889, in *Die Grosse Politik, op. cit.,* IV, 409.

34 Tyler, *Foreign Policy, op. cit.,* p. 227.

35 *Cf.* Tyler, *Foreign Policy, op. cit.,* pp. 247-49; Bailey, *Diplomatic History, op. cit.,* p. 464.

36 Vagts, *Deutschland und die Vereinigten Staaten, op. cit.,* I, 692-93.

37 A further decision was reached in 1900, when it was agreed that Great Britain should withdraw from Samoa, that the United States should have the island of Tutuila, an area of seventy-seven square miles with the harbor of Pago Pago, and that the rest of the islands should go to Germany.

38 Robert Louis Stevenson, *Valima Papers and a Footnote to History* (New York, 1925), p. 268.

39 Stevenson, *Footnote to History, op. cit.,* p. 90.

40 Vagts, *Deutschland und die Vereinigten Staaten, op. cit.,* 1, 694.

41 *Ibid.*

42 *Frankfurter Zeitung,* January 29, 1890.

43 *Berliner Tageblatt,* March 29, 1890. On November 29, 1850, King Frederick William IV of Prussia, faced with the prospect of Austrian and German intervention, was forced to submit at Olmütz and accept the old German Confederation of 1815. To Prussian patriots this was the most humiliating episode of their history, because it meant a renewal of Austrian domination in their affairs.

44 *Die Grosse Politik, op. cit.* IV, 51.

45 *Ibid.,* IV, 54-55.

46 *Ibid.,* IV, 55-56

47 Lord Edmond Fitzmaurice, *The Life of Granville, George Leveson Gower Second Lord Granville* (London and Bombay, 1905), II, 351.

48 *Die Grosse Politik, op. cit.,* IV, 56.

49 *Ibid.,* IV, 409.

50 *Ibid.,* IV, 413.

51 *Ibid.,* IV, 407-408.

52 Otto von Bismarck, *Gedanken und Erinnerungen, op. cit.,* pp. 691-93.

53 Joachim Kürenberg, *The Kaiser: A Life of Wilhelm II, Last Emperor of Germany,* trans. by H.T. Russell and Herta Hagen (New York, 1955), p. 415.

CHAPTER 9

1 Quoted in a letter from Count Helldorf, leader of the Conservative Party, to Hans Delbrück, who was close to government circles. (Hans Delbrück, *Government and the Will of the People,* trans. by R.S. MacElway [New York, 1923], p. 49.)

2 Erich Eyck, *Bismarck and the German Empire* (London, 1950), p. 323.

3 *Ibid.*

4 The Imperial Rescript on the Labor Question, which led to the first quarrel between Bismarck and William II.

5 William II.

6 Moritz Busch, *Bismarck: Some Secret Pages of His History* (London, 1898), III, 307.

[7] Prince Chlodwig of Hohenlohe-Schillingfürst, *Memoirs,* ed. by Friedrich Curtius and trans. by George W. Chrystal (London, 1906), p. 243.

[8] Maximilian Harden, *"Bismarcks Sohn," Die Zukunft,* XLVIII, (1904), p. 4.

[9] Lucius Freiherr von Ballhausen, *Bismarck-Erinnerungen* (Stuttgart and Berlin, 1921), p. 518.

[10] Philipp zu Eulenburg-Hertefeld, *Aus 50 Jahren* (Berlin, 1923), p. 293.

[11] *Memoirs of Prince von Bülow* (Boston, 1932), IV, 461-62.

[12] *Ibid.*

[13] *Letters of Empress Frederick,* ed. by Sir Frederick Ponsonby (New York, 1930), p. 413.

[14] *Ibid.,* p. 414.

[15] Eulenburg, *Aus 50 Jahren, op. cit.,* p. 247.

[16] Johannes Haller, *Aus dem Leben des Fürsten Philipp zu Eulenburg-Hertefeld* (Berlin, 1924), p. 52.

[17] General-Feldmarschall Alfred Grafen von Waldersee, *Denkwürdigkeiten,* ed. by Heinrich Otto Meisner (Stuttgart and Berlin, 1923), II, 129.

[18] Waldersee, *Denkwürdigkeiten, op. cit.,* II, 87.

[19] Haller, *Eulenburg-Hertefeld, op. cit.,* p. 55.

[20] Bülow, *Memoirs, op. cit.,* I, 262.

[21] *Ibid.*

[22] Haller, *Eulenberg-Hertefeld, op. cit.,* p. 55.

[23] *Ibid.*

[24] Bülow, *Memoirs, op. cit.,* I, 262.

[25] Emil Ludwig, *Bismarck,* trans. by Eden and Cedar Paul (Boston, 1928), pp. 567-68.

[26] On Bismarck's dismissal, see K.F. Nowak, *Kaiser and Chancellor* (London, 1930); W. Mommsen, *Bismarcks Sturz und die Parteien (Stuttgart, 1924); W. Schüssler, Bismarcks Sturz* (Leipzig, 1921); E. Gagliardi, *Bismarcks Entlassung* (Tübingen, 1927); Emil Ludwig, *Kaiser Wilhelm II,* trans. by E.C. Mayne (London, 1926); and H. Delbrück, *Vor und Nach dem Welkriege* (Berlin, 1926). For Bismarck's version, see Otto von Bismarck, *Gedanken und Erinnerungen,* vol. III (Stuttgart and Berlin, 1921). For William II's account, see William II, *The Kaiser's Memoirs,* trans. by T.R. Ybarra (New York, 1922).

[27] Stoecker was dismissed from his post by William II. See Louis L. Snyder, *From Bismarck to Hitler* (Williamsport, Pa., 1935), pp. 13-24.

[28] Eyck, *Bismarck and the German Empire, op. cit.,* p. 312

[29] Siegried von Kardorff, *Bismarck in Kampf und sein Werk* (Berlin, 1943), II, 44.

[30] Georg Freiherr von Eppstein, *Fürst Bismarcks Entlassung* (Berlin, 1920), p. 65. Bismarck had additional cause for complaint against Boetticher: "When Boetticher's assistant insinuated to the Emperor that I had become incapable of transacting business through the immoderate use of morphine, His Majesty queried my son Herbert about the matter, and was rebuked by him and Prof. Schweninger, from whom the Emperor learned that the suggestion was a pure invention." (Otto von Bismarck, *Gedanken und Erinnerungen, op. cit.,* III, 84.).

[31] Eyck, *Bismarck and the German Empire, op. cit.,* p. 313.

[32] Hohenlohe, *Memoirs, op. cit.,* p. 243.

[33] The Three Emperors' Conferences (1872-1878) (William I of Germany, Francis Joseph of Austria, and Alexander II of Russia); the Austro-German Alliance (1879); the Three Emperors' League, (1881-1887); the Triple Alliance (1882, renewed in 1887, 1891, 1903, and 1912) (Germany, Austria-Hungary, and Italy); and the Reinsurance Treaty (1887-1890).

[34] The elder Bismarck has been responsible for Eckardstein's diplomatic career. "He is over six feet tall, can drink without getting drunk, and is otherwise suitable, so we'll make a diplomat of him." (*Cf.* Baron von Eckardstein, *Ten Years at the Court of St. James, 1895-1905,* trans. and ed. by George Young [New York, 1922], p. 27.)

[35] Hermann Freiherr von Eckardstein, *Lebenserinnerunge und politische Denkwürdigkeiten* (Leipzig, 1919), I, 107-09.

[36] E. Brandenburg, *From Bismarck to the World War, A History of German Foreign Policy, 1870-1914* (London, 1927), p. 23.

[37] Karl Friedrich Nowak, *Germany's Road to Ruin,* trans. by E.W. Dickes (London, 1932), pp. 5-6. For Herbert Bismarck's account see *Die Grosse Politik der Europäische Kabinette, 1871-1914,* ed. by J. Lepsius, A. Mendelssohn Bartholdy, and F. Thimme (Berlin, 1922), VII, 3, 4.

[38] William II was willing to renew the Reinsurance Treaty even though he believed that the Bismarcks intended to abandon the Triple Alliance and instead, obtain an understanding with Russia. *Cf.* Hohenlohe, *Memoirs, op. cit.,* p. 412.

[39] Quoted in Nowak, *Kaiser and Chancellor, op. cit.,* p. 6. After Bismarck's fall, Herbert Bismarck made an attempt to obtain the document on the Reinsurance Treaty from the archives of the Foreign Office. "With his usual brutality, he [*Herbert Bismarck*] demanded that the official in charge give it to him, but the latter said: 'Your Excellency is no longer my chief, and I don't have to listen to you any longer,' whereupon Herbert, most cynically, dismissed him." (Ludwig Bamberger, *Die Geheimen Tagebücher* [Frankfurt-am-Main, 1932], p. 482.)

[40] For the text of this order see Eppstein, *op. cit., Fürst Bismarcks Entlassung, op. cit.,* note 62.

[41] Otto von Bismarck, *Gedanken und Erinnerungen, op. cit.,* III, *650-54, passim.* On April 14, 1890, William II and his new Chancellor, Count Leo von Caprivi, announced suspension of the Order of 1852, which Bismarck had been unwilling to do. For the text of the order, see O. Gradenwitz, *Bismarcks letzter Kampf, 1888-1898, Skizzen nach Akten* (Berlin, 1924), p. 114.

[42] Bismarck's letter of resignation was published in a Berlin newspaper on the day of the retired Chancellor's death in 1898. A copy of the letter was given to the newspaper by Moritz Busch. The communication was thus publicized as the dead Chancellor's indictment of the living Emperor. (*Cf.* Eyck, *op. cit., Bismarck and the German Empire, op. cit.,* p. 322.)

CHAPTER 10

[1] *Memoirs of Prince von Bülow* (Boston, 1932), IV, 641.

[2] *William II, My Memoirs, 1879-1918* (London, 1922), p. 12.

[3] This was indicated in the memoirs of Count Waldersee, who was close to the Emperor. "The Kaiser wants, when the Chancellor goes, to hold on to the son as Foreign Minister. He must be convinced of that: the thing will look better before the world, if Count Herbert follows his father after a while. There can be no doubt that this would have to happen,

because every Chancellor must hold leadership over foreign affairs in his own hands." (General-Feldmarschall Alfred Grafen von Waldersee *Denkwürdigkeiten,* ed. by Heinrich Otto Meisner [Stuttgart and Berlin, 1923], II, 103.)

[4] Philipp zu Eulenburg-Hertefeld, *Aus 50 Jahren* (Berlin, 1923), pp. 290-91.

[5] *Ibid.,* p. 291.

[6] Waldersee, *Denkwürdigkeiten, op. cit.,* II, 114.

[7] Eulenburg, *Aus 50 Jahren, op. cit.,* p. 237.

[8] *Ibid.*

[9] *Ibid.,* p. 249.

[10] Otto von Bismarck, *Gedanken und Erinnerungen,* (Stuttgart and Berlin, 1921), III, 655.

[11] Siegfried von Kardoff, *Bismarck im Kampf und sein Werk* (Berlin, 1943), II, 79.

[12] Otto von Bismarck, *Gedanken und Erinnerungen, op. cit.,* III, 658.

[13] Moritz Busch, *Bismarck: Some Secret Pages of his History* (London, 1898), III, 314. Apparently, Bismarck believed that Boetticher had been selected as his successor, and knew nothing as yet about the choice of Caprivi.

[14] R.A. Müller, *"Die Entlassung," Süddeutsche Monatshefte,* December, 1921, p. 163.

[15] Ludwig Bamberger, *Die Geheime Tagebücher* (Frankfurt-am-Main, 1932), pp. 541-42.

[16] Müller, "Die Entlassung," *op. cit.,* p. 163 *ff.*

[17] Kardorff, *Bismarck in Kampf, op. cit.,* II, 79-80.

[18] Quoted in Joachim von Kürenberg, *The Kaiser: A Life of Wilhelm II, Last Emperor of Germany,* trans. by H.T. Russell and Herta Hagen (New York, 1955), p. 102.

[19] Count Johann Friedrich von Alvensleben (1836-1913) started his work as a diplomat as attaché in Brussels in 1861; then Legation Secretary in Munich, Stuttgart, Dresden, The Hague, and Washington; Embassy Councillor in St. Petersburg, 1872; General Consul in Bucharest, 1876; Prussian Ambassador at Darmstadt, 1879; Imperial Ambassador at The Hague, 1882; Imperial Ambassador at Washington, 1884; and Minister Plenipotentiary in Brussels, 1888. Later in 1901, he was Imperial Ambassador at St. Petersburg.

[20] Otto von Bismarck, *Gedanken und Erinnerungen, op. cit., III, 659-60.* [The fallen Chancellor added some significant remarks: "On March 26th I took my leave from the Emperor. His Majesty said that 'only worry for my health' had moved him to take part in the resignation. I answered that in the last few years my health had seldom been better than in the past winter." (*Ibid.,* III, 660.)]

[21] Lord Crewe, *Lord Rosebery* (New York, 1931), p. 293. The reference is to Adolf Hermann Freiherr Marschall von Bieberstein (1842-1912), Ambassador of the Grand Duchy of Baden at Berlin.

[22] Kardorff, *Bismarck im Kampf, op. cit.,* II, 79.

[23] Johannes Ziekursch, *Das Zeitalters Wilhelms II, 1890-1918* (Frankfurt-am-Main, 1930), pp. 3-4. Eulenberg testified similarly to this attitude of Herbert Bismarck: "Herbert, whom I saw daily – the echo of his father – considered the situation as the beginning of the end – for the collapse (*Zusammenbruch)* of Germany, which could be avoided only by the personal leadership of the Chancellor, his father." (*Cf.* Eulenburg, *Aus 50 Jahren, op. cit.,* p. 228.)

[24] Edmond Vermeil, *Germany in the 20th Century, A Political and Cultural History of the Weimar Republic and the Third Reich* (New York, 1956), p. 9.

25 Count Georg Leo von Caprivi (1831-1899), Prussian general and statesman, had a brilliant military career. In 1888 he became Commanding General of the Tenth Army Corps in Hanover. In 1890 he succeeded Bismarck as Reichs Chancellor and Prussian Minister-President and Minister of Foreign Affairs. An able soldier, he turned out to be a weak Chancellor.

26 Johannes Haller, *Aus dem Leben des Fürsten Philipp zu Eulenburg-Hertefeld* (Berlin, 1924), p. 156.

27 Ziekursch, *Das Zeitalters Wilhelms II, op. cit.,* p. 156.

28 William II, *Memoirs, op. cit.,* p. 15.

29 William Walter Phelps to James G. Blaine, April 2, 1890, No. 93, *Confidential,* quoted in Otto zu Stolberg-Wernigerode, *Germany and the United States during the Era of Bismarck* (Philadelphia, Pa., 1937), p. 316.

30 *Cf.* Kardorff, *Bismarck in Kampf, op. cit.,* II, 85; and Bülow, *Memoirs, op. cit.,* I, 10.

31 Busch, *Bismarck, Secret Pages, op. cit.,* III, 341. Herbert never forgave those he held responsible for wrecking his father's career and his own. "I have often spoken with him, but never did he find one word of forgiveness for the men he held responsible for the catastrophe that broke over his father." (Paul Liman, "Herbert Bismarck," *Westermanns Monatshefte,* 97 [1904], pp. 429-33.)

32 Bülow, *Memoirs, op. cit.,* IV, 641. On May 3, 1890, Herbert Bismarck wrote to Bülow again: "The day after tomorrow I am going to England for three weeks.... I do not think I shall come back to the service...and probably I shall not be asked to. I have no faith in the public prosecutor from Baden [*Marschall*]. (*Ibid.,* IV, 643.)

33 Lord Crewe, *Lord Rosebery, op. cit.,* p. 292.

34 S. Gwynn and G.M. Tuckwell, *The Life of the Rt. Hon. Sir Charles Dilke, Bart.* (London, 1917), II, 307.

35 Prince Chlodwig of Hohenlohe-Schillingfürst, *Memoirs,* ed. by Friedrich Curtius (London, 1906), p. 417.

36 From a letter of Count Münster (then German Ambassador in Paris but apparently on leave in London) to Count Waldersee, London, June 4, 1890. Münster ended this information with a fervent "*Donnerwetter!*" (General Feldmarschall Alfred Grafen von Waldersee, *Aus dem Briefwechsel,* Vol. 1: *Die Berliner Jahre, 1886-1891,* ed. by Heinrich Otto Meisner [Berlin and Leipzig, 1923], p. 379.)

CHAPTER 11

1 *Cf.* Max Weber, *Politische Schriften* (Munich, 1921), p. 138. This paragraph appeared originally in 1917 in the *Frankfurter Zeitung.*

2 Heinrich von Poschinger, *Conversations with Bismarck* (New York, 1900), p. 261.

3 C. Grant Robertson, *Bismarck* (London, 1918), p. 465.

4 Schönhausen was Bismarck's birthplace and the Bismarck ancestral estate. Kniephof, Varzin, and Friedrichsruh were family mansions.

5 Otto von Bismarck, *Die Gesammelten Werke (Friedrichsruher Ausgabe)* (Berlin, 1924 *ff.),* XIV-2, 1001.

6 Poschinger, *Conversations, op. cit.,* pp. 174-75.

7 *Memoirs of Prince von Bülow* (Boston, 1932), I, 532.

8 Dr. Karl Peters, colonial explorer and propagandist, founder of the *Gesellschaft für Deutsche*

Kolonisation in 1884 and first president of the *Alldeutscher Verband,* in 1891, was an active agent of an energetic colonial campaign for Germany.

⁹ *Hamburger Nachrichten,* November 17, 1891, morning edition.

¹⁰ Johannes Haller, *Aus dem Lebensbild des Fürsten Philipp zu Eulenburg-Hertefeld* (Berlin, 1924), p. 95.

¹¹ *Ibid.,* pp. 95-96.

¹² *Letters of the Empress Frederick,* ed. by Sir Frederick Ponsonby (New York, 1930), p. 427.

¹³ General-Feldmarschall Alfred Grafen von Waldersee, *Denkwürdigkeiten* (Stuttgart and Berlin, 1923), II, 188.

¹⁴ *Ibid.,* II, 77

¹⁵ *Ibid.,* II, 174. Waldersee reported this story from what he called "quite trustworthy sources." He regarded these telegrams as "the first gestures of reconciliation to the Emperor by the Bismarck family."

¹⁶ Haller, *Eulenberg, op. cit.,* p. 96. Apparently William II was angered by the action of Prince Bismarck in revealing that Karl Heinrich von Boetticher (1833-1907), court favorite and high official in the Foreign Office , had at one time withdrawn a large sum from the *Welfenfond* in order to hide the debts of his father-in-law. The Bismarcks regarded Boetticher, once a devoted friend and co-worker, as partly responsible for their downfall.

¹⁷ Haller, *Eulenburg, op. cit.,* p. 253.

¹⁸ Bülow, *Memoirs, op. cit.,* I, 262.

¹⁹ *Cf.* Poschinger, *Conversations, op. cit.,* pp. 258-59; and F.P. Stearns, *The Life of Prince Otto von Bismarck* (Philadelphia, Pa., 1899), p. 412.

²⁰ Waldersee believed that his error was made when the clerk added Herbert Bismarck's name as one of the current Ministers *a(usser) D(ienst) [out of service].* (*Waldersee, Denkwürdigkeiten, op. cit.,* II, 304). Eulenburg, on the other hand, explained that the invitation was not to Herbert but his cousin, and that the clerk, without further reflection, made the mistake of adding Herbert's name as a member of the *Reichstag.* (Philipp zu Eulenburg-Hertefeld, *Aus 50 Jahren* [Berlin, 1923], p. 258.)

²¹ Waldersee, *Denkwürdigkeiten, op. cit.,* II, 304.

²² Eulenburg, *Aus 50 Jahren, op. cit.,* p. 256. *Cf.* Prince Chlodwig of Hohenlohne-Schillungfürst, *Memoirs,* ed. by Friedrich Curtius, trans. by George W. Chrystal (London, 1906), II, 451.

²³ Hohenlohe, *Memoirs, op. cit.,* II, 401. See also Waldersee, *Denkwürdigkeiten, op. cit.,* II, 304.

²⁴ Eulenburg, *Aus 50 Jahren, op. cit.,* p. 256.

²⁵ *Ibid.*

²⁶ *Ibid.,* p. 259.

²⁷ Waldersee, *Denkwürdigkeiten, op. cit.,* II, 305.

²⁸ Waldersee was certain that Herbert Bismarck was the guilty one. See Waldersee, *Denkwürdigkeiten, op. cit.,* II, 375.

²⁹ Siegfried von Kardorff, *Wilhelm von Kardorff, Ein Nationaler Parliamentarier im Zeitalter Bismarcks und Wilhelm II, 1828-1907* (Berlin, 1936), p. 313. According to Kardorff, Herbert Bismarck had nothing to do with the revelation of the Reinsurance Treaty in the *Hamburger Nachrichten* and was himself surprised by it. *(Ibid.,* p. 315.)

30 *Ibid.,* p. 315.

31 Haller, *Eulenburg, op. cit.,* p. 253. See also Bülow, *Memoirs, op. cit.,* I, 411.

32 William II, *My Early Life* (New York, 1926), pp. 209-13, *passim.*

CHAPTER 12

1 Joachim von Kürenberg, *Johanna von Bismarck* (Berlin, 1935), p. 260.

2 For a brief account of the Arnim affair see Erich Eyck, *Bismarck and the German Empire* (London, 1950), pp. 210-13.

3 Otto von Bismarck, *Gedanken und Erinnerungen* (Stuttgart and Berlin, 1898, 1919), pp. 461-66.

4 *Memoirs of Prince von Bülow* (Boston, 1932), IV, 459.

5 *Ibid.,* IV, 548.

6 *Ibid.,* 1, 252.

7 *Ibid.,* IV, 459.

8 Kürenberg, *Johanna von Bismarck, op. cit.,* p. 260.

9 Bülow, *Memoirs, op. cit.,* I, 252.

10 E. Brandenburg, *From Bismarck to the World War, A History of German Foreign Policy, 1870-1914* (London, 1927), p. 23.

11 *Ibid.,* p. 23.

12 Baron von Eckardstein, *Ten Years at the Court of St. James, 1895-1905* (New York, 1922), pp. 62-63.

13 See Chapter 9.

14 A.J.P. Taylor, *The Course of German History* (New York, 1946), p. 141.

15 Bülow, *Memoirs, op. cit.,* IV, 607.

16 *Ibid.,* IV, 645-46. Bülow, himself, Chancellor from 1900-1909, retained Holstein in service.

17 Johannes Haller, *Aus dem Leben des Fürsten Philipp zu Eulenburg-Hertefeld* (Berlin, 1924), p. 383.

18 Eckardstein, *Ten Years, op. cit.,* p. 11.

19 Moritz Busch, *Bismarck, Some Secret Pages of His History* (London, 1898), III, 341.

20 *Ibid.,* p. 343.

21 Bülow, *Memoirs, op. cit.,* 1, 7.

22 The details of the incident are from a letter sent by Philipp Eulenburg to Emperor William II from Munich on March 4, 1894. (*Cf.* Helmuth Rogge, ed., *Friedrich von Holstein: Lebensbekenntnis* in *Briefen an eine Frau* [Berlin, 1932], pp. 167-70.)

23 Councillor in the Foreign Office.

24 *Neue Freie Presse,* March 1, 1894.

25 Rogge, *Holstein, op. cit.,* pp. 169-70.

26 *Ibid.,* p. 168.

27 Haller, *Eulenberg, op. cit.,* p. 167.

28 *Ibid.*

[29] Hermann Freiherr von Eckardstein, *Lebenserinnerungen und politische Denkwürdigkeiten* (Leipzig, 1919), II, 42. Eckardstein reported further: "Since the funeral services for the dead Prince Bismarck [*1898*], Herbert Bismarck has gradually come to normal relations with William II, and he as well as his friends have been working on the Emperor as well as in the *Reichstag* for the Imperial Chancellor's post." *(Ibid.)*

[30] Bülow, *Memoirs, op. cit.,* I, 330.

CHAPTER 13

[1] *Memoirs of Prince von Bülow* (Boston, 1932), IV, 587.

[2] F.P. Stearns, *The Life of Prince Otto von Bismarck* (Philadelphia, Pa., 1899), p. 405.

[3] Quoted in Siegfried von Kardorff, *Wilhelm von Kardorff: Ein nationaler Parliamentarier im Zeitalters Bismarcks und Wilhelm II, 1827-1907* (Berlin, 1936), p. 267.

[4] O. Gradenwitz, *Bismarcks letzter Kampf, 1888-1898* (Berlin, 1924), p. 243.

[5] Koppel S. Pinson, *Modern Germany* (New York, 1954), p. 284.

[6] Gradenwitz, *Bismarcks letzter Kampf, op. cit.,* pp. 242-43.

[7] *Ibid.* Gradenwitz claims that Bleichröder was the source for the rumor that Bismarck intended to visit Vienna on a political mission. According to Gradenwitz, Bleichröder was in Friedrichsruh at the time, hence he obviously was the guilty one.

[8] *Memoirs of Prince Chlodwig of Hohenlohe-Schillingfürst*, ed. by Friedrich Curtius (New York, 1905), II, 446.

[9] See Horst Kohl, *Denkwürdige Tage aus dem Leben des Fürsten Bismarcks* (Leipzig, 1898), p. 83; and Karl Wipperman *Deutsche Geschichtskalendar* (Leipzig, 1775 *ff.*), 1892, II, 26.

[10] *Reichsanzeiger,* July 7, 1892.

[11] Johannes Haller, *Aus dem Leben des Fürsten Philipp zu Eulenburg-Hertefeld* (Berlin, 1924), p. 110.

[12] O. Gradenwitz, *Akten über Bismarcks grossdeutsche Rundfahrt, Sitzungsberichte der Heidelberger Akademie der Wissenschaft, Philosophisch-historische Klasse,* vol. XIII (Heidelberg, 1921), p. 23. On Holstein's role in the Vienna dispatch see also Hans Delbrück, "Von der Bismarck-Legende," *Historische Zeitschrift,* 133 (1926), p. 80; H.O. Meisner, *Der Reichskanzler Caprivi. Eine biographische Skizze* (Tübingen, 1955), 713-17; and Helmuth Rogge, *Holstein und Hohenlohe* (Stuttgart, 1957), p. 387.

[13] For the full text see O. Gradenwitz, *Bismarcks letzter Kampf, op. cit.,* pp. 240-42.

[14] William II's letter to Francis Joseph was not published until 1919, when it appeared in the *Österreichsche Rundschau, LVIII* (1919), 109-10, and then only in fragmentary and toned down form. Bismarck, however, as he revealed quickly in the *Hamburger Nachrichten,* learned about the Kaiser's letter shortly after it was sent. (See Gradenwitz, *Bismarcks letzter Kampf, op. cit.,* pp. 244-45.)

[15] Later, Bismarck told a guest at Friedrichsruh: "I still have a sharp eye up to 100 meters." (A.O. Meyer, *Bismarck: Der Mensch und der Staatsman* [Stuttgart, 1949], p. 693.)

[16] "Letter of Uriah" (2 Sam.xi. 15), a treacherous letter, importing friendship but in reality a death warrant. It refers to the Biblical story of Uriah the Hittite, a captain in David's army, who was sent to the most dangerous area of the battle line, where he was killed. David then took as his wife Bathsheba, who had been Uriah's spouse.

[17] On the Bismarcks' journey to Vienna, see Hans Blum, *Fürst Bismarck und seiner Zeit*

(Munich, 1895), IV, 445-64; Kohl, *Denkwürdige Tage, op. cit.,* pp. 95 *ff;* Meyer, *Bismarck, op. cit.,* pp. 691-93; and Adolf von Westarp, *Fürst Bismarck und das deutsche Volk,* Munich, 1892, *passim.*

[18] Blum, *Fürst Bismarck, op. cit.,* IV, 445.

[19] *Ibid.,* IV, 446. See also Kohl, *Denkwürdige Tage, op. cit.,* p. 94.

[20] Blum, *Fürst Bismarck, op. cit.,* IV, 446.

[21] Johannes Zierkursch, *Politische Geschichte des neuen deutschen Kaiserreiches,* vol. 3: *Des Zeitalters Wilhelms II, 1890-1918* (Frankfurt-am-Main, 1930), III, 71.

[22] Stearns, *Bismarck, op. cit.,* p. 405

[23] Hohenlohe, *Memoirs, op. cit.,* II, 446.

[24] Arthur von Brauer, *Im Dienste Bismarcks* (Berlin, 1935), p. 354. Crown Prince Rudolf, who was invited to the wedding, suddenly was "called away" on a journey. (See Blum, *Fürst Bismarck, op. cit.,* IV, 448.)

[25] Otto von Bismarck, *Die Gesammelten Werke, op. cit.,* XIV-2, 1005.

[26] Brauer, *Im Dienste Bismarcks, op. cit.,* p. 354.

[27] Kohl,*Denkwürdige Tage, op. cit.,* p. 94.

[28] *Ibid.*

[29] Otto von Bismarck, *Die Gesammelten Werke, op. cit.,* XIV-2, 1006.

[30] *Ibid.* Bismarck was so angered that he made the subject of uniforms the sole subject of his letter to William. A postscript added: "If the ban exists, then it must be for street wear only, not for indoors, otherwise gentlemen from many lands would have to make more daily changes than they possibly could." (*Cf. Bismarcks Briefe an seinen Sohn Wilhelm,* ed. by Wolfgang Windelband [Berlin, 1922], p. 24.)

[31] Blum, *Fürst Bismarck, op. cit.,* IV, 446.

[32] Kohl, *Denkwürdige Tage, op. cit.,* p. 94; see also Blum, *Fürst Bismarck, op. cit.,* IV, 447.

[33] Blum, *Fürst Bismarck, op. cit.,* IV, 447.

[34] *Ibid.*

[35] *Ibid., p. 448.*

[36] For the full text, see Hermann Robolsky, *Bismarck, 1888-1898* (Berlin, 1899), pp. 278-76.

[37] For Bismarck's enmity with Richter, see H. Röttger, *Bismarck und Eugen Richter im Reichstage, 1879-1890* (Bochum, 1932).

[38] Robolsky, *Bismarck, op. cit.,* pp. 286-87.

[39] Blum, *Fürst Bismarck, op. cit.,* IV, 449-63.

[40] Hans Blum, *Persönliche Erinnerungen an den Fürsten Bismarcks* (Munich, 1900), p. 198. See also Ziekursch, *Politische Geschichte, op. cit.,* III, 71.

[41] Gradenwitz, *Akten, op. cit.,* p. 51.

[42] Blum, *Fürst Bismarck, op. cit.,* IV, 459.

[43] *Ibid.,* IV, 463.

[44] *Cf.* Raymond J. Sontag, *Germany and England, Background of Confict 1848-1894* (New York, 1938), p. 276.

[45] Ziekursch, *Politische Geschichte, op. cit.*, III, 71.

[46] *Ibid.*

[47] *Norddeutscher Allgemeine Zeitung,* June 27 and 28, 1892.

[48] *Hamburger Nachrichten,* July 4, 1892.

[49] *Cf.* Paul Liman, *Fürst Bismarck nach seiner Entlassung* (Berlin, 1904), p. 112.

[50] *Cf.* Fritz Hellwig, *Carl Ferdinand Frhr. v. Stumm-Halberg, 1838-1901* (Heidelberg-Saarbrücken, 1936), p. 442.

[51] Paul von Hatzfeldt to Holstein, July 1, 1892. (See *The Holstein Papers,* ed. by Norman Rich and M.H. Fisher [Cambridge, Eng., 1961], III, 413.)

[52] Paul Liman, "Herbert Bismarck: Ein Gedenkwort," *Westermanns Monatshefte,* 97 (December, 1904), p. 431.

CHAPTER 14

[1] Paul Liman, "Herbert Bismarck, Ein Gedenkwort," *Westermanns Monatshefte,* 97 (December, 1904), p. 430.

[2] Johannes Penzler, ed., *Fürst Herbert von Bismarcks politische Reden* (Berlin and Stuttgart, 1905), pp. 81-98.

[3] *Ibid.,* p. 88.

[4] *Ibid.*

[5] *Ibid.,* pp. 88-89.

[6] *Ibid.* p. 92.

[7] *Ibid.* p. 85

[8] Herbert's maiden address took place on July 14, 1893, in what was to be a long session of the *Reichstag.*

[9] Penzler, *Herbert von Bismarck, op. cit.,* pp. 96-110.

[10] Siegfried von Kardorff, *Wilhelm von Kardorff, Ein nationaler Parliamentarier im Zeitalters Bismarcks und Wilhelm II, 1828-1907* (Berlin, 1936), p. 224.

[11] *Ibid.,* p. 284.

[12] Penzler, *Herbert von Bismarck, op. cit.,* pp. 111-30.

[13] *Ibid.,* pp. 134-45.

[14] Siegfried von Kardorff, *Wilhelm von Kardorff, op. cit.,* p. 168.

[15] The Progressives, or left liberals, the oldest of the *Reichstag* political parties, underwent an almost bewildering series of rifts. The *Fortschrittspartei,* founded in 1861, lasted until 1884, when it combined with the *Freisinnige Partei,* secessionists from the National Liberal Party. The *Freisinnige Partei* had been founded in 1880 by Richter and others. Richter's opposition to the army measures of 1893 finally split his own party: the left wing became the *Freisinnige Volkspartei* and the right wing emerged as the *Freisinnige Vereinigung.* In 1910 all the left-liberal groups combined to form the *Fortschrittliche Volkspartei,* which after 1919, became the Democratic Party.

[16] *Cf.* Maximilian Harden, *World Portraits* (London, 1911), p. 122.

[17] *Ibid.,* p.134.

[18] Penzler, *Herbert von Bismarck, op. cit.,* pp. 146-64.

[19] *Ibid.*, p. 165.

[20] The Exceptional Laws, orginally enacted for a period of two and a half years, and thereafter extended every two years, were allowed to expire in 1890, the year of Bismarck's retirement. During this period over 1,500 persons were arrested and some 150 periodicals and 1,200 non-regular publications were suppressed. (*Cf.* Otto Atzrott, *Sozialdemokratische Druckschriften und Vereine verboten auf Grund...* [Berlin, 1886].)

[21]

Year	Votes	No. Socialist deputies in the *Reichstag*
1871	123,975	2
1874	351,952	9
1877	493,288	12
1878	437,158	9
1881	311,961	12
1884	549,990	24
1887	763,128	11
1890	1,427,298	35
1893	1,786,738	44
1898	2,107,076	56
1903	3,010,771	81
1907	3,259,029	43
1912	4,250,401	110

(*Statistisches Jahrbuch, Statistik des deutschen Reichs, Vierteljahrshefte für Statistik des deutschen Reichs.*)

[22] Sickness Insurance Act of 1883, Workmen's Compensation Act of 1884-1885, Old Age Pension Act of 1889.

[23] Penzler, *Herbert von Bismarck, op. cit.*, p. 187.

[24] *Ibid.*, pp. 187-88.

[25] *Ibid.*, p. 196.

[26] *Ibid.*, p. 194.

[27] *Ibid.*, pp. 202-06.

[28] For the texts of these speeches, see Penzler, *Herbert von Bismarck, op. cit.*, pp. 214-368.

[29] *Ibid.*, p. 220.

[30] *Ibid.*, pp. 218-20.

[31] *Ibid.*, pp. 244-47.

[32] *Ibid.*

[33] *Memoirs of Prince von Bülow* (Boston, 1932), I, 210.

[34] *Ibid.*, I, 327.

[35] The four successors to Prince Bismarck as Chancellor were: General Leo von Caprivi (1890-1894); Prince Chlodwig zu Hohenlohe-Schillingfürst (1894-1900); Prince Bernhard von Bülow (1900-1909); and Theobald von Bethmann-Hollweg (1909-1917).

[36] Baron von Eckardstein, *Ten Years at the Court of St. James, 1895-1905*, trans. and ed. by George Young (New York, 1922), p. 136.

[37] Lord Crewe, *Lord Rosebery* (New York, 1931), p. 448.

[38] *Ibid.*, p. 448.

[39] Helmuth Rogge, ed., *Friedrich von Holstein: Lebensbekenntnis in Briefen an eine Frau* (Berlin, 1932), p. 215.

[40] *Ibid.*,

[41] Eckardstein, *Ten Years at St. James, op. cit.*, p. 137.

[42] Penzler, *Herbert von Bismarck, op. cit.*, p. 365.

[43] *Cf.* Johannes Penzler, ed., *Fürst Bismarck nach seiner Entlassung*, 7 vols. (Leipzig, 1897).

[44] Penzler, who also edited Herbert Bismarck's speeches, later stated that the elder Bismarck's speeches on the Polish question appeared word-for-word in his collection. (*Cf.* Penzler, *Herbert von Bismarck, op. cit.*, p. 294.)

[45] On July 30, 1898, on the death of his father, Herbert assumed the family title of Prince, which had been bestowed upon the elder Bismarck after the Franco-Prussian War. Along with the title, Herbert inherited ownership of Friedrichsruh.

[46] In the preface of Penzler, *Herbert von Bismarck, op cit.*, p. 2.

CHAPTER 15
[1] See Maximilian Harden, *"Herbert Bismarck: Ein Gedenkwort," Die Zukunft*, 48 (October 1, 1904), pp. 470-81.

[2] *Memoirs of Prince von Bülow* (Boston, 1932), I, 267.

[3] Paul Liman, "Herbert Bismarck," in *Westermanns Monatshefte*, 97 (December, 1904), p. 432.

[4] *Ibid.*

[5] *Ibid.*

[6] *Ibid.*

[7] Prince Chlodwig zu Hohenlohe-Schillingfürst (1819-1901), Bavarian leader, uncle of William II, and Chancellor from 1894 to 1900.

[8] Bülow, *Memoirs, op. cit.*, I, 453. From a letter from Herbert Bismarck to Bülow dated October 18, 1900.

[9] *Ibid.*, II, 59, 60.

[10] *Ibid.*, I, 607-09.

[11] *Hamburger Nachrichten*, June 22, 1903.

[12] *Ibid.*, October 14, 1903.

[13] There is ample evidence to show that the third Prince Bismarck was anti-Nazi in sentiment. See *The Van Hassel Diaries* (New York, 1947), pp. 87, 160; and *The Ciano Diaries, 1829-1943* (New York, 1947), pp. 357, 369, 402, 453, 456, 470, 474, 489, 491, 547, 551.

[14] Gottfried von Bismarck honored the Bismarck name by his active opposition to Hitler and the Third Reich. He was arrested by the *Gestapo* after the failed attempt on Hitler's life on July 20, 1944, tried before the dreaded People's Court, acquitted, and transferred to Sachsenhausen concentration camp.

[15] Heinrich von Poschinger, *Aus Grosser Zeit, Erinnerungen an den Fürsten Bismarcks* (Berlin, 1905), p. 171.

[16] Harden, "Herbert Bismarck," *op. cit.,* p. 470.

[17] Poschinger, *Aus Grosser Zeit, op. cit.,* p. 169.

BIBLIOGRAPHY

Apeler, Alfred, *Otto von Bismarck* (New York, 1968).

Aydelotte, William Osgood, *Bismarck and British Colonial Policy* (Philadelphia, Pa., 1937).

Bailey, Thomas A., *A Diplomatic History of the American People* (New York, 1946).

Ballhausen, Freiherr Lucius von, *Bismarck-Errinerungen* (Stuttgart and Berlin, 1921).

Bassman, Walter (ed.), *Staatsschriften Graf Herbert von Bismarck: Aus seiner politischen Privatskorrespondenz* (Göttingen, 1964).

Baumgardt, Rudolf, *Bismarck: Licht und Schatten eines Genies* (Munich, 1951).

Bergstraesser, Ludwig, *Geschichte der politischen Parteien in Deutschland* (7th ed., Munich, 1952).

Berlebach, Hans Hermann, *Kaiser Wilhelm II. und Fürst Bismarck* (Berlin, 1922.)

Beust, Friedrich Ferdinand Graf von, *Aus Drei-Viertel-Jahrhunderten, Erinnerungen und Aufzeichnungen,* 2 vols. (Stuttgart, 1887).

Bismarck, Herbert (ed.), *Fürst Bismarck an seiner Braut und Gattin,* rev. by Horst Kohl, 2 vols. (Stuttgart, 1914), English ed. *The Love Letters of Bismarck, 1846-1889,* trans. under supervision of Charlton T. Lewis (New York, 1901).

    – Korrespondenz, by Klaus-Peter Hoepke, in *Fürst Bismarck Archiv,* Friedrichsruh.

Bismarck, Otto von, *Die gesammelten Werke (Friedrichsruher Ausgabe),* ed. by Herman von Petersdorf; Friedrich Thimme; Werner Frauendienst; Willy Andreas; Wilhelm Schüssler; Wolfgang Windelband; Gerhard Ritter; and Rudolf Stadelmann, 15 vols. (Berlin, 1924-35), especially vols. 3, 6b, 6c, 7, 8, 14-I, and 14-II.

    – Gedanken und Errinnerungen, 3 vols. in one (Stuttgart and Berlin, 1898, 1921).

Bismarcks Parlamentarische Reden, ed. by Wilhelm Böhm, 16 vols. (Stuttgart, Berlin and Leipzig, n.d.)

Blowitz, Henri Stephan de, *My Memoirs* (London, 1903).

Bosbach, Heinz, *Fürst Bismarck und die Kaiserin Augusta* (Cologne, 1936).

Brandenburg, Erich, *From Bismarck to the World War, a History of German Foreign Policy, 1870-1914,* trans. by Annie Elizabeth Adams (London, 1927).

Bülow, Prince von, *Memoirs,* trans. by Geoffrey Dunlop and F.A. Voigt, 4 vols. (Boston, 1932).

Busch, Moritz, *Bismarck, Some Secret Pages of His History* (New York, 1898).

– *Our Chancellor,* trans. by William Beatty-Kingston (New York, 1884).

Bussmann, Walter (ed.), *Staatssekretär Graf Herbert von Bismarck, Aus seiner politischen Privatkorrespondenz* (Göttingen, 1964).

Cornwallis-West, Mrs. George, *The Reminiscences of Lady Randolph Churchill* (London, 1908).

Crewe, Lord, *Lord Rosebery* (New York, 1931).

Darmstaedter, F., *Bismarck and the Creation of the Second Reich* (London, 1948).

Dawson, William H., *The Evolution of Modern Germany* (London, 1908).

– *The German Empire, 1867-1914,* 2 vols. (London, 1919).

– *The German Workman* (London, 1906).

Die Grosse Politik der Europäischen Kabinette, 1871-1914. Sammlung der Diplomatischen Akten des Auswärtigen Amtes. Im Auftrage des Auswärtigen Amtes herausgegeben von Johannes Lepsius, Albrecht Mendelssohn Bartholdy, Friedrich Thimmes, 40 vols. (Berlin, 1922-27).

Eckardstein, Herman Freiherr von, *Lebenserinnerungen und politische Denkwürdigkeiten,* 3 vols, (Leipzig, 1919-20).

Ellison, Joseph Waldo, "The Partition of Samoa: A Study of Imperialism and Diplomacy," *Pacific Historical Review,* VIII (September, 1939), pp. 268 *ff.*

Eppstein, Georg Freiherr von, ed. *Fürst Bismarcks Entlassung* (Berlin, 1920).

Eulenburg-Hertefeld, Philipp zu, *Aus 50 Jahren, Erinnerungen, Tagebücher und Briefe,* ed. by Johannes Haller (Berlin, 1923).

– "Herbert Bismarcks Tragödie," *Deutsche Rundschau,* 194 (1923), pp. 225-48.

Eyck, Erich, *Bismarck,* 3 vols. (Zürich, 1941-44).

– *Bismarck and the German Empire* (London, 1950).

– *Das persönliche Regiment Wilhelms II* (Zürich, 1948).

– *Gladstone* (Erlenbach-Zürich and Leipzig, 1938).

Fitzmaurice, Lord Edmond, *The Life of Granville, George Leveson Gower, Second Earl Granville,* 2 vols. (London and Bombay, 1905).

Flenley, Ralph, *Modern German History* (London, 1953).

Flex, Walter, *Zwölf Bismarcks* (Berlin, c. 1925).

Frederick III, *The War Diary of 1870-71,* trans. and ed. by A.R. Allinson (London, 1927).

Fuller, Joseph Vincent, *Bismarck's Diplomacy at its Zenith* (Cambridge, Mass., 1922).

Gagliardi, Ernst, *Bismarcks Entlassung* (Tübingen, 1927).

Gooch, G.P., *Franco-German Relations, 1871-1914* (London, 1928).

Grossrichard, Yves, *Les cents visages de Bismarck* (Paris, 1970).

Gwynn, S. and G.M. Tuckwell, *The Life of the Rt. Hon. Sir Charles W. Dilke, Bart.,* 2 vols. (London, 1917).

Hagen, Maximilian von, *Bismarcks Kolonialpolitik* (Stuttgart, 1923).

Hahn, Ludwig and Carl Wippermann, *Fürst Bismarck, Sein politisches Leben und Wirken,* 5 vols. (Berlin, 1878-91).

Haller, Johannes, *Aus dem Leben des Fürsten Philipp zu Eulenburg-Hertefeld* (Berlin, 1924).

Hammann, Otto, *Der missverstandens Bismarck: Zwanzig Jahre Deutscher Weltpolitik* (Berlin, 1921).

Harden, Maximilian, *Köpfe* (Berlin, 1911)
    – "Herbert Bismarck: Ein Gedenkwort, *Die Zukunft,* 48 (October 1, 1904), pp. 470-81.

Headlam-Morley, J.W., *Bismarck and the Foundations of the German Empire* (New York, 1899, 1930).

Henderson, F.A., *A Short History of Germany,* 2 vols. (New York, 1916).

Hobson, J.A., *Imperialism: A Study* (Ann Arbor, Mich., 1965).

Hoffman, Hermann, *Fürst Bismarck, 1890, 1898* (Stuttgart, Berlin, and Leipzig, 1914).

Hohenlohe-Schillingfürst, Prince Chlodwig of, *Memoirs* ed. by Friedrich Curtius, trans. by George W. Chrystal, 2 vols. (London 1906).

Holborn, Hajo, *A History of Modern Germany, 1840-1945* (New York, 1969).

Kardorff, Siegfried von, *Wilhelm von Kardorff, Ein nationaler Parliamentarier im Zeitalter Bismarcks und Wilhelm II, 1828-1907* (Berlin, 1936).
    – *Bismarck in Kampf und sein Werk,* vol. 2 [*Feldpostausgabe*] (Berlin, 1943).

Kennedy, Paul M., "German Colonial Expansion," *Past and Present,* 54 (1972). pp. 134-41.

Kissinger, Henry A., "The White Revolutionary; Reflections on Bismarck," *Daedalus,* 97 (1968), 888-924.

Knaplund, Paul, *Gladstone and Britain's Imperial Policy* (New York, 1927).
    –*Gladstone's Foreign Policy* (New York, 1935).

Koschitzsky, Max von, *Deutsche Kolonialgeschichte,* 2 vols. (Leipzig, 1888).

Kranz, Herbert, *Bismarck und das Reich ohne Krone* (Stuttgart, 1960).

Kürenberg, Joachim, *Johanna von Bismarck* (Berlin, 1935).
– *The Kaiser: A Life of Wilhelm II, Last Emperor of Germany,* trans. by H.T. Russell and Herta Hagen (New York, 1955).
Langer, William L., *The Diplomacy of Imperialism,* 1890-1902, 2 vols (New York, 1935).
Letters of the Empress Frederick, ed. by Sir Frederick Ponsonby (New York, 1930).
Liman, Paul, *"Herbert Bismarck, Ein Gedenkwort,"* *Westermanns Monatshefte,* 97 (December, 1904), pp. 429-33.
Linde, Fritz, *Bismarck, Grösse und Grenze seines Reiches* (Leipzig, 1939).
Lowe, Charles, *Prince Bismarck, An Historical Biography,* 2 vols. (London, 1886).
Ludwig, Emil, *Bismarck, The Story of a Fighter,* trans. by Eden and Cedar Paul (Boston, 1928).
– *Kaiser Wilhelm II,* trans. by E.C. Mayne (London, 1926).
Mehring, Franz, *Geschichte der deutschen Sozialdemokratie,* 4 vols., 12th ed. (Stuttgart, 1922).
Meinecke, Friedrich, *Die Idee der Staatsräson in der neueren Geschichte* (Munich, 1924).
–*Weltgeschichte und Nationalstaat,* 7th ed. (Munich, 1928).
Mommsen, Wilhelm, *Bismarcks Sturz und die Parteien* (Stuttgart, 1924).
– *Bismarck* (Munich, 1954).
Moon, Parker Thomas, *Imperialism and World Politics* (New York, 1926).
Naumann, Friedrich, *Die politische Parteien* (Berlin, 1910).
Nowak, Karl Friedrich, *Germany's Road to Ruin,* trans. by E.W. Dickes (London, 1932).
– *Kaiser and Chancellor* (London, 1930).
Oertzen, Dietrich von, *Adolf Stoecker, Lebensbild und Zeitgeschichte* (Schwerin-in-Mecklenburg, 1912).
Oncken, Hermann, *Das Deutsche Reich und die Vorgeschichte des Weltkrieges,* 2 vols. (Leipzig, 1933).
– *Das Zeitalter des Kaisers Wilhelm* (Berlin, 1890).
Paul, Gustav, *"Hildebrands Bismarckdenkmal,"* *Kunst und Künstler,* 9 (1910), pp. 98-101.
Penzler, Johannes, ed., *Fürst Herbert von Bismarcks politische Reden* (Berlin and Stuttgart, 1905).
Pflanze, Otto, *Bismarck and the Development of Germany* (Princeton, 1963).
Pinson, Koppel S., *Modern Germany: Its History and Civilization* (New York, 1954).

Poschinger, Heinrich von, *Aus Grosser Zeit, Erinnerungen an den Fürsten Bismarck* (Berlin, 1905).
— *Conversations with Bismarck* (New York, 1900).
Rachfahl, Felix, *Deutschland und die Weltpolitik, 1871-1914,* vol. 1: *Die Bismarck'sche Aera* (Stuttgart, 1923).
Rich, Norman and M.H. Fischer (eds.), *The Holstein Papers,* vols. 1-3 (Cambridge, Eng., 1955-61).
Richter, Eugen, *Im alten Reichstag, Erinnerugen,* 2 vols. (Berlin, 1896).
Richter, Günther, *Friedrich von Holstein: Ein Mitarbeiter Bismarcks* (Lübeck and Hamburg, 1966).
Robertson, C. Grant, *Bismarck* (London, 1918).
Rogge, Helmuth, ed., *"Friedrich von Holstein: Lebensbekenntnis in Briefen an eine Frau* (Berlin, 1932).
Röhl, John L., *Germany Without Bismarck: The Crisis in Government in the Second Reich, 1890-1900* (Berkeley, Cal., 1967).
Rothfels, Hans, *Bismarcks englische Bündnispolitik* (Berlin and Leipzig, 1924).
— *Bismarck-Briefe* (Göttingen, 1955).
Rottger, H., *Bismarck und Eugen Richter im Reichstage, 1870-1890* (Bochum, 1932).
Ryden, G.H., *The Foreign Policy of the United States in Relation to Samoa* (New Haven, 1933).
Schierbrand, W. von, *The Kaiser's Speeches* (New York, 1903).
Schnabel, Franz, *Deutsche Geschichte im 19. Jahrhundert,* 4 vols. (Freiburg-im-Breisgau, 1929-37), rev. ed., 1948-51.
Schüssler, W., *Bismarcks Sturz* (Leipzig, 1921).
Seeley, J.R., *The Expansion of England* (London, 1883).
Simon, Walter Michael, *Germany in the Age of Bismarck* (New York, 1968).
Simpson, J.Y., *The Saburov Memoirs, or Bismarck and Russia* (Cambridge, Eng., 1929).
Snyder, Louis L., *Die persoenlichen und politischen Beziehungen Bismarcks zu Amerikanern* (Darmstadt, 1932).
— *From Bismarck to Hitler* (Williamsport, Pa., 1935).
— *German Nationalism: The Tragedy of a People* (Harrisburg, Pa., 1952).
— "The American-German Pork Dispute, 1879-1891," *The Journal of Modern History,* XVII (March, 1945), pp. 16-28.
— *The Blood and Iron Chancellor* (Princeton, N.J., 1967).
Snyder, Louis L. and Ida Mae Brown, *Bismarck and German Unification* (New York, 1966).
Sontag, Raymond J., *Germany and England: Background of Conflict, 1848-1894.*

Stearns, F.P., *The Life of Prince Otto von Bismarck* (Philadelphia, Pa., 1899).

Steinberg, S.H., *A Short History of Germany* (New York, 1945).

Stern, Fritz, *Bismarck, Bleichröder, and the Building of the German Empire* (New York, 1977).

Stevenson, Robert Louis, *A Footnote to History* (New York, 1895).

Stoecker, Adolf, *Christlich-Sozial, Reden und Aufsätze* (Bielefeld and Leipzig, 1885).

Stolberg-Wernigerode, Otto zu, *Germany and the United States during the Era of Bismarck* (Philadelphia, 1937).

Stolper, Gustav, *Germany Economy, 1870-1890* (New York, 1940).

Sybel, Heinrich von, *Die Begründung des deutschen Reiches durch Wilhelm I,* 7 vols. (Munich, 1889-95).

Taylor, A.J.P., *Germany's First Bid for Colonies, 1884-1885* (London, 1938).
– *The Course of German History* (New York, 1946).
– *Bismarck: The Man and the Statesman* (New York, 1955).

Temperley H. and L.M. Penson, *Foundations of British Foreign Policy* (Cambridge, Eng., 1938).

Townsend, Mary Evelyn, *The Rise and Fall of Germany's Colonial Empire, 1884-1918* (New York, 1930).

Tyler, Alice Felt, *The Foreign Policy of James G. Blaine* (Minneapolis, Minn., 1927).

Vagts, Alfred, *Deutschland und die Vereinigten Staaten in der Weltpolitik,* 2 vols. (New York, 1935).

Valentin, Veit, *The German People* (New York, 1946).

Vallonton, Henri, *Bismarck et Hitler* (Paris, 1954).

Vermeil, Edmond, *Germany in the 20th Century, A Political and Cultural History of the Weimar Republic and the Third Reich* (New York, 1956).
– *Germany's Three Reichs, Their History and Culture,* trans. by E.W. Dickes (London, 1944).

Waldersee, General-Feldmarschall Alfred Graf von, *Aus dem Briefwechsel,* vol. 1: *Die Berliner Jahre, 1886-1891,* ed. by Heinrich Otto Meisner, 3 vols. (Berlin and Leipzig, 1928).
– *Denkwürdigkeiten,* ed. by Heinrich Otto Meisner, 3 vols. (Stuttgart and Berlin, 1923).

Ward, A.W., *Germany, 1815-1890,* 3 vols. (Cambridge, Eng., 1916-18).

Weber, Max *Politische Schriften* (Munich, 1921).

Weissbuch Samoa, February 15, 1889, No. 37.

Wertheimer, Eduard von, *Bismarck im politischen Kampf* (Berlin, 1930).

Wertheimer, Mildred, *The Pan German League* (New York, 1924).

William II, *My Early Life* (New York, 1926).

    – *My Memoirs, 1878-1918* (London, 1922).

Windelband, W., *Herbert Bismarck als Mitarbeiter seines Vaters* (Stuttgart, 1921), 28 pp.

Zeuner, Hans Joachim, *Bismarcks Begegnungen mit Wilhelm II nach seiner Entlassung* (Göttingen, 1961).

Ziekursch, Johannes, *Politische Geschichte des neuen deutschen Kaiserreiches,* vol. 3: *Das Zeitalters Wilhelms II, 1890-1918* (Frankfurt-am-Main, 1930).

Zimmer, Alfred, *Geschichte der deutschen Kolonialpolitik* (Berlin, 1914).

INDEX

163, 164, 167, 172, 209 *n*.25, 215 *n*.35

Carola, German corvette, 60

Carolath-Beuthen, Elizabeth von, 44, 53, 55, 60, 71, 83, 89, 120, 167

Carolath-Beuthen, Prince von, 44, 77

Carolath-Schleinitz-Loë cabal, 67

Caroline Islands, 105, 106

"Cartridge Prince" (later William I), 122

"Central Ox" (Otto von Bismarck), 62, 64, 66, 67, 99, 106, 107, 114, 115, 116, 142

Chamberlain, Joseph, English politician and imperialist, 101, 112

Charles of Prussia, Prince, 47

Charles II, of Spain, 105

Chelius, Lieut. von, 42

Chlumetzki, Baron von, 165

Christian-Social Workers' Party, 77, 79

Churchill, Lord Randolph, English Chancellor of the Exchequer, 1886; 93

Churchill, Lady, 93

Churchill, Randolph, son of Winston Churchill, xi, 179

Churchill, Winston, xi, 115, 179

Civil War, American, 84

Cohen, Dr. Eduard, Chancellor von Bismarck's physician, 35-36, 49, 50, 82

"Combination" at Friedrichsruh, 141-50, 159

Congo Free State, 56

Congress of Berlin, 1878; 31, 98, 104

Cramb, J.A., British imperialist, 101

Crimean War, 1853-56; 32

Crispi, Francesco, Italian Minister-President and Foreign Minister, 1887-89; 41, 98

Crowe, Joseph, 108

Cuirassiers, 20

Damarsland, 59

Dardanelles, 30

Darmstadt, 21

Delbrück, Hans, professor, historian, and publicist, 205 *n*.1

Denmark, Prussia's war against, 1864; 19-20

Derby, Edward Henry Stanley, Earl of, British Colonial Minister, 1882-85; 60, 64, 65, 66, 68, 90-91, 111

Dias, Bartholomeu, Portuguese explorer, 58

Dias, Paulo, 58

Dilke, Sir Charles Wentworth, Under Secretary in the British Foreign Office, 1880-83; 38, 39, 66, 90, 91, 93, 94, 111, 139, 202 *n*.27.

Disraeli, Benjamin, Earl of Beaconsfield, 31

Dönhoff, Countess Marie, 53-54

Dönhoff-Friedrichstein, Count Carl von, 157, 158

Dornberg, Baron, 120

Dragoons, 20, 21, 22, 23, 24

Dresden, 164

"Dropping the Pilot," *Punch* cartoon, 139

Drummond, Henry, 84

East African Convention, 1890; 110

Eckardstein, Baron Hermann von, 41, 154-55, 159, 176-77, 207 *n*.34, 212 *n*.29

Egypt, Chancellor Bismarck's policy on, 57, 62, 64, 65, 66, 67-68

Egyptian Fairy Tale, Eulenburg's, 146

Einkreisungspolitik (encirclement policy), 155-56

Eisendecher, Karl von, 10, 188 *n*.30

Elbe, 111

Milton, John, 12

Moltke, Count Kuno, 147-48

Moltke, Gen. Helmuth, Count von, 24, 25

Monroe Doctrine, 67, 106

Morier, Sir Robert, English Ambassador in Madrid, 1871-85; in St. Petersburg until 1893; 95, 96

Motley, John Lothrop, historian, 10

Münster-Ladeburg, Georg Herbert, Count zu, German Ambassador in London, 1882-84, in Paris until 1900; 59, 61-62, 64, 66, 68, 69, 91, 111, 112, 209 *n*.36

National unification, Bismarck's three wars of, 19-20

Nauheim, 23, 24

Nepotism, 60, 72, 119, 142

New Course, 180

New Guinea, 91

New Zealand, 102

Newdegate, 39

Norddeutsche Allgemeine Zeitung, 166-67

Nordic gods, 42

Obrigkeit, die, 35

Olmütz, humiliation of, 110, 205 *n*.43

Ordensfest, 147

Order of 1852; 127-28

Pago Pago, 101, 103

Palazza Modena, 53

Palffy von Erdöd, Count, 165

Palmerston, Henry John Temple, 3rd Viscount Palmerston, British Prime Minister, 57

Panama Canal, 106

Papists, 39

Paradise Regained, 13

Paris, 38, 41

Paris, Peace of, 1856; 31

Pemba, 113

Pendleton, George Hunt, 103, 204 *n*.18

Penzler, Johannes, 177, 216 *n*.44

People's Court, 216 *n*.14

Peters, Dr. Karl, 209-10 *n*.8

Phelps, William Walter, 108, 109, 137

Pitt, William the Elder, xi
– William the Younger, xi

Pius IX, Pope, 48

Pless, Prince, 117

Plessen, Lieut. Col. von, 75

Polish question, 177

Pomerania, 4, 5

Pont-à-Mousson, 21, 23, 26

Posen, 183-84

Potsdam, 46, 75

Pourtalès, Count Friedrich von, Councillor in the Foreign Office, 157, 158

Powell, Consul, 92

Prince of Wales, brother of Empress Frederick III, 118, 133

Progressive Socialists, 72

Progressives, 214 *n*.15

Puttkamer, Heinrich von, father of Johanna von Bismarck, 4

Puttkamer, Robert von, Prussian Minister of Culture, 1879-81, Minister of the Interior until 1888; 80

Radolin, Prince, 72